Engaged Spirituality

Social Change and American Religion

GREGORY C. STANCZAK

RUTGERS UNIVERSITY PRESS
New Brunswick, New Jersey, and London

Library of Congress Cataloging-in-Publication Data
Stanczak, Gregory C., 1967–
  Engaged spirituality : social change and American religion / Gregory C. Stanczak.
    p. cm.
  Includes bibliographical references (p.   ) and index.
  ISBN-13: 978-0-8135-3835-8 (hardcover : alk. paper)
  ISBN-13: 978-0-8135-3836-5 (pbk. : alk. paper)
1. Spirituality—Social aspects—United States.   2. Religion and social problems—
United States.   3. Social change—Religious aspects.   4. Social change—United
States. I. Title.
  BL2525.S72 2006
  306.60973—dc22   2005024944

A British Cataloging-in-Publication record for this book is available from the British
Library.

Manufactured in the United States of America

For my parents

Contents

Preface

What sustains ongoing social action? The answer to that question is not a simple one and it is not a singular one, but it is one that nags and often eludes social activists, social service directors, and flagging volunteers alike. Participation of the rank and file in social movements, for example, is almost always event based rather than an ongoing lifestyle or career built upon social change. This conclusion need not be disheartening. After all, the most dynamic and effective social change is often born out of the participation of great numbers of everyday individuals who occasionally get pushed beyond the limits of what they deem acceptable. Indeed, this has been the success of suffragists, gay and lesbian marchers, and innumerable others who have collectively stepped into the streets to make their voices heard. Solidarity, compassion, and righteous efficacy can sustain these networks for significant, although limited, periods of time before the typical participant returns to her normal or other life.

Yet this conventional view of sporadic activists as agents of social change came up against a different perspective as I conducted research at the Center for Religion and Civic Culture at the University of Southern California. Through the center I had exposure to seemingly endless overlapping projects in which religious institutions as well as religiously motivated individuals across southern California were devoting significant amounts of their time to making changes in their immediate surroundings or within the increasingly globalized world. Although most of my participation in social change has been with secular organizations by design, and my interactions with others who also participate seems equally secular, it became increasingly evident through this work that perhaps one of the answers to my original question about what sustains social action might be found in religion and more specifically the subjective elements of spirituality.

This idea took getting used to at first, even as an examinable hypothesis for study. Although religious institutions have driven social change in the United States from abolition through the Promise Keepers, spirituality does not typically crop up as an analytical variable in research on social change. This analytic thinness was compounded by my own relationship with the topic, as I do not consider myself religious or spiritual in any sense that is used in this study. However, as my early research merged with religious communities and spiritually inspired individuals, I gained a new respect and wider appreciation for the ways that religion and spirituality function in everyday life around me. It soon became abundantly clear that religion and spiritual experiences in the United States can and do have profound effects not only on conservative social action but also in progressive, liberal, and sometimes even radical reform.

I began listening more carefully and taking seriously these feelings that seemed to prompt service work and foster social change. Not only that, I began asking pointedly about the connections between spiritual experiences and motivation and between spiritual practice and sustainability. By the time this project emerged, I was deeply curious about the ongoing and sometimes unspoken spiritual connection that motivated and sustained social action. The connections are profound and result in the stories that fill these pages.

Beyond the intimate and compelling stories of spiritual experiences, I also explore what kinds of social influences shaped, prodded, and sustained these beliefs in action. Clearly interlocking social factors—social networks, material resources, social structures, and individual agency—significantly impact the kind of spiritually inspired action that is possible. These interlocking factors pose methodological, epistemological, and theoretical puzzles. Asking "does your spirituality influence your social commitments" is simply not enough. What concerns me here is the way in which spirituality is embedded within lived experience and in concert with communities of believers and communities of activists that reinforce and provide outlets for their values.

In telling these stories, I hope to stay true to the intent with which they were told to me. This is no simple task, especially when it comes to telling spiritual narratives of which I have little experiential knowledge. At the same time, as a sociologist I have tried to maintain an analytic perspective. This was often quite easy when my views did not meld with those promoted. For the most part, however, I was continually and somewhat surprisingly seduced by the interviewees' infectious passions. They most likely do not know this, since my interactions with many of them lasted only the length of our interview. While our meetings were brief, I feel I came to know the participants intimately through hours upon hours spent with their voices, their videos, and their transcripts. And now I would like to acknowledge and thank them for their honesty and for their struggles.

This book is primarily an academic look at the way in which spirituality is a social resource in the lives of people working for social change. How is it that those with a spiritual engagement in the world are motivated toward, sustained within, and creatively transforming of the actions that bring about social change? In asking this type of question, I hope that I have not bled the experiential content out of these stories. Instead, I imagine that this volume could also be read by those interested more in the stories than the theories. Since my objective is primarily an academic one, I want to call to attention various points in which I temper what might be construed as a normative read on spirituality. When I do so, I intend this to be about spirituality as a social resource rather than any one type of spirituality or the theological questions about spirituality in general.

As the individuals' stories attest, no one does much in their lives without the explicit and implicit help and support of those around them. Although conducting research, analyzing data, and writing draft upon draft can seem like a solitary experience, I could not have done this alone. The Center for Religion and Civic Culture was central to this final product. It was through a post-doctoral research fellow at the Center that I was able to explore these questions within a stimulating and supportive environment. More than just the academic and administrative support that is essential, I was lucky to also find a great deal of social support through my colleagues. Donald Miller played an instigating role in acquiring a substantial grant from the Ford Foundation that made this work possible. I am indebted to Don's generosity for helping birth this project and then setting it loose once I found my footing. Jon Miller, often through example, provided invaluable mentoring on how to do top-notch scholarship. Grace Dyrness's energy, exuberance, and sincere connection with the interfaith community in Los Angeles opened many doors that I otherwise would not have known existed. Timothy Sato worked thanklessly on format on earlier drafts of this work and helped ground me and pick up my slack when I needed it.

I have been lucky enough to have a strong network of colleagues and, more important, friends who have shepherded me through the peaks and valleys of this project. Ernestine Avila shared useful insights on sticky ethnographic issues, Michele Dunbar encouraged critical writing, while Michael Blackie and Shelly Peffer unflaggingly commiserated and celebrated by my side. Last but not least, Clark Collins gave me focus, support, and direction and kept my eye on the bigger pictures in life.

Introduction

"I DON'T THINK I've ever been asked that," Ann confessed with a puzzled tone in her voice. She knitted her forehead and repositioned herself in her chair. "You would think I would have, but . . . ." Ann had devoted her early adult years to a Catholic religious order, but in the 1970s, like many of the other nuns that she served with, she came to a long-thought-out conclusion that her talents and her dreams could be better developed outside of her order. This transition involved fits and starts along different paths. For years during the 1980s she worked with nuclear freeze activists, where she utilized and thrived upon her political passions, but she still did not experience the fulfillment or extensive sense of community that her order had provided. Eventually she settled into a longer term career in Catholic social services in northern California. Her entire adult life had been a mix of unwavering social action and deep religious devotion, both to varying degrees at varying times. Yet it had taken years before someone had asked her specifically about the deeply rooted biographical turning points that generated her life of conviction and dedication. By the end of our interview, during which we both experienced emotional highs and lows as her story unfolded, Ann confessed that revisiting childhood memories and the emotional junctures of compassion and caring somehow felt cathartic, therapeutic, and even spiritual. And all it took was one simple question that too often remains unasked.

This book emerged out of an extensive research project constructed to identify and examine unasked questions about the connection between spirituality and social change. In the spring of 2001, the Ford Foundation selected the Center for Religion and Civic Culture to explore these questions among mainstream American religious traditions. "Mainstream" in this sense includes all religious traditions that are not, for lack of a better term, new age spiritualities. This initially included Muslims, Jews, Hindus, Protestants, and Catholics. A parallel project that focused on alternative spiritual traditions and practices was conducted by the Center for the Contemplative Mind in Society. Donald Miller and I were the principal investigators of this project, which spanned two collaborative and productive years. During that time, the project grew in ways that I had not expected at the outset. The interview process itself constantly provided elements of the unexpected.

Indeed, Ann's response was profound but by no means uncommon. The interview process was at times quite emotional. Childhood lessons of discrimination loomed heavily in several memories. Others relived experiences of personal growth and collective empowerment. Still others revealed the chain of idiosyncratic events that together comprised a surreptitious route to their present spiritual, personal, and professional position. Some related remarkable mystical experiences of hearing a divine guiding voice through the wind in the trees or physically feeling the energy of the Holy Spirit course through their body during notable episodes of spiritual transformation. Others appreciated a more mundane and relatively static understanding of spirituality through private prayer routines or contemplation. Still others were prominent religious leaders who had told their stories countless times and, although speaking passionately and expressively, did not have to dig deeply to uncover their testimony.

These stories, the narrative data for this essay, are taken from seventy-six in-depth interviews with exemplary individuals who articulated a connection between spiritual practice and a commitment to social justice. The sample began with the extensive southern California interfaith community contacts developed over years through the Center for Religion and Civic Culture. Additional contacts were generated through snowball sampling techniques that included recommendations from civic organizations, movement activists, religious organizations, seminaries, and rabbinical schools, as well as recommendations from the participants themselves following each interview. The final sample includes individuals predominantly within southern California; however, I conducted additional interviews in northern California, Pennsylvania, New York, and Washington, D.C. Of the seventy-six interviews, thirteen of the participants were Jewish, thirty-three were Protestant, fourteen were Catholic, six were Muslim, four were Buddhist, five were Hindu, and one was Jain. The sample consisted of forty-two men and thirty-four women.

Interviews were very conversational and followed an open-ended, semi-structured, narrative-based protocol, the belief being that it was important to uncover the widest variety of ways that people interpret spirituality and the perhaps unacknowledged ways that they implemented spirituality into their everyday lives and service work. As part of this approach I asked broad questions that invited personal reflection rather than following a rigidly structured interview protocol that might limit a participant's responses and introduce my own researcher biases about the nature, shape, or direction of spirituality. This open-ended approach at times revealed surprisingly novel insights. Yet, while conversational and semistructured, these interviews systematically addressed several core elements, beginning with descriptions of the types of social action in which respondents were currently engaged and followed by questions regarding the motivations, turning points, or influences that they felt affected their line of work or volunteerism. These reflective questions created compact life histories that formed the basis for follow-up discussion and pointed exploration of specific issues.

With regard to spirituality, I asked to what degree, if any, they found connections between their spiritual life and their service work. Based on these responses I asked further about when these connections were first felt or established. Much like the social service life histories, this line of questioning produced similar spiritual life histories. As these stories unfolded, I further asked if they could characterize their religious upbringing and how they viewed their spiritual evolution to where they are today, focusing on any salient turning points or experiences that impacted their work. Finally, I specifically asked about each individual's daily spiritual practice or routine. At times, this took the form of describing a typical day in their life and the various points in which spirituality emerged.

Interviews lasted, on average, one hour but ranged from half an hour to two and a half hours, and one even included singing as a form of spiritual connection and activism. All of these interviews were either audiotaped or videotaped with the written permission of the participants and then transcribed verbatim. Throughout the book I use the real names of the participants and the real projects that they are involved in. The one exception is Ann, quoted above. I drew this passage from my conversation with Ann after the interview officially ended. Because of this fact, and because of the emotional tone of the interview, I changed the name this one time.

Religious Institutions and Organizations

As the interviews unfolded, I also conducted detailed research of seminaries, rabbinical schools, religious and civic organizations, and online communities. I considered Catholic and Protestant seminaries from an online database of 193 accredited institutions affiliated with the Association of Theological Schools. The sample of rabbinical schools consists of the five accredited institutions in the United States: Hebrew Union College's three campuses, the University of Judaism, Jewish Theological Seminary, Yeshivah University, and the Reconstructionist Rabbinical College. I studied each school's mission statement, degree requirements for higher education, and catalog of classes. I contacted each school that offered either a specific degree or specialized program in spirituality or offered at least three explicit classes on spirituality. From this smaller sample I requested departmental literature, reading lists, and syllabi.

Based on my review of the curricula, as well as conversations with students, faculty, and administration, the dialog of renewed spirituality and a spiritually informed social service is already occurring across campuses, although not necessarily through curricular channels. A new, inquisitive generation of rabbinical students, for example, is privately revitalizing the ritual purifying bath known as the Mikvah as a way of exploring the experiential aspects of the theology they learn in the classroom. However, these creative and individual appropriations taking place on campuses are not yet institutionally reflected. Admittedly, spirituality may be introduced within various courses in religious education, but the emphasis does not yet match the extracurricular demand. In fact, some educational leaders bluntly admitted that one of the reasons that spirituality was not more fully embraced within more religious schools was that it was potentially disruptive and too difficult to funnel without losing its experiential efficacy. I was surprised to find that in an era of the politicized classroom, spirituality and, more specifically, spirituality as a tool for identity exploration and social critique was not incorporated more systematically into the curricula. This is at a time when, even within many of these rabbinical schools and seminaries, feminist contributions made substantial inroads to radically revising classroom dynamics, power relationships, and the very language used to express social thoughts and the relationship between personal issues and broader social patterns.

Many students as well as others find the connection between spirituality and social action in faith-based organizations. In looking through these groups, I initially relied heavily upon larger, publicly known organizations such as the Muslim Public Affairs Council (MPAC), Habitat for Humanity, the Jewish Council on Urban Affairs, and Pax Christi. From these better-known organizations, I drew together samples from Web page links and online searches as well as personal recommendations from other organizations and participants in this project. While the organizations I contacted had a relatively high public profile, I also included lesser-known organizations that either had a unique approach to spirituality or to social action. Thousands of organizations exist and online organizations are notoriously mercurial. Therefore, my sample was never exhaustive or complete. Nevertheless, I feel that this organizational context provides a reasonable background of the work being done across the country and a fair footing for the interviews I conducted.

Searching for Words

Talking about spirituality is difficult and hindered by the variety of ways in which it is defined colloquially and academically. I spent a good deal of time researching approaches to spirituality in places that I was often quite frankly surprised to find. I used these definitions as background for thinking through my approach to spirituality. When reviewing the literature on spirituality across disciplines, the one field that I did not draw upon was theology. These well-argued and thorough considerations of spirituality have a different analytical base than the types of literature that I am most concerned with here. Of course this debate is an active one in theology and such in-depth consideration of that field would require a project in itself.

There appears to be a therapeutic model emerging. Pockets of psychology and psychotherapy, for example, now allow spirituality into the therapist's office if it is a preexisting source for comfort and meaning-making in the patient's life.[1] As Patricia Sermabeikian points out, a transcendent power provides clients with "courage, strength, and willpower" when coping with change or conflict and is significant in producing personal transformation.[2] Similarly, segments of social work are exploring individual and community-based approaches to spirituality as one legitimate source for seeking resolutions to family or community problems.[3] Finally, medicine and occupational therapies utilize a more clinical approach, looking at rates of recovery and acquisition of skills when patients and clinicians tap spiritual motivations and frameworks.[4]

Beyond therapeutic approaches, oddly enough, business schools have repositioned spirituality at the center of innovative research projects, ethnographic fieldwork, and best-practice models. The business model spans the corporate and private spectrum, providing some of the most creative and proactive applications of spirituality in ways that circumvent alienating business cultures while remaining virulently focused on successful business practice. These applications alter shifts in organizational management styles and reconfigure workplace environments, experimenting with what is known as the "spiritual workplace." The articulation and implementation of spirituality in the business model is not often discussed in reference to denominational religious dogma or even transcendent ideals such as God or salvation,[5] although such direct sentiments do surface at times.[6] Instead, the business model employs a more diffuse, ecumenical definition of spirituality that favors the nonspecific spirituality of popular inspirational speakers or business gurus such as Stephen R. Covey and M. Scott Peck.[7]

Elements of business spirituality vary across the needs, size, and composition of different workspaces but might include recognizing the worth and value of people through employee-centered management; facilitating a working climate that demands high levels of personal integrity in all interactions; creating an environment of trust, faith, respect, and love in each other individually and collectively; and meeting both the economic as well as the individual needs of employees.[8] Prescriptive recommendations from the business model argue that such a holistic approach to improving morale, integrity, and the integration of the entire individual into the workplace is not only morally beneficial to the internal dynamics of the company, but also results in increased productivity and profit. While on the surface this may seem counterintuitive in an era tainted by high profile corporate scandal and the globalization of impersonal corporate sprawl, the business model holds fast to its claim that increasing morale and increasing profit are complementary and mutually reinforcing rather than paradoxical and incompatible.

Spirituality, while sometimes viewed as being a strictly inward, even narcissistic activity, has, according to these developments, infiltrated very public and collective realms. Indeed, as the interviews all suggest, spirituality is a vital resource, sustaining people in the hard work of social change and, on regular occasions, inspiring them to imagine possibilities that exceed realistic expectations. As Stephen L. Carter suggests, "People to whom religion really matters, people who believe they have found answers to the ultimate questions, or are very close to finding them will often respond to incentives other than those that motivate more secularized citizens."[9] While not as much has been written about spirituality as a social resource in social change, the work that has been done views spirituality as multidimensional in its applications to life's problems and approaches to solving these problems. Laurel Kearns for example suggests that in times of upheaval or normative uncertainty, spirituality becomes essential in forging new social meaning systems and strategies for action.[10] As these various applications indicate, shifts are beginning to emerge regarding the acceptable role of spirituality in everyday life, and not only as a comfort.

Talking about Spirituality

Conducting research on the feelings and ephemeral personal qualities of social change can be inspiring, challenging, and at times frustrating. Admittedly, variations in definitions slow down the way that spirituality is incorporated as an analytical component of social change. One way of getting closer to these meanings is to share stories. I have tried to reconstruct in detail, depth, and emotional sensitivity the narratives from these interviews. My project maps individual stories as experiential nodes—points on a national map connecting instances of spirituality and its attempts to make the world a better place. Both of these criteria, spirituality and social action, were broadly defined in these interviews to allow for a wide range of interpretation. By doing so, the testimonies reveal the diversity within the contemporary American landscape.

What remains beyond the scope of this project is the way in which particular narrative structures, bound by religious tradition, local history, or ethnic affiliation affect the retelling of these stories in patterned, recurrent, and meaningful ways. Christian witness, for example, especially among theologically conservative sectarian movements, publicly emphasizes the sins of the past, the point of salvation, and the new purified self in Jesus, in God, or in the Holy Spirit, whereas publicly voicing profound spiritual experience within Hindu culture can count as pride, resulting in destructive, presumed hierarchies of proper or desirable mystical experience. However, a particular narrative form emerges that, while imposed by the interview process, felt very natural and amenable to the way that most participants framed their experiences and their commitments. Moments of profound spiritual experience for each person in this sample reoriented relationships with the world and propelled action. The way this relationship is articulated is always deeply embedded in sacred textual interpretations, ecclesiastical doctrine, or lived social traditions and practice. Yet at the same time, the patterns of connection between spirituality and social action often transcend the specificity of these scripts.

Seventy-six stories that vary across faith tradition, biographical experience, community ties, emotional involvement, and access to resources could easily produce an indecipherable maze of interesting but eclectic minutia. In the chapters that follow, I have sifted through these stories in a way that provides an interpretive account of the range of experience and action that I believe captures the nature of these narratives as a whole. Throughout these pages I present a smaller subset that more readily reveals their points of convergence. Opting for one story over another is a difficult task when each tale is so personally poignant. However, selecting a subset of interviews stylistically improves the narrative flow while also analytically highlighting the main points about spirituality and social action.

While much of this book will paint a somewhat rosy picture of spirituality as a salient social resource in bringing about change, I should also preface this analysis with a brief caveat. Many of these participants were engaged in a vision of social transformation that, while not often explicitly stated in political terms, could be characterized as progressive. These men and women are fighting for immigrant rights, a living wage for the working poor, healthcare for those who fall through the insurance gap, and AIDS counseling that embraces lesbian, gay, bisexual, straight, and transsexual populations. Of course, others were not. Spiritual experiences and religious institutions still clearly and frequently act as conservative forces in our society, in a general way by defending the status quo or by contributing to inaction and in a more specific way by implicating personal responsibility for what may be structural problems. Political reads on feeding the hungry, for example, differed in intentions across these interviews. Some interpreted this work as serving those who are structurally discriminated against by historical policy decisions and contemporary corporate political greed, while others saw it as serving those who need to be fed as a precursor to them pulling themselves up by their bootstraps and out of a position that their individual choices and personal sins had produced.

These positions are not mutually exclusive, but even so it is these latter interpretations that troubled me politically as a teen and young adult and that are still troublesome to my personal politics today. I admit that I am supportive of some applications of spirituality for action and to some degree those biases have affected the sample of people interviewed here. Yet what these interviewees did share, independent of their politics, was a spiritual connection to this work, and it is this spiritually informed social action that I want to highlight. Beliefs and mandates for acting for change in the world can be explicitly understood—"God told me directly in a dream to work alongside the homeless"—or implicitly inferred—"Islam at its core is about peace and compassion to others."

I hope this book will serve as a starting point for looking at spirituality as a social resource that can, and already is, applied in a variety of social settings for a variety of ends. It is not, however, intended to be read as a political statement about the particular applications of spirituality in social action and service.

Engaged Spirituality

Chapter 1   Bridging the Gap

The Split between Spirituality and Society

Oɴ ᴀɴ ᴜɴᴜsᴜᴀʟʟʏ ʜᴏᴛ California morning, I met with Rabbi Steven Jacobs inside the cool yet bustling administrative wing of his temple in the San Fernando Valley. A scan of his office walls confirmed Jacobs's reputation as a formidable veteran of the civil rights era. International press clippings, a photo-op with his close colleague the Reverend Jesse Jackson, and mementos from a recent excursion to Israel mark a lifetime of passionate commitment to social justice and peaceful resolution. Much like others I interviewed throughout the two years of collecting data for this project, Jacobs believes that human beings are cocreators with God and therefore equally responsible for making the universe a better place. As cocreators, Jacobs explained, humans work collaboratively in the world, looking out for each other and acknowledging their interconnectedness. Using a contemporary example based on the traditional Jewish spiritual practice of blessing the bread before a meal, Jacob explains:

> When I thank God for the food, and I'm talking about a *cocreator*, I'm talking about the Earth as the Lord's and you have nature and you plant and you grow wheat and you harvest your crop. God's not gonna harvest your crop. We're the ones who are taking God's earth and we're going to plant and we're going to harvest it. It's going to be our hands that make the bread. It's going to be our hands that put it on the table. So that's what I mean by cocreator. When I think of the people who put the food on my table—migrant workers and others— I'm very conscious of things that I think most people aren't because

they go to supermarkets and everything's packaged. They don't have any sense of the toil that went into that product—from whence it came. So I have a different sense and relationship to food and poor people. And the migrant workers and the strawberry—the people who pick the very food that goes onto our table. So I'm very aware of what it means to be a cocreator. It takes us as human beings to make God's influence real.

While relatively few respondents used the term "cocreator," the resonance with an active approach to spiritually motivated social change was resounding. Jacobs's spin on blessing the bread reveals the way in which casting the world in a spiritual light involves an internal shift in perspectives, in conscience, in practice, and in affective connection to social relationships that pattern the world. But to what degree does a spirituality of social justice already exist in the internal, interpersonal, and perhaps even corporate environments in which social change agents work each and every day? More fundamentally, what does this spirituality look like, how does it feel, how does it function, and how is it sustained? Just what do people mean when they talk about spirituality?

Spiritual but Not Religious

It is hard not to slip into talking about spirituality and religion in dichotomous ways. One might imagine Jacobs's blessing of the bread as a religious ritual, while his unique rearticulation of the migrant worker's role as a cocreator involves spiritual retooling. Once seen as complementary components of an integrated whole, religion and spirituality are increasingly interpreted as two distinct phenomena that may share occasional overlap but, for the most part, represent two diametrically opposed philosophies or feelings. The ubiquitous phrase "I'm spiritual, not religious" is most likely heartfelt for scores of Americans; however, it has become reified by detractors of spiritual individualism as a new foreboding standard, a cultural idiom of an individualized and rootless society.[1]

Robert Bellah and his colleagues in *Habits of the Heart* crystallize this perception around a new prototype dubbed "Sheilaism" after one of their interview subjects, Sheila Larson. From this perspective, church and community appear less important than experience and feeling.[2] Sheilaism soon became symptomatic of a social and cultural eclecticism in which spirituality was offered, perhaps more enticingly, in bookstores, coffee shops, television shows, and even diet fads. The gloomy prognosis was that institutional religion would wither.[3] When given these dichotomous options, it seems that spirituality would have slim potential for social change beyond its effects on religious competition and self-help hucksterism.[4] But can individuals really support such a nihilistic view of individualistic spiritual motivations among their fellow Americans? One empirically convincing answer is that they may not have to.

In a thorough evaluation of survey questions and responses, Penny Long Marler and C. Kirk Hadaway agree that social trends have, in part, produced a demonstrable shift from religiosity to spirituality.[5] Yet they also argue that the presumed sharp divide between spirituality and religion reported in quantitative survey data is a result of the way in which surveys were conducted and questions were listed (or omitted) across various surveys; in other words, the divide was more an effect of polling than of practice.[6] In fact, rather than religion and spirituality being polarized opposites on the same continuum, the more resent research suggests that the most religious Americans also tend to be the most spiritual.[7] The unbridgeable gap, then, is actually much smaller than earlier warnings suggest. Of course, while this does not discount the earlier assessments of what increased spirituality may mean, it does open the door to exploring the connections between the two and getting around the somewhat stultifying characterization of spirituality as overly narcissistic and private.

These findings ring true for each of the individuals that were interviewed here. As Jacobs's short insight points out, while they were spiritually adroit and often had uniquely tailored individual practices, they were also deeply attached to a longstanding religious community. Undoubtedly, spirituality for social change cannot be understood without an interpretive religious framework, nor can it be experienced exclusively within the space of sacred community alone. So, while this is a book primarily interested in spirituality, it also at times must take a close look at the religious communities in which spirituality was learned, fostered, and maintained with the help of a community of others.[8]

Defining Spirituality

If spirituality and religion overlap, and those who are spiritual tend to also be the same as those who are religious, what is the analytical difference between the two? How might one distinguish between spirituality and religion without artificially segregating them from each other? While undoubtedly these types of questions are batted around with much more frequency and eloquence in rabbinical schools, seminaries, and religion departments, a recently renewed debate is taking place in the social sciences, where some of the most significant definitional exploration is fomenting.[9] Summarizing a decade of conceptual work, spirituality is very often discussed as a "search for the sacred."[10] This phrase may sound overly simplistic, but it elegantly captures the core elements of a quest and of a transcendent order without adding too many doctrinal or social parameters. Of course, under this broad umbrella fall a diverse spectrum of practices, rituals, beliefs, and social contextual influences through which individuals negotiate a personal connection.

A more specifically active definition suggests that spirituality involves the "paths people take in their efforts to find, conserve, and transform the sacred in their lives."[11] Spirituality, as a search for the sacred, is not static but multi-dimensional, not only about finding but also about sustaining and sometimes creatively re-creating one's construction of the sacred. What is also compelling about this definition is the way spirituality is identified across binaries that previously coincided with the split between spirituality and religion, binaries such as individual and institutional or traditional and nontraditional.

Additionally, while nearly all of the current conceptual definitions of spirituality allow for or even expect a compatibility with religion, they also acknowledge the broad ways in which the sacred can be perceived in, or extended to include, otherwise mundane objects, interpersonal relationships, or even, as these cases here will attest, social structural patterns such as poverty or racial discrimination. As such, spirituality, whether found in the synagogue or on the beach at sunset, has seemingly limitless applications and sources. Spirituality, then, is the active and sometimes creatively fluid attempts by individuals and groups to connect with the sacred.

There are two other dimensions to consider as well. First, spirituality is often pragmatic. Robert Wuthnow, in his study of spirituality throughout the second half of the twentieth century, argued that practice-oriented spirituality—the spirituality of the day-to-day, disciplined, and focused attempts at connection with the sacred—salvages the individual quests from the often disparaging "seeker" phenomenon of contemporary religious homelessness.[12] Practice concretizes this wandering, selfish search in practical ways that give spiritual substance, beyond moods and whims, to the profound experiences of individuals in their everyday lives. Wuthnow's practice-oriented emphasis acknowledges that through this practice day-to-day life fuses with spirituality in ways that provide a greater integration of the sacred into mundane activities or spaces.

Second, spirituality is affective or emotionally felt. In certain ways, the affective component of spiritual connection parallels the faddishly popular argument for emotions as a form of intelligence. Spiritual intelligence allows for useful traits beyond the rational standards of traditional intellectual intelligence.[13] As with intelligence, emotional resources can be crafted and honed in ways that provide an extra edge in finding meaning and developing creative solutions to life's challenges. Emotions and feelings provide one additional link between individuals and their perceptions and actions within the social world around them.[14] This affective level can be surprisingly unexpected in practice and can produce surprisingly unexpected consequences in action.

All of these threads can be drawn together in ways that contribute to the understanding of socially active spirituality. First, spirituality is *transcendent,* or at least somehow directed toward communicating with something subjectively perceived to be sacred. Second, spirituality is an *active and ongoing* process that not only seeks out the sacred but also maintains and even changes it in one's life. Third, spirituality is *multidimensional*—traditional and/or creative, individual and/or collective. Fourth, spirituality is *unlimited* in its experience and is bound neither to time nor place nor objects, but rather is accessible in all aspects of life. Fifth, spirituality is *pragmatic*. It is both a resource and is resourceful, and as such it can be honed and utilized through active practice by individuals throughout their lives. Finally, spirituality is *emotional*, connecting individuals to their lived environments in deeply affective ways.

Defining Social Change

The remainder of this book is devoted to unpacking the connections between the flexibility and situatedness of spirituality as it relates to social change. For the purposes of this study, "social action," "social activism," "social change," and at times "social justice" are all colloquial shorthand terms that respondents used to refer to different levels of the same basic principle: service work in society—whether on the local, the institutional, the regional, the state, or the global level—that is strategically focused and at times mandated by deeply held transcendent values to bring about change in this world. The term "social action" is most often applied to the classically considered direct service work of volunteer agencies, such as feeding the hungry, serving the poor, and administering to the sick. Of course, these somewhat cliché phrases at times take on highly complex organizational casts when dealing with the complicated issues that face modern communities.

When discussing spirituality in more general terms, I will reference the spiritualities directed toward social action in the interviewees' lives, unless specifically noted. Spirituality directed toward social action is similar in many ways to other forms of spirituality, yet not all spirituality is engaged for social action and change—at least not in the way they are conceptualized here. In other words, I am not considering evangelical spiritualities that strictly profess that saving individual souls through conversion will change the world. Whether or not they are right, my interest falls upon those who act upon their spirituality explicitly to bring about changes in communities, in social or religious policies, in social services, or individually, even when it does not assume religious conversion. This form of spirituality is uniquely constructed through various social and subjective influences that merge a spirituality of the soul with a spirituality of the streets. Although the convergence of spirituality and the streets fits a contemporary social milieu, considering an earlier example grounds this analysis as more than a current trend.

The Bridge across the Rhine

On a bone-chilling, dreary December morning, I asked John and Denise Woods, both now in their eighties yet notably active, if they could tell me the story about their participation in rebuilding Europe following the Second World War. Gracious and keen to details, they happily agreed, telling this tale in tandem.

Shortly after the end of World War II, the Woods, not married at the time, joined a group of others who were going to Europe as part of a Moral Re-Armament (MRA) contingent. Their objective was to establish a center in Switzerland where a simple principle, founded by Frank Buchman, could be implemented. The principle was a populist combination of world affairs and individual spirituality that claimed that a change of heart was possible in any human being, out of which can flow consequential social, political, and economic developments. The MRA, in pursuit of this end, had acquired what had once been a posh resort in the Swiss town of Caux, nestled deep within in the Alps overlooking Lake Geneva. Neutral Switzerland was well suited as a common ground for the political, economic, and moral work that had to be hammered out between nations.

John Woods, a close aide and confidant to Buchman during this period, recalls that the movement was off to a good start except for the glaring omission of the Germans. Germans, of course, were prohibited from crossing their national borders immediately following the war. Beyond the legalities were the deep-seated animosities between the Germans and much of Western Europe. However, Buchman optimistically challenged this notion. As a consequence, MRA representatives were deployed to Germany to meet with the heads of the occupying forces to request a relaxation of the conventions that limited German travel in order to work toward European reconciliation in Caux. Somewhat surprisingly, the MRA contingent returned with an approval directly from George C. Marshall, the U.S. Secretary of State and architect of the Marshall Plan. Marshall was well aware of the work being done by the MRA and, as John Woods conveys, believed in the unfolding amalgam of spiritually motivated politics. Subsequently, for the first time since the end of the war, Germans left their country.

The tension as well as the potential was dramatic and palpable. Germans now came face to face with Europeans of all stripes who had stood up to the unrelenting Nazi destruction of their hometowns, their friends, and their families. Individuals could express themselves openly to their captors and their executioners, but, as might be expected, this was not easily achieved in straightforward, unmitigated conversation. Emotional buffers and bridges were required. Keeping in mind that reconciliation was the first step to rebuilding a European community, the MRA employed creative techniques beyond collective and private dialogue. Musicals and plays, for example, told the stories of loss and shame from various points of view, thereby complicating the process of individual blame and blanket accusations.[15]

One of the major mediating techniques Buchman contributed was an introspective, meditative spiritual practice that he learned years ago at Oxford. Resonating with Quaker traditions, Woods recalls, Buchman held to a basic premise that there was a voice inside each person that is of God (here loosely defined). Buchman suggested to his guests, "Take time to listen to that voice and if you believe in God you can experiment. Listen to the deepest thing in your own heart and ask for truth about yourself and act on it in a constructive way."

The reflective reconciliation played out in a particularly striking way with Ingrid Law, a friend of Denise Woods, and, in John's words, "a great, very courageous resistance leader herself in the war." Law was the leader of the Socialist Women of France in 1946 when the MRA was seeking participants, and she took part wholeheartedly, Denise said, until it was announced that the German envoys were on their way. Denise recalls, "Ingrid just froze. There was no question in her mind that she was going to stay in the building with Germans in it. [Ingrid] said, 'If I heard that language spoken I would vomit.'" Denise was taken aback by the response that Ingrid had, admitting that she never experienced such a reactive and visceral depth of feeling about a group of people. With short notice, Ingrid packed her things and approached Buchman to say her goodbyes. "He looked at her and said, 'Madam, how do you expect to rebuild Europe and leave out the Germans?'" At this point, Ingrid "turned on her heels," retreated to her bedroom, and didn't come out for three days. Each day, Denise brought her dinner on a tray, which Ingrid accepted through a crack in her door, leaving the dirty dishes in the corridor when she finished.

During these tense days with her friend, and for a long time before that, Denise had the practice of praying first thing in the morning before she did anything else. Her practice was conversational and focused upon setting the priorities of the day based upon this spiritual reflection. During her prayer, she finally addressed Ingrid's three-day seclusion. "The thought I had that morning was—this is the day to put before her this burning question; would you like to meet a German? So I trusted [that feeling] . . . . I think that helps in the electricity of an occasion. You're not forcing something but you're turning a light on." Denise, motivated by what she called an "inner sense," knocked on Ingrid's door and asked, "I wonder if you'd like to meet a German today?" To which Ingrid simply replied, "Oui." Denise continued, "Shall I arrange it?" Ingrid, "Oui." Denise prodded further, "Shall I arrange it for lunch?" Ingrid, "Oui." Denise turned, elated, saying, "We were committed."

When lunchtime arrived, Denise approached Ingrid's room and the door finally opened. They walked to the dining hall, where they gathered their food, cafeteria style on trays, and proceeded to a small table in the outdoor garden, where a German woman and her translator were seated, waiting. Ingrid did not touch her food; instead, she leaned forward on the table and said, "I had to speak to you today. I had to find a way to talk to you because somewhere I've got to get free of my hatred. It's too much." All at once, Ingrid's story poured out. Sickening details about the torture of her son by German soldiers and the crippling malnutrition of her two youngest children emerged accusatorily. Denise recoiled, at least internally, at the bottled-up anger that understandably erupted from Ingrid. Denise, glancing around the table, asked herself, "My goodness, what have we done? We've subjected this German woman, who's barely arrived, to the intense hatred of a French woman. That isn't fair. She just got here." But the German woman sat stoically, absorbing the intensity of the moment and the rage of a mother whose children had been unimaginably harmed.

When Ingrid finished, the German woman, through her interpreter, quietly added, "Well I'd like to tell you something about myself. My husband took part on the plot on Hitler's life and, as you know, that failed. But the men who took part in the plot were killed and he was one of them. And I'm alone in the world, raising our two daughters, and since coming here I've had to face the fact that we in Germany did not resist in time nor did we resist on a scale that would have made a difference . . . . And I can only ask for your forgiveness." The table fell silent.

Eventually the women rose and went farther out into the garden overlooking the pristine Alpine lake, where they could get some privacy from the activities of the conference. What happened there shocked Denise. She recalls, "All of the sudden, this Marxist, Socialist friend of mine, I heard her saying, 'I think if we prayed about it, God would free me from my hatred.'" Ingrid began to pray very simply. "Oh Father, free me from my hatred for the sake of the future." While the conversation up until that point had all transpired through translations from German to French and back again, the German woman joined Ingrid, praying in flawless French. She had understood the dialogue in French all along but was unwilling to speak it until that moment of prayer. Denise explained that throughout her life Ingrid would always refer to that moment in the garden, when the Socialist French feminist prayed with the German, as the moment at which the bridge across the Rhine was built—and it never broke.

Midcentury Moderns

As this powerful story illustrates, the natural affiliation between individual spiritual experiences and social change is by no means a recent development.[16] Across millennia and throughout cultures, radical social shifts have been the products of divinely interpreted revelations or collectively defended definitions of the transcendent "Truths" about the universe. Even within the presumably "secular" twentieth century, when conventional social wisdom championed modernism's reign and rationality characteristically shaped the United States' domestic technological and scientific development, the Woodses' perspective on European reconstruction reveals a very different trajectory and set of guiding principles that set the texture of social and political affairs.

When I began conceptualizing how this book about individual spirituality and social change would open, I never expected that I would turn to the Woodses. However, I feel as if they lift us out of our own peculiar time and space and help cleanse the palate of our contemporary assumptions about the nature of spirituality and its connection to social change. Through their story we are able to step back from the often cynical, new age, or individualistic stereotypes of contemporary spirituality and look more closely at the social contributions of spirituality, to ask if and how these might still be at work today.

To use a newly conceived label, the Woodses are part of the Greatest Generation. As a whole, this cohort is characterized as deeply sacrificial for family and nation, courageously fighting a noble war or selflessly contributing in other ways at home. Symbolically they collectively personify and embody the staid prosperity that followed the hard times of the Great Depression. They are reconstructed through our mediated memory nostalgically and monolithically as conventional white suburban families that upheld consensual American values such as hard work and community.[17] We do not often think of this Greatest Generation as a spiritual generation in today's terms. Religious, yes, but spiritual, no.[18]

While religious affiliations were strong, members of the Greatest Generation, broadly speaking, were not known as being expressive with their personal feelings or indulgent with their experiences. Tom Brokaw's best-selling book

The Greatest Generation set as its sole objective the documentation of personal stories by the aging members of this generation, particularly stories of war and sacrifice.[19] These stories have had an impact among family members who were often unable to draw out emotional recollections from their own parents, grandparents, aunts, or great uncles.

The same may be suggested of stories of intimately personal spiritual experiences.[20] For many of the people that I interviewed, their religious upbringing was very formulaic—a social duty performed on Saturdays or Sundays or in the form of a prayer before meals. Few had deeply expressive or individually compelling experiences growing up and fewer still witnessed, either in person or through stories, the connection between spiritual experience and social change.

However, the Woodses' story points to the real possibility that a socially directed spirituality was present among an active and influential set of individuals during the middle part of the century. Not only was it present, for some it was actively applied to efforts of great proportion. That a form of spirituality in the 1940s might be used by a French feminist Socialist in reconciling the unimaginable pains the Germans inflicted on her family and her country was striking, although not completely surprising to me, when I first heard this story. After all, spiritual experiences have been bubbling up throughout the history of the United States, and it stands to reason that other cyclical patterns, whether publicly acknowledged or not, effect change in other times and other places as well.[21]

After two years of listening to stories and experiences that span decades of social service work, I came to realize that the Woodses' story was by no means an anachronistic anomaly or simply a creature of its time, when civic participation and responsibility was high and spirituality occasionally found its way into this endeavor. Clearly, the remarkably unique time and place of this story greatly affected the experiential details of spirituality, as well as its contribution to the work of social transformation. Yet if we think of applied spirituality—or "engaged spirituality," as I will refer to it throughout this book—conceptually the Woodses remind us, or at the very least raise the question, about the private/public dichotomy of religion and the active role of spirituality as a motivation and catalyst for change.

A Spiritual Resource

Apart from the seemingly broad social and historical shifts in spirituality and religion that mark reawakenings or organizational schisms in religious institutions, it is equally important to understand spirituality in its everyday manifestations that incrementally foster change locally and, at times, globally. From this perspective, spirituality is an individual and collective social resource that, while shaped and molded by social and cultural contexts, exists in the hearts and minds of some people in ways that are similar to other cultural tools used to make sense in the world and to make choices about how to act within that world. Spirituality is more aptly considered an internal yet socially shaped variable that affects individual motivations and creative innovations in actively striving for social change.[22] At times throughout history, spirituality has been constituted and wielded as a mighty tool, as was the case with the outstanding revolutionary figures of the twentieth century. More often, the effects of this spiritual tool have been local and the efforts not always so dramatically successful, although no less profound.

Spiritual Markets

If we consider spirituality as a social resource, contemporary contexts provide a rich backdrop for accumulating these resources. One common contemporary metaphor compares the diverse religious landscape and the competition between Christian churches (and even non-Christian organizations) to a marketplace where rationally informed shoppers browse around until they find what religion they want to consume.[23] Consumption of religion from this point of view is rationally determined; the costs and benefits of attending one religious congregation are weighed much like any other decision that we make in everyday life, such as where to send our children to school or which medical insurance plan would best serve our needs.[24] Religion, in this case, is a far cry from the irrational and overly emotional delusions that early social theorists suggested. For some, religion in this marketplace becomes trivialized, reduced to whims and fads alongside any number of other lifestyle accessories.[25] Religion as an institution becomes a commodity in the service of a therapeutic society, interested primarily in self-development, expressive individualism, and a narcissistic quest for personal satisfaction.[26] Self-help groups, popular psychology, and spiritual products become booming industries in a society that continually seeks to reinvent itself one person at a time.[27]

The residual effects of this cultural trend toward therapeutic consumption spill throughout society as spirituality becomes a cultural currency. We can see this in the marketing of tell-all autobiographies, the hawking of confessional talk shows, and even in the advertising of political campaigns; all emphasize openness, sharing, and publicly exposing the wounds of our lives in an effort to heal them with the balm of full disclosure. When former President Bill Clinton released an autobiography detailing his childhood as well as his personal and public life while in office, it was touted as the most intimately revealing self-examination of any past president. Clinton was both derided and championed as a creature of his times, a new introspective public figure who discussed personal demons openly. To his critics, this was nothing but self-indulgent egoism, while his supporters credited his vulnerability and forthrightness.[28] Not surprisingly, in an act of synchronicity that illustrates the overlap of this trend between politics, media, and commodities, one of the former president's first stops on his book tour was the Oprah Winfrey show, a show that at its apex regularly dedicated portions of the hour to "Finding Your Spirit." In a market where competing daytime television programs include a show in which a self-proclaimed "medium" speaks to deceased relatives of audience members, Winfrey's introspective feel-good spirituality more closely defines the cultural, and now political, mainstream.

The spirituality of therapeutic pop culture, if we think back to the multidimensional and pragmatic aspects of our working definition, cannot be thought of as universally trivialized or universally revitalizing. While the question "What would Buffy do?" shouts out one particularly contemporary meaning,[29] the dangling keychain question of "What would Jesus do?" is equally as telling of the way in which spirituality is both a faddishly individual fashion accessory and an individual imperative to constantly remind oneself of the spiritual considerations in life's choices.[30] Whether Christian punk rockers, primetime demons, or Deepak Chopra's latest best seller are discussed jokingly, derisively, or concertedly, contemporary spirituality seems to be an unavoidable part of the popular culture detritus about which all of us can contribute our own two cents.

Confessions and self-reflections—both secular and spiritual—are part of the ubiquitous backdrop in contemporary culture and have created an atmosphere that allows for and perhaps even encourages a very public exploration of the experiential, emotional, and spiritual elements of life. The stories that I have collected illuminate one small corner of this broader arena and give voice to the ongoing ways in which a very different, critical spirituality has always been part and parcel of the American religious, civic, and popular experience.[31] Although hard to imagine from this current milieu, openly expressing that spiritual component was—and sometimes still is—seen as unbecoming, inappropriately intimate, or a matter to be relegated to private and even hidden moments of life.[32] Yet the current expressive backdrop of mainstream culture allows for greater empirical exploration of the ways in which spiritual connections are utilized in everyday life.

Shifting Spiritual Borders

In the incredibly hot and dry eastern communities of greater Los Angeles, I met up with Werner Marroquin, an organizing member of La Asociacion Nacional Slavadorena Americana, or SANA. SANA was created as a civic organization among Salvadorians living in southern California but, much more than that, Marroquin envisions SANA as a cultural repository of Salvadorian art, music, poetry, and dance, as well as a place to sustain the stories of migrants who fled the civil war at home. He explains, "We want to be able to be reminding our community that once we were persecuted. Once we were hungry. Once we were cold, and there were good hands that opened their hearts to us, and feed us, and treat us well, and gave us a space to sleep, and gave us food to eat." This history not only provides a sense of rootedness to his children and others growing up in the United States, and increasingly being born here, it also provides a moral lesson. Marroquin adds, "I think it's important for my kids to know that they were persecuted once and they have to be sensitive to future generations of immigrants, to future conflicts that are going to come, because I don't think they're going to end. And they have to have a sense of solidarity."

While having one foot still planted metaphorically in El Salvador, Marroquin is firmly committed to civic participation in his new home. He intimately knows the struggles of living underground in the United States from the days before he became a citizen. But being a citizen does not mean renouncing this past identity. Marroquin says, "We don't want to jump [into being American] with no first name or last name and with not a face and with not a history. We want to jump in there by saying who we are."

A large part of who Marroquin is involves his spiritual ties to the blended identity of the national and transcendent aspects being Salvadorian. Although Marroquin is Protestant, he feels a keen affiliation with the Catholic culture that is inseparable from his sense of Salvadorian identity. Part of this identity is symbolically represented through the World Savior statue of Jesus that stands in the national cathedral in San Salvador. Marroquin sees this as neither Catholic nor exclusively Salvadorian, but rather as a representation with which all Christians can affiliate. However, the iconic role of this statue as a Salvadorian representation of both national and spiritual identity inspired a group of patrons in Los Angeles to fund a replica of the statue, hand crafted in El Salvador. When it was complete, the Salvadorian artisans said they would ship it to Los Angeles by air. Yet Marroquin asked, "What would Jesus do in our times?" He continued, "Would he take an airplane or would he walk a path that thousands of sisters and brothers have taken?" The answer to that question by the migrant and religious community in Los Angeles was resounding. He would walk.

Marroquin took part in the overland journey to bring the replica of the World Savior to Los Angeles across the path that migrants and displaced Salvadorians traveled not that long ago. This, Marroquin said, would be the migrants' vindication. When the statue finally arrived, SANA planned a massive event in a downtown park. Thousands attended. Cultural identity blended with spiritual feelings of awe and the blossoming of a new form of civic community that Marroquin had envisioned all along. Not only was this a moment of raising self-esteem within the Salvadorian community, Marroquin said, "it reminds us of the work that we need to do, the challenges that we also oppose, the bitterness of our human condition that we need to be striving [against] every day. It's all kinds of specific and concrete things." When asked what his experience of this event felt like spiritually, Marroquin replied, "there's an energy that glows and nobody can escape it . . . . The energy is very positive and kind of cleans you out."

Marroquin, in trying to establish a new network of civic participation among Salvadorians now living in America, utilized a spirituality of in-betweeness. This spirituality, while drawing upon Catholic traditions in El Salvador, resonated beyond that strictly religious group as a potent symbol of nation, of community, and of common experience and produced a new sacred effervescence within the community. The statue pulled in symbolic representations that were not seen as gross commodities or secular tricks to attract attendance. As Marroquin claimed, "It's no longer, 'Ah, this [statue] is just a piece of wood.' That's the cynical piece in our hearts." Instead, this piece of wood transformed into a new representation of past and future, of old and new, of spirituality and civic society, and the broader social historical trends of war and migration that continually overlap with spiritual and religious change. The qualitatively distinguishing addition of this diffuse spirituality is both personally affective as well as communally integrative, fostering community bonds and civic engagement, as well as promoting social change.

Feeling Connected

If, as Marroquin's example illustrates, the spiritual and the civic are inseparable in the ways they are lived, why is it that they are often discussed separately? In many ways—as with the discussion of religion and spirituality—some find it easier to think in specifics, in blacks and whites and binary codes, about how the world or how spirituality actually works. Perhaps this is because of the simplicity of this design, or, more likely, it is because so much of our world has been, and to a large degree still is, interpreted along a series of gross distinctions. Dichotomies such as culture and religion, sacred and profane, individual and collective, rational and nonrational, public and private, even male and female have shaped and, for many people, constrained the direction and extent of spiritual experiences.

One compelling binary tension that has received attention throughout the past generation is the private versus public role of religion in political and civic life. This distinction is particularly salient when considering stories of spiritually engaged social action. There is a notable and somewhat schizophrenic disjuncture between spirituality and the public sphere that is affected primarily by modern public discourse—of secular governments, intellectuals, and religious bodies. There are sound reasons for remaining cautious of overlapping church and state sympathies. Yet while there is a considerable amount of attention paid to maintaining a divisional purity between religious spheres and the sphere of civil society, underneath this discourse the connections continue to be made both by individuals and organizations alike. In fact, the frameworks that establish a binary model of secular society versus spirituality simply do not fit the experiences of the people that I spoke with or the ways in which their spirituality was acted upon. Instead, spirituality, as an individual resource, is better equipped to navigate and negotiate both miniscule and monumental decisions.

The individuals interviewed in this study engaged in subtle yet profound ongoing actions within their communities that produced a society that, on one level, retained the veneer of a division between religion and society while, on another level, actively pursued connections between the two. SANA, for example, hosted an event that through some eyes may have appeared profoundly religious. Yet Marroquin's assessment of the role of the World Savior replica was that, while it clearly centered around religious symbolism, it was inseparable from the civic community that took root around the event and could be read as a social event by community members of all faiths. These interpretations vary, but the distinct split between what is religious and what is social is no longer clear.

The French theorist of science Bruno Latour addressed this split, cautioning that as modernists we still try to get the world to fit into an empirically readable order that privileges binaries and artificial distinctions between the natural world and human-made culture.[33] Spirituality and God coexist nicely in this modern framework, partitioned away and having little implication for either science or social and political cultures.[34] Yet by doing so, the multiple examples of social processes or outcomes that do not fit these strict typologies—"hybrids," as he put it—get pushed underground, where they proliferate outside of our social purview. When these anomalies or hybrids eventually reemerge, they seem inexplicable. Elements of spirituality or God that do not act according to a dichotomous framework do not disappear, but rather continue to develop in ways that are surprising or even shocking when they surface. New "tribalisms," particular definitions of militant jihad, intelligent design, or, more broadly, socially engaged spiritualities are all examples of hybrids that do not fit within an overarching Western, modern approach that keeps God at bay within a private metaphysics. Since these hybrids do not fit, they must be publicly wrestled with when they finally emerge. Rather than accepting these hybrids as normal realities, individuals condense them into their modern framework by denouncing them as primitive, regressive, or sometimes even superstitious.[35]

In fact, many of the people interviewed for this project understood this framework intimately and subsequently tailored their public presentations in ways that downplayed their spiritual motivations. Even so, connections were fused whether they were publicly expressed or not and remained personally profound all the while. Ingrid Law, for example, surprised Denise Woods when she unexpectedly revealed that she drew significantly upon Catholic reserves in ways that affected her interpersonal reconciliation in the hotel at Caux and ultimately altered her future political understandings of a newly emerging Germany and the role that she should take in that collaborative reconstruction. Still today, for the most part, one can only speculate about the extent to which spirituality functions as a motivation for participation in or instigation for progressive social change—a particularly timely hybrid for examination.

While there may be only a small but growing academic interest in this connection, the lack of analysis does not imply that such a connection is not occurring but instead may suggest that it is occurring subterraneously. The research questions in this study and the participants' individual reports of experiences were often self-edited in ways that pulled spirituality out from the accepted and expected research model. However, by listening to these stories over the course of two years, I learned a great deal about the synergy between experience and tradition, between feeling and history, between innovation and consistency, between individual insight and collective efforts, in the broadest of terms, between spirituality and religion.[36] More to the point, no one felt quite comfortable specifying spirituality without reference to a variety of other elements of everyday life, from religion, to family, to work, to, surprisingly often, traffic.

As the boundaries of our society begin to blur, the ongoing subterraneous connections between spirituality and social action reemerge publicly in creative and examinable ways. If we acknowledge that spirituality can be more than just private, individualized narcissism with little connection to social life—and it seems much of the concern over contemporary spirituality is actually a veiled concern for individualistic spirituality—then, as these preliminary vignettes reveal, spirituality must also be considered in its hybrid form as a social, shared, and potentially consequential resource for social change.

Inspiring a Change

When turning more directly to social change, it should be kept in mind that this discussion of spirituality does not deny or preclude the organizational strengths of religion. Although the focus will be on spirituality, the contributions of religion have slipped substantively into the academic vernacular for understanding the way in which institutional agents usher in social change or stabilize social equilibrium and are complementary to this argument.

The civil rights movement was one notable episode of dramatic social change in which religious organizations played a central role. Aldon Morris, in his rich chronicling of the movement, suggested that the Southern Christian Leadership Conference acted in many ways as a decentralized network of southern black churches.[37] As such, it had at its disposal the various organizational resources that churches as social institutions provide, resources such as church halls, communication networks, and trained leaders. These were invaluable assets in the successful mobilization of the participants and the economic feasibility of thrown-together volunteers who needed physical spaces in which to meet and social networks through which to solicit support.[38]

Yet spirituality infused this process. Beyond the organizational resources such as leadership networks or meeting halls, churches had a significant amount of moral authority within society that conferred legitimacy upon the movement as a whole as well as the civil disobedience that movement volunteers orchestrated and implemented throughout the South. The perceived transcendence of religion that leaders so powerfully conjured up and that traditional hymns so gently impart—in other words, the spiritually felt component of religion—sets religious indignation apart from the legal-rational, institutional authority of jurisprudence and politics. For those who take this transcendence as real, religion can both stabilize and legitimize some actions while standing in judgment of others in ways that prompt or even necessitate change. This transcendent mandate was something the Reverend Martin Luther King Jr. was well aware of, and his personal charisma carried this religious call in ways that could capture the religious and the nonreligious alike. In the revival-style meetings that followed in the footsteps of the social gospel movement generations earlier, King preached an inner-worldly, moral command for social engagement, suggesting that "any religion that professes to be concerned with the souls of men [*sic*] and is not concerned with the slums that damn them, the economic conditions that strangle them, and the social conditions that cripple them is a dry-as-dust religion."[39]

The transcendent components of the civil rights movement were particularly consequential on an individual basis, in part, because of the charismatic dexterity of King for inspiring personal passions, but also (especially for many of the white participants who had discovered their calling for social justice issues) because it was the first time in their lives that religion had been connected to a dramatic confrontation with society rather than simply a private and subtle confirmation of the status quo. Religion, through spiritual experience, became much more internally charged and externally active for these individuals.

Just as the emotional energies that religion at times elicits can be used collectively to mobilize mass constituencies and create a sense of moral authority and shared identity, the same may be true on the individual level. It is this individual resource that will be explored here as motivation for, sustainability in, and creative innovation of social change.[40] In fact, it has been suggested that out of these spiritual experiences, individuals may interpret a sense of efficacy in their efforts, an elevated confidence, or a feeling of personal control over external circumstances that is qualitatively different from other forms of experience.[41]

A sense of efficacy or control is a crucial component in understanding why people decide whether or not to take action over a particular issue. Both apathy and engagement often hinge upon the perception of efficacy. As mentioned earlier, shifts in contemporary society have created a perceived narcissistic individualism that has led to the fragmentation of self-involved spirituality. In fact, it has been argued that Americans do not participate in civic life to the same degree as past generations.[42] Interestingly, the two casualties of the so-called self-indulgent turn in culture—spirituality and civic participation—may actually benefit from each other in discernable and regenerative ways.

First, spirituality has not been fully explored as a significant spark for the shift in perspective toward personal and collective efficacy within social movement analyses or social change in general. Yet this is crucial for success. Frances Piven and Richard Cloward, in their contemporary classic, *Poor People's Movements,* argue that "the social arrangements that are ordinarily perceived as just and immutable must come to be seen as unjust and mutable."[43] When individuals can turn this corner in their heads, new actions, previously thought untenable or out of reach, now appear quite achievable and even necessary.[44] Seen from this perspective alone, the creative potential of spirituality for social action can be read as a distinct subjective resource that, while often embedded within other institutional religious resources, requires additional attention as a significant variable in its own right.

On the other hand, while individual spiritual experience can spark the vision of a better society, acting upon this experience confers an authenticity of action itself and expunges doubts and uncertainties. Just as the blurred dichotomies discussed above have allowed for various hybrids such as spiritually informed social action to reemerge both publicly and academically, they also produce destabilizing questions. Today's social and, to an extent, existential struggle may be with what Anthony Giddens terms "radical doubt." Humans question various aspects of their previously taken-for-granted social knowledge, such as religious institutional doctrine and history, and their understanding of the world becomes a set of hypotheses rather than known Truths.[45] For some, this may result in apathy about civic or religious participation, while for others it opens up possibilities for the newly directed social action that can provide actual embodiments of a more stable rather than destabilized ontological grounding.

In the stories that follow, spirituality and social change are intricately intertwined and mutually reinforcing. Social service, social action, and civic participation that promotes change motivates, sustains, and transforms individual spirituality, just as spirituality motivates, sustains, and transforms social change.

Engaging Spirituality

Transformative spiritual moments are difficult to classify along commonly expressed differences such as public/private, religious/secular, or individual/collective. In my estimation, they are all of these or, looking at it from another perspective, they are none of them. Indeed, very few interviewees felt comfortable using such confining distinctions. Spiritual experiences with social mandates shoot right through the center of these categories. By using the term "engaged spirituality," I hope to capture the holistic ways in which these transformations were felt. Rather than simply constructing a neologism that blurs boundaries between binary distinctions, I suggest that these points of origin, or transformative moments in which engaged spirituality crystallizes in peoples' experiences, comprise border positions that allow for an integration of each of these pairs. Spiritual experience for social action sits at the intersections where the public becomes private or the religious spills onto the secular. In other words, profound experiences offer points at which individuals can move across the borders that artificially separate these distinctions. Spirituality has always allowed for individual mediation, appropriation, and at times improvisation that collective, traditional, religious institutions by their very constitution constrain or at least impinge upon. Engaged spirituality functions similarly, permeating the boundaries and allowing for creative innovation for negotiating between private experience and public action or between spiritual transcendence and social praxis.

The perceived bifurcation of spirituality and religion has produced a divide that pits private spirituality against many other social or productive elements of modern life, including civic participation and working for social change. In other words, religions do social services and spirituality does the soul. This divide is not completely an artificial one, but it is an overstated one. Whereas religion is primarily collective, public, and shared, spirituality is simultaneously collective *and* individual, public *and* private, shared *and* internally intimate. Spirituality is neither one nor the other of these pairings, but both. It is this fluid quality that, if understood as an already occurring, individually nurtured social resource, has vast potential socially and analytically.

Throughout this book, I will use the term "engaged spirituality" to encapsulate these connections. In the most literal sense, engaged spirituality is the social juncture between the transcendent, active and ongoing, multidimensional, unlimited, emotional, and pragmatic aspects of spirituality that motivate actions for social change. In contrast to a solely personal spiritual quest of self-exploration, engaged spirituality is always directed outward with the intention of making a discernable difference in the social world.

Admittedly, as the members of SANA point out, spirituality is always caught up in its social context. However, it is not a cloak for more fundamental issues such as immigration patterns, denominational definitions, ethnic affiliation, or nationality. Interpretations of spirituality are shaped and constituted by individual choices, social structures, and transcendent experiences of the social world that surrounds it—including religious institutions, politics, and economics. At the same time, spirituality remains an indisputable, although sometimes unrecognized, force for acting upon that complex world in creative and passionate ways, ultimately affecting one's identity as well as one's ongoing choices and actions.

| | Biography, Behavior, |
| Chapter 2 | and Belief |

The Sources of Spirituality

IT IS A REMARKABLY short walk southwest from the trendy tourist hub of Union Square in San Francisco to an adjoining neighborhood that has been dubbed the "killzone" by local media. This six-block area in the heart of the Tenderloin district has more homicides per year than any other neighborhood in San Francisco. The ringing of the trolley cars is replaced by police sirens. The designer shops and historic hotels only blocks away are abruptly exchanged for strings of liquor stores and one-room residential hotels, where tattered drapes billow from several open windows overhead. Behind the doors of these inexpensive hotels, many residents are dually diagnosed with more than one mental and/or physical disorder. Back on the street, prostitution, drug use, and drug dealing are conducted in broad daylight, bringing along high rates of associated petty and violent crime. Sadly, HIV rates also skyrocket, and the Tenderloin claims the desperate distinction of being the most heavily impacted area for HIV infection in San Francisco.

The thirty linear blocks that make up the entire Tenderloin neighborhood are home to an incredibly diverse mix of approximately twenty-five thousand people. Many Southeast Asians settled in the area as immigrants or refugees throughout the 1980s and most of the children of the Tenderloin come from these households. The white population tends to be elderly, predominantly living in one-room apartments or hotels and participating in communal meal plans. Latino and African Americans make up equal parts of the community and a small number of Native Americans, Pakistanis, Indians, and Palestinians

complete the mix. Many others are homeless, driven out from the more affluent areas of the city as the gentrification of these other neighborhoods attempts to sweep away the less aesthetic and less conscionable reminders of
urban life. In the Tenderloin, the common ground among such a diverse population is that they are all equally poor. While many others come for the day
to engage in illegal activity, few who live here have made the choice to live
here—few except the Reverend Glenda Hope.

For the past thirty years, Glenda Hope has made her home among the
families and the elderly, the refugees and the prostitutes. Hers is not a story of
judgmental missionary zeal or handing down charity from a lofty vantage point.
Hope is an active and integrated member of a community with whom she has
built a life, although, admittedly, not a life she would have envisioned for herself years earlier.

Glenda Hope grew up in Georgia with the career goal of someday teaching physical education. Years of athletic training toward that end, however,
took their toll, straining her knees and refocusing her goals to something less
physically strenuous. While these career shifts were taking place and Hope
struggled with choosing a new path, she was also shifting her denominational
affiliation. Raised a Southern Baptist, Hope became a member of the Presbyterian Church while attending college. These overlapping changes converged
when Hope received a religious calling during her senior year to serve her newfound church after graduation. She explained feeling an inner sense of clarity
to pursue a church vocation within the Presbyterian Church, although she had
little idea what form that would take. During the 1950s, the Presbyterian
Church did not ordain women, and Hope admits that she had never met a female Presbyterian minister, or a female minister of any religious background
for that matter.

Within this cultural framework, the option of pastoring a church never
entered her mind. Instead, Hope attended a seminary in Virginia, where she
earned a master's degree in Christian education, and then returned to Georgia,
where she spent several years working as the director of Christian Education
at a large parish outside of Atlanta. Working in a parish setting was never
something that Hope thought she would like, yet she remembers being "totally
startled how much I really enjoyed being there." In 1965 the Presbyterian
Church began ordaining women. Fueled by her newfound passion for ministry
work, Hope enrolled in the San Francisco Theological Seminary with the
ambitious intention of getting a Master's of Divinity degree and then settling
down at the helm of a local parish.

Hope completed her ministry training and coursework rather easily and
even got married along the way. Now all she needed was a job offer from a

parish and the Presbyterian Church would finalize her ordination. However, while the administrative body of the Presbyterian church was ready to ordain women at this time, local parishes were not. There was little masking the issue, Hope recalls. Although today such blatant comments would never be made so explicitly, in 1969 Hope heard, "You've got everything we want, except you're the wrong gender." She recounts, "It never occurred to me that there would be people who wouldn't want me because of my gender. I mean, if God wanted me, why wouldn't they?" Today, Hope looks back at her response and realizes it was rather naive considering the sociohistorical context. However, that re-action foreshadowed the innocent yet headstrong way she would engage her spirituality to shake up social conventions and restrictive barriers for herself and others throughout her life.

Eventually, the prestigious Old First Presbyterian Church in San Francisco extended a half-time call and the now-ordained Rev. Glenda Hope began work-ing within a special ministry for young adults. After three years in congrega-tional youth ministry, however, Hope became convinced that God was calling her to reach out to the unchurched young adults. Realizing that this would not happen within a traditional parish, Hope resigned from Old First Presbyterian and started the Young Adult Network on the edge of the Tenderloin. Along with their house church, the open doors of the new ministry offered cheap but good coffee and a variety of homemade treats. With little other effort, the res-idents of the Tenderloin quickly came to them. Their open-door hospitality beckoned the homeless and the poor who were beginning to characterize the neighborhood.

Today, that coffeehouse ministry is the multifaceted San Francisco Net-work Ministries and is often the first and last door through which many in the Tenderloin find help and respect. Founded and still under the direction of Rev-erend Hope, the San Francisco Network Ministries encompasses a vast array of services, including SafeHouse, a residential program with twenty-four-hour staff offering counseling, educational programs, health care, vocational skills, and money management; the Listening Post, a drop-in ministry at the Am-bassador Hotel for people living with HIV or full-blown AIDS; family residence programs, in conjunction with Asian Neighborhood Design, offering thirty-eight apartments for the working poor; and a sixteen-hundred-square-foot computer training center, a community center for email connections and job skills training. Hope's groundbreaking work includes the first and only street-access AIDS clinic in the Tenderloin and the first program for transgendered people who are HIV positive. This innovative entity that Hope and her staff designed, implemented, and organized has now, in Hopes words, "spun off to be its own thing." Hope clarifies, "We're not empire building, we're model building—getting things started [and then] cutting them loose or giving them over to somebody else and then we do something nobody's doing."

The lifelong social commitment that Reverend Hope's story conveys stems from her similarly lifelong spiritual commitment, which stays strong through emotional resonance with everyday activities. In fact, Hope's social and spiritual commitments are indistinguishably fused in her ongoing partnerships that she maintains with her community and the common vision that they share for a better future. Similar local stories of committed lay and religious leadership— although of varying degrees—are common across neighborhoods throughout the country. Yet these stories often go unarticulated, unquestioned, or unexamined. Even during times when the status of religious leadership has slipped considerably among pockets of the general public, alternative examples of Catholic nuns running an abused women's shelter or Muslims operating a food bank might, without contradiction, produce an internal reasoning that "this is what religious people do." This assumption is derived from individual experiences of directly seeing religion in action or indirectly learning about religion through local media or word of mouth. Indeed, this assumption is a popularly touted, underlying basis for political agendas supporting charitable choice.[1]

However, embedded ideas or coded implications of religious service in American public life leave the origins and motivations of certain actions unexamined. If that is what religious people do, then the question of why they do it is left unasked; the answer is tautologically assumed in the statement itself. In this loop, religion becomes a diffuse and sufficient reason for social service. But that misses the biographical, contextual, and organizational complexities found among religious leaders involved in social service activities as well as the spiritual motivations that guide many others who are not in formal religious positions and do not publicly disclose their spiritual experiences in social or secular settings. Moreover, it does not address why some religious individuals or institutions engage in social change while others do not. When listening to the stories here, it is in these nuances where spirituality plays its hand.

When asked directly about how, when, and where these social and spiritual commitments fused together, some of the people I interviewed had pat and practiced testimonies that detailed points of individual transformation or potent transcendent communion. Others wove more convoluted stories of childhood impressions, family relationships, political awakenings, or community experiences. A few concertedly reflected on the origins of these motivations and uncovered deeper influences that they had not even realized themselves. Whatever their individual bent within these stories, no one ever simply suggested that "this is what religious folk do" and that is the beginning and end of the discussion. In fact, some had to overcome stagnant ideas of what religious people do in order to discover the social motivations that were beginning to develop in their own spiritual and political consciousness.

There are four main categories of formation or transformation that characterize the ways in which individuals develop a spiritually motivated commitment to social change. As the title of this chapter suggests, this formation is a unique product of personal spiritual biographies—those peculiarities of individual life that reconstruct behaviors and beliefs in ways that privilege or even require a social action component of spiritual life. While personal biographies always retain a distinct imprint, it is possible to talk more generally about four main clusters of experiences by which ideas fused: inherited engagement, learned engagement, social encounters, and spiritual epiphanies.

Inherited Engagement

Several people explained that they learned the connections between social and spiritual commitment from family practice or long-term involvement within religious institutions that had deeply entrenched social commitments. For these people, the combination of social commitments and spirituality seems natural, the only way to express or experience their faith. Passing down spiritually informed understandings of one's role and responsibility in the world makes sense when considering the patterns of religious transmission in general.

Not surprisingly, parents play a large role in the way that individuals learn about religion. Their influence on the types of communities their children join, the kinds of practices and beliefs they maintain, and the very religious identity that they claim, tends to stick as they pass into adulthood and often linger long throughout their lives as they eventually become distinctively theirs.[2] Rabbi Leonard Beerman, for example, is one of the most prolific individuals I interviewed with regard to social activist commitments. Well beyond the age that most people retire, Beerman is still affiliated with countless local, national, and international organizations, all committed in some way to social justice. He is cofounder of the Interfaith Center to Reverse the Arms Race, cochairman of the Los Angeles Jewish Commission on Sweatshops, and a member of the Blue Ribbon Committee for Affordable Housing in Los Angeles, and is involved in countless other projects about which he is deeply convicted.

Most of Rabbi Beerman's convictions regarding social justice are intertwined within a lifetime of welcoming the Sabbath with his family. For generations, the Beermans have been integrally connected to an understanding of a greater community and a greater struggle, not only with other Jews but with innumerable others who struggle against seemingly impervious forces that impinge upon life. This sense of struggle and connection is rooted in Beerman's own upbringing in a small Michigan town of fourteen thousand people in the deepest lows of the Great Depression. Life in this and many other regions in the United States, Beerman notes, was rarely untouched by the painful taint of anti-Semitism and acts of blatant discrimination. Beerman recalls that welcoming the Sabbath and especially honoring the holy days of the Jewish calendar provided the entirety of his religious education in a town with only seven other Jewish families. It was over these meals that he learned of the historical struggles, the great sense of compassion, and the integral role of peace in the stories that comprised Jewish heritage and identity.

During the Great Depression, the Beerman family witnessed the collapse of the factories around them and the ruin that befell their neighbors, including neighbors who harbored prejudices against the young Jewish family. The Beermans did not emerge unscathed from the economic forces that were crippling so many other families at that time. In fact, it was through these shared struggles that their weekly Sabbath took on an added, albeit bittersweet, celebration of an American identity that the Beermans were passionately cultivating. This identity, while drawn deeply from Jewish tradition, also incorporated the active challenge that the current American struggle called for. Rabbi Beerman recalls, "We wanted to be part of a larger society, and at the same time we were dissatisfied with that society and what it was doing to human beings." It is this intimate wrestling with society's effects upon its members that produced an unflagging positive outlook, fused with action, that Beerman calls Jewish optimism. He explains, "Jewish optimism is rooted in the profound contempt for life as it is. If you don't have that contempt for life as it is, you are not an optimist. Because you can imagine the way of life different from the one you live in, that's optimism."

Today, the traditional weekly observance of the Sabbath continues not only in ritual but in its connection to justice. Each week, Beerman gathers together with his wife, his three daughters, and his five grandchildren. They begin each evening by welcoming the Sabbath and lighting the Sabbath candles. Beerman says a blessing over the wine, symbolic of the wine drunk for centuries of similar observances. A blessing is then said over the special braided bread. The family members kiss each other and the rabbi, using the same blessing that Jacob used for his family in the Hebrew Bible, blesses his children and his grandchildren. Finally, the meal begins. Rabbi Beerman recalls, "When I divide or cut the bread for my grandchildren and then we pass it around the table, I look at their hands and I look at my own hands and I become aware of something." Beerman rephrases a passage attributed to sociologist Robert Bellah, noting that the hands of others that lift us from the womb will ultimately lay us in the grave. Beerman smiles and says, "The hands of others make our lives possible." He reflects on the hands that have brought this bread to this table. There is his grandchild, who offers a piece to her mother; the hands of his wife, who bought the bread in the market; the bakers, who produced the bread from its raw ingredients; and, finally, echoing Jacobs, the workers, perhaps migrant day workers, who labored in the fields so that the bread could nourish the rabbi's loved ones. Beerman thinks of the other workers in Los Angeles, the garment workers, for instance, who help to make his life possible and to whom, in turn, he dedicates many of his working hours.

Rabbi Beerman's intimate portrayal of the most spiritual moment of his week melds together various dimensions of spirituality. His spiritual reflection is holistic through its incorporation of the rabbi's family life, his religious calling, and his work in social activism. Beerman explains that the blessing he bestows connects him to a transcendent, sacred tradition of generations upon generations of fathers—both real and imagined—as far back as Jacob in the Torah, who passed along the same blessing to his children. The weekly ritual provides connection and unity among his present family around the table while drawing on the traditions learned from his family as a child. At the same time, Beerman sees the ritual as projecting spiritual, social responsibility and healthy, critical dissatisfaction with the world into the future by imprinting the ritual upon his grandchildren. Considering current trends in American religious participation, Beerman is probably right in imagining this projection into the future. Most likely his children and grandchildren will continue similar practices and retain similar identities, even though the shape and flavor of these practices may change to fit the changes around them.[3]

While connection across generations of families remains a strong contributing element in religious and collective identities that constitute inherited engagement, religious switching or dabbling in other practices undoubtedly occurs. Families relocate, denominations reassign pastors, resources dry up within one congregation and are reapplied for new practices or worship styles within another.[4] Yet given these various external influences on religious switching, when different choices are made people still tend to remain within the same religious tradition or family of traditions with which they were raised.[5] In fact, even though the contemporary religious landscape is metaphorically compared to a marketplace in which people shop for the religious community that suits their needs, Rodney Stark and Roger Finke have made the point that even considering the vast options from which to select, only 1 percent of Americans switch to a completely new religion.[6] When the Reverend Hope, for example, switched from her Southern Baptist roots to the Presbyterian Church while in college (a switch that, depending upon congregation, could have been substantially different in styles of practice), she stayed within the Protestant family that she inherited from her parents.

Beyond the large role that parents and family activities play in extending religious traditions and participation into adulthood, friends and new social networks eventually eclipse the role of family in affecting the choices individuals make.[7] In many ways, that parallels the changes in politics and activism that can bubble up during late adolescence and early adulthood. For example, participation in what became known as "Freedom Summer" during the civil rights era depended on a variety of overlapping factors.[8] Much like with religious perspectives, most of the young adults that volunteered during that summer had inherited similar shared values and ideological support from their parents. Beyond staying within the political family of values of their parents, most had a potent sense of their individual and collective efficacy in bringing about the changes that they set out to accomplish and the social and economic ability to take a summer off to volunteer.[9]

However, the individuals I spoke with rarely attributed their socially active spirituality to the traditions of their family or the religious institutions in which they were raised. Of course, some, like Beerman, acknowledged the influence that their parents had upon their social politics and spiritual development, but, unlike Beerman, most tended to see their parents' influence as an indirect connection. More often than not, people would nostalgically laugh when thinking back to the nominal nods that their family, church, or mosque made to the annual canned food drive or the cardboard origami rice bowl that collected pocket change around the dinner table of many Christian families in the 1970s. Regardless of the extent of social engagement, the transmission of service work or volunteerism into adulthood, as with the transmission of religious attachment into adulthood, seems to have various dimensions and an idiosyncratic mix of influences.[10] Inherited engagement, therefore, can be seen as a subjective position that depends upon one's recollection of family practices and the socialization of social justice values alongside spiritual practice.

Beyond the cumulative effects of childhood socialization and peer group development in adulthood, many people could articulate a specific experience, a sudden crystallization of purpose, or a rereading of the appropriate lines of action for their lives. Even though individuals may have had extremely different moments of transformation—from a vivid dream in which God speaks directly to them to a slow evolution cycling through meditation and everyday experiences—the remaining three categories can be identified as ones that typify a personal transformation of purpose and action.

Learned Engagement

"First of all, it's natural and then it's historical," Pastor Isaac Canales explained of the solidifying role that religious education had on his spiritual development. "Naturally, I came to an encounter with Christ and His spirit. And His spirit is all about love, helping others, transforming the world. That's just raw power. But then, when I got to college, I got saved again . . . . It almost seemed like I had another conversion experience when I entered into the conversation of all the great thinkers in our Christian heritage." Up until his college years, Canales had only been exposed to religion through "natural" experiences of spiritual connection and the osmosis of living within a setting where church and family were inseparable. In fact, for Canales, visions were powerful but expected, the natural way that religion worked as inherited from his family and Pentecostal community. Even though Canales danced around the periphery of the Pentecostal community as a youth and even at one point attempted to turn his back on the moral Christian life that his parents envisioned for him, he was still deeply influenced by the culture of that religious tradition. When he entered college, a new world of great thinkers throughout history provided a different vocabulary for his experiences and, by Canales's own account, functioned as his second conversion. This was not the taken-for-granted religion of his youth but rather a new and vibrant form of intellectually engaging in the role of religion in the world.

Most would agree that education, done well, can be a transforming secular experience. But examples from these conversations suggest it can be spiritually transforming as well. At first blush, this idea may seem incongruous with the widely held assumption that for a variety of reasons the college or university experience is a secularizing period of young adults' lives. New ideas and new identities, shaped by individual choices and increasingly diverse peer influences, affect how young adults express themselves through clothes, food, theories, and even religion and spiritual experience. Perhaps for the first time in their lives, students must decide on their own whether or not to attend synagogue, Sunday service, or Friday prayers, and those who decide to do so must seek out a suitable space in which to practice. It is somewhat difficult to assess in aggregate whether changes in weekly participation actually reflect subjective beliefs and values regarding religion. However, studies indicate that weekly religious participation often decreases during college.[11]

The pluralism and diversity of collegiate independence can also open up different religious options that previously had not been considered and, with them, a renewed sense of spirituality and service. Reverend Hope, for example, changed from the Southern Baptist tradition of her family to the Presbyterian church while in college. It was also in college when she first perceived the strong sense of clarity from God to pursue a vocation in church service. Others told similar stories of learning new ways of practice, studying histories of social engagement, or hearing new philosophies about spiritual commitments to social change while in college, rabbinical school, or seminary. This new knowledge reaffirmed and crystallized belief for some who already had a substantial religious base. For others it provided a new direction in which to enact the beliefs that they already had, while still others learned of new traditions that they had never known existed.

Brother Ed Dunn's experiences were not as clearly punctuated as Pastor Canales's, but they were similarly tied to his educational experience. When asked if he had a calling to his work in the Franciscan order, Dunn replied, laughing, "Like in the night, right? Lightning and thunder?" Evidently, this was not the case for Brother Dunn. Dunn's understanding of spirituality is a lived praxis of working closely with those who are economically less fortunate or somehow disenfranchised. Instead, Dunn's spirituality is the spirituality of Gustavo Gutierrez.

Raised in an Irish Catholic home in Philadelphia, Dunn does not remember getting from his family a strong connection between his religious tradition and broader social issues. Although he does remember with a quixotic smile that "my mom says I always loved Saint Francis." The link between faith and social practice to which Dunn now devotes his life developed over three summers while he was in college. During summer breaks, Dunn volunteered in the Appalachia Mountains of Eastern Kentucky at a Catholic camp for children. Outside of the daily routines of the camp, Dunn followed the camp priest into the tiny mountain towns where the priest would street preach. Dunn recalls, "He'd do a preaching and set up his loud speakers and we'd sing a couple songs—"What a Friend We Have in Jesus." And then, what was great is, we would go and spend an hour visiting folks. And uh, it wasn't pressing them to become Catholics. It was just to listen to them and their stories." For the first time Dunn remembers actually hearing, face to face, the stories of the different lived realities of people far removed from his own experiences. He listened as well to other religious groups that were assisting in the area, such as the Quakers, Catholic nuns, and another Christian church that was helping the United Mine Workers Union. Each of these groups had denominational differences in theology and doctrine, but what impacted Dunn was the common social ministry. He says, "Those summers were my real education about how religion and social practice comes together."

After completing his college degree, Dunn continued his education at the Mexican American Cultural Center in San Antonio, Texas. While there he had the opportunity to take a course on liberation theology with Gustavo Gutierrez that, in his own words, "absolutely blew my mind. . . . It was one of the classes I would run to every morning, because he was giving me words for some senses—like from Appalachia—that I had had about who God is and what the options for the poor is and how you put your faith into practice in the social realm, but he gave me a vocabulary for it that I never had before." This vocabulary concretized the experiences of living out one's religious beliefs in socially active ways and allowed Dunn to pursue feelings that previously did not have a name. Learning this vocabulary within the bounds of academia for Dunn, as well as for Pastor Canales, conferred an additional institutional legitimacy to act upon these ideas and impulses that were beginning to stir.

Learning, however, does not always come simply through the halls of the academy. Sara Desh Arpana had a different experience of Learned Engagement. Sara Desh Arpana grew up in the Church of England in Australia. Throughout her childhood she strongly believed as an unquestioned matter of fact in the apostolic succession of the Anglican Church. No other church, let alone religion, had the direct line to God. This changed unexpectedly when Latter-Day Saint missionaries came to her small and somewhat provincial town. Although neighbors slammed doors in their faces, Sara Desh Arpana, at twelve years old, let them in out of the heat of an exceptionally sweltering summer day and offered them two tall ice-cold glasses of juice. Even at this early age and after listening intently to their compelling pitch, she knew the Church of Latter-Day Saints was not the church for her. Nevertheless, she had been profoundly impressed and simultaneously unsettled by their passionate conviction. It was these sensations that stuck after the young men stepped back out into the shimmering heat.

For some time following that visit, Sara Desh Arpana began asking very "twelve-year-old questions," such as "Is there a religion that is right and if so, what is it for me?" Mahatma Gandhi, whom she had learned about in school, presented a particularly puzzling conundrum for a young girl who had not questioned the salience of alternative beliefs before. Could Gandhi have been wrong in his faith when he did such good in the world? Sara Desh Arpana's curiosity was sparked and she read anything she could get her hands on, from the I Ching to the Koran. Ultimately, she says, "I just happened to find that one." That one was the Christopher Isherwood translation of the Bhagavad-Gita. She recalls immediately thinking, "This answered all of my questions." It was an "ah ha" moment.

At the back of the book was a note inviting those who wanted to learn more to write to the Vedanta Center of southern California. Sara Desh Arpana set pen to paper as soon as she finished the final page. The center responded promptly with a recommended reading list and encouraging her to explore these ideas more deeply through her local library, which she did. "This was my faith. There was no question of it. This was what I wanted out of religion." By the age of twenty-two, Sara Desh Arpana had left Australia and was in southern California on her way to monastic ordination. She explained, "It's as though the circle is broken so the circle can expand. . . . You give up all family ties or society ties because you belong to the world. You serve the world and the whole world is in effect your family."

Spiritual awakenings through education can be unexpected revelations, such as with Sara Desh Arpana, or they might be undoubtedly powerful moments of extension, confirmation, and legitimation, as with Canales and Dunn. While these particular experiences were radically transformative in the lives of these three, others found that spiritual education was more likely conservative, limiting, or even inhibiting of spiritual exploration and development. In fact, this perspective led one rabbi to develop an organization that reintroduced spiritual diversity into what had become, for many, rote patterns of belief and practice.

Rabbi Rami Shapiro creates and orchestrates a variety of workshops and retreats for religious leaders as part of his umbrella Jewish ministry, Metivta. One of the workshops offered through Metivta is specifically pitched toward Jewish rabbis of different denominations, with the intention of introducing them to spiritual texts of the great mystical teachers of their own religious traditions. As Rabbi Shapiro claims, "The seminaries don't teach spiritual material specifically and they don't teach the contemplative at all usually." At the time of our interview, Metivta was in the second cycle of a two-year program and had seventy rabbis at various stages of immersion with the contemplative models. It appears to be having an effect. Shapiro notes, "They come out of it saying, 'I never knew these texts existed. I didn't get this in school. Five years of rabbinic seminary and nobody told me that we had these mystical books. I mean, I had them somewhere, but I never read them.'"

Texts are only one part of Metivta's workshop training. Contemplative practices are also necessary components. Shapiro makes it clear that "if it's just an intellectual thing, it doesn't go too far. If you can tie it into a meditative practice, chanting practice, some kind of ongoing daily spiritual work, then I think you really transform the individual and the individual can go out and transform the world." While education can be a transforming agent, broadening one's perspectives through the collective ideas of historical discourse and

contemporary application, in many other instances mainstream canonical education can be, and often is, conservative with regard to fostering spiritual
experience. Private institutes such as Metivta act upon this system with new
educational tools specifically designed to reshape the taken-for-granted expectations of congregational religious life.

Social Encounters

Reverend Glenda Hope built her life around a very progressive commitment
to social change. While in many ways Hope's path to her current position involved a series of accidents, blocked avenues, and serendipitous circumstances,
a deep spiritual stirring gave her solid direction for the next thirty years. Hope
reported that her call to church service occurred in college; however, her
career-long dedication to spiritually informed social service awoke during
Dr. Martin Luther King Jr.'s funeral in 1968—an event that (using the biblical reference to the conversion of the apostle Paul) she refers to as her "Damascus Road" experience.

> I was out here when Doctor King was assassinated. I was in San Fran-
> cisco. I was just devastated by that. Friends of mine took up a collec-
> tion to send me back to Atlanta, my hometown, for his funeral. That
> was a true conversion experience. That was the closest to a Damascus
> Road sort of thing I ever expect to have. Being in that group of people,
> about a hundred thousand people I guess, and probably 85 percent
> were black. And everybody was together. Truly there was no sense of
> separation of races or whatever—Mahalia Jackson singing those old
> pious songs, "Take My Hand Precious Lord," and it was all put to-
> gether in that movement for true love and justice—that major trans-
> formation in my life. I don't know what would have become of me if
> that hadn't happened.

The confluence of social justice and spirituality that Hope felt at that
service was a catalyst for her own convictions. For Hope and others, the connection between spirituality and social engagement occurs during or after a
particularly salient social encounter or experience. Not simply religiously spiritual and not simply progressively ideological, the particular combination of
each fuses in ways that are unattainable to the same degree through Sunday
service and contemplative prayer or marches and sit-ins on their own. While
each of these other practices or events may produce profound intimations of
spiritual connection, the culmination of the social import of King's funeral,
the integration of the crowd, the spirituals sung by a world-renowned voice,
and the sheer numerical power of the turnout was overwhelming—particularly

for a white Christian woman raised within the segregated culture of the mid-century South. A new sense of community solidified through the emotions and collective actions of those taking part. Such moments are what Emile Durkheim described as the universally fundamental building blocks of religious sentiment and meaning.[12] In these overwhelming moments of collective union, emotions bubble up, or effervesce, to use Durkheim's term, in ways that transcend the individual and even the collective. As with others who have experienced a transformative social encounter, these moments are interpreted as a spiritual sign or reflected upon as the agent for giving substance to otherwise abstract spiritual or political messages and beliefs.

Of course, not all profound social encounters are so specifically delineated in space and time. For Alice Linsmeier, a sense of social commitment built slowly for years before a trip to El Salvador in the 1980s crystallized her feelings. Linsmeier was raised Catholic by parents with a strong Jesuit background. However, the schools that Linsmeier attended and the upper-middle-class parish did not have a particularly Jesuit ring. Instead they were conventional, emphasizing rich liturgical tradition—"a very Catholic Catholicism," as Linsmeier remembers with a smile. Rather than giving up religion based upon her parent's version, Linsmeier felt she had to "find another way of looking at things and to have it match a little bit more of what my own personal stirrings were to do."

After college Linsmeier was, as she puts it, luckily declined by the Peace Corps and ended up pursuing the Jesuit Volunteer Corps (JVC) on the advice of a Jesuit family friend. This path turned out to be precisely what Linsmeier was seeking. She recalled that being part of the JVC "helped to give a whole perspective of the faith that does justice and working in communities and that urgency and struggle." Her experience with JVC clarified what she wanted to do with her life. As she put it, "They say with JVC that you're ruined for life. So, it really worked in my case."

After her stint in JVC, Linsmeier got a job working for Jesuit Refugee Service (JRS) in Los Angeles. During her first years there, Salvadorians were fleeing from the battles at home and making their way across the United States border in large numbers. Through the JRS, Linsmeier recalls being "horrified by the stories of the war but amazed at the popular movement, their faith, their goodness." She heard through volunteers on the ground and from new immigrants to the United States that the Salvadorians who stayed behind were creating grassroots organizations while still in refugee camps, mobilizing their displaced communities and setting plans for repopulating their massacred villages. All of this was taking place even though the government had not formulated or approved an official policy for their return. Both outraged at the stories of the devastations of war and deeply encouraged by the resilient community response, she decided she had to go to El Salvador to see with her own eyes what was happening.

Linsmeier got the opportunity in 1987. What was scheduled to be a brief tour of refugee camps sponsored by JRS turned into a six-year stay for Linsmeier. "Just by going there and being very moved, I think there is a lot of people who have gone to El Salvador and had been transformed. I was one of many, because it was so clear what was going on and what the people's response was— was just so incredible." When asked what sustained her during this time in the face of such dire conditions, she replied, "The community was so solid, unified, full of faith . . . . the community would have its own, what is it called, celebration of the word. And where they would all reflect on biblical things. So, yeah, it was definitely a whole part of the people and what they had seen and their struggle."

This communal faith was also practical and pragmatic in the contentious and violent context of El Salvador. While Linsmeier admits to feeling only relatively safe in the area—after all, the United States was backing the soldiers who were committing most atrocities—those around her were rarely safe, and she recalls times when the community would risk their lives for each other. In one case, soldiers entered the camp from time to time attempting to arrest a mentally retarded boy who sought shelter there. "The whole community would surround him and say, 'You know what, we are all children of the same god. You don't have permission to hurt your brother like this.'" Since some of the soldiers were forced recruits who were merely children themselves, these tactics often worked. What's more, as Linsmeier points out, the whole country was deeply Catholic and this conferred a resonant transcendent and nationalist authority upon the community's claims. She concludes, "It was pretty easy in some ways being there because the people were just so clear. The community that I lived with and the whole movement that was going on made it pretty clear what we were there for and how to keep their spirits up in all of it."

It is not difficult to understand that witnessing the community solidarity and sense of faith against the backdrop of palpable life-and-death circumstances, far from home and familiarity, could have a transformative effect on Linsmeier's life. Events such as Linsmeier's and even Hope's have an almost exotic or fantastic element to them. Their experiences are individual brushes with social and cultural phenomena that all Americans shared, albeit from a sanitized distance of media news reports and collective history. Many might recall the coverage of the violent turmoil in El Salvador, the newsreel of King's funeral procession, or, more diffusely, the drug wars and the scourge of HIV/ AIDS that continue to plague inner-city environments such as the Tenderloin. These biographies reveal intimate connections to social landmarks that are out of the scope of everyday experiences. Yet social encounters that spark personal transformation do not have to entail such dramatic locales or harrowing stories. They can be much more parochial or mundane yet still retain the power and impact necessary for individual transformation. Similarly, transformation is not just for the pioneers, the leaders, or the organizers on the forefront of social issues. Just as often, the leaders see these transformations taking place among their volunteers.

Javier Stauring is one of twenty-three chaplains assigned to the Central Juvenile Hall in downtown Los Angeles. Tucked back among stockyards and warehouses in the shadow of the adjacent downtown skyline is an expansive detention center in which over six hundred children are imprisoned at any given time. The ages of these inmates range from eight to eighteen, with the vast majority being boys and ethnic minorities. Segregated units within the institution hold nearly two hundred of these children as they wait to be tried in the courts, some as adults.

Stauring is involved in a variety of programs within the Central Juvenile Hall in Los Angeles, including advocacy, education of churches on criminal justice and social justice issues, and, most immediately, direct ministry to incarcerated youth. Stauring admits that the direct ministry is the foundation for everything else that he does. It is in this interpersonal interaction that correctional statistics become flesh-and-blood boys and girls. In part because of the personal testimonies that Stauring is able to communicate regarding the conditions and personalities of the inmates, direct ministry at the detention center is able to attract a significant number of volunteers both from local churches and from colleges and universities in the surrounding area.

Volunteers assist in a variety of activities such as accompanying minors to mass on Sundays, but the core activities of the ministry is group conversation and relationship building. In small circles of four or five, volunteers ask the kids about their experiences in the center, the day-to-day challenges that they face, the mundane ups and downs, outside relationships with family or with their own children, or struggles with their schoolwork inside the detention program. Eventually the volunteers turn the conversation toward integrating a selected religious reading for the week. These group sessions with the Catholic ministry are entirely optional for the inmates; however, there is typically a strong turnout and lively participation in the reading and reflection. Demographics of the incarcerated population help explain part of the high turnout rate for this Catholic ministry. By Stauring's account, 80 percent of the detained kids are Latino, many of whom come from neighboring East Los Angeles, and, even if they are not self-identified as Catholic, most have strong cultural connections to the Catholic religious traditions and their sense of community.

In getting to know the volunteers over the years, Stauring says with a smile that most sign up, as he puts it, "believing that they're going to have an effect on *somebody else's* life." Yet, "what happens over and over again is the people that come and visit are the ones that go through the transformation." This is not to suggest that the children may not benefit from the direct ministry. However, the fact that volunteers, believing they will be the one's providing for others, are the ones who have a significant spiritual experience in their service work is a fascinating turn. Stauring suggests that these visits are moments in which volunteers "see the face of Jesus in these kids." This is facilitated by making a connection to biblical mandates, further solidifying the experience of the volunteers. Stauring quotes from the Bible the clear message that, he argues, informs these volunteers' experiences: "I was in jail and you visited me." Through this connection, it becomes less difficult to discern who is learning from whom or who is being transformed. Stauring gives a general example by saying, "You build a relationship with the kid and many, many times you come to admire their resilience; you come to feel a lot of compassion for their life stories."

From the grandmothers that volunteer with Stauring to Linsmeier's example of being in the midst of a raging civil war or Canales reading theology at Harvard, the common thread that weaves through these narratives is that individual transformation occurred as these people came to see their relationship with and in this world somewhat differently. Education and social encounters became moments of transcendent change through which the definitions of the way the world worked also changed. No longer were the daily routines routine or inevitable or concrete. Each transformative moment slid these individuals toward a perception of the world that was malleable, unjust, and in need of new or continued action. The potentials of what should be replaced the fixed realities of what always already is. These moments in which individuals turn ideological corners and see the world differently are the crucial and required elements for motivating action to bring about change in the world. Many times these are cognitive processes through which potential members weigh the costs and benefits of participation, the likelihood of success, or the resonance with their own worldviews or values.[13]

But as these stories attest, making that turn involves more than a cost-benefit analysis. In addition, shifts in social perspectives and activism are experientially based in profoundly emotional and often morally compelling ways. James Jasper notes that subjective shifts are many times shifts away from predominantly cognitive views of the world and toward moral views in which change is both necessary and plausible.[14] Many of these narratives support this idea and suggest that transformations often develop organically or sponta-

neously from a deeply impacting interactive and experiential process that is
at once social and spiritual.

Indeed, many of the people interviewed already had either a developing
social political concern or a spiritually informed desire to make the world a
better place. What they required was an experiential moment in which these
became clearly and practically linked together. Brother Dunn, for example,
was already seeking out a ministry through which he could extend the type
of community-based model that he learned about in the Appalachians. His
education with Gutierrez provided the additional transcendent imperative of
exigency that heightened the cognitive shift in defining what should be done.
This spiritual vocabulary, along with Gutierrez's charisma, provided what Dunn
needed to act upon these ideals that, until then, were just knocking around in
his head. Now they became his life's work. Similarly, Hope already had been
called to service in the church and had already been involved in the civil
rights movement for some time when she attended King's funeral and, through
that emotionally powerful and effervescent public ritual, realized that the social world could—and, more important, should—be changed through continual
spiritually based activism.

Education or social encounter in these cases was not overly determining
or the sole basis for either social justice politics or religious service. Rather,
these social, educational, and spiritual motivations congealed in a salient moment of transcendent synergy that the participants could readily identify years
later as significant turning points in their lives. Running to class, feeling swept
up in the community of mourners, or visiting war-torn communities in El Salvador all produced emotional resonances that for these people made transcendence palpable in this world.

Spiritual Epiphanies

"I met the Lord Jesus Christ as my savior on drugs and an LSD trip." When the
Reverend Isaac Canales began his testimony about his first conversion experience, I knew I was probably not in for a typical story of finding personal salvation. And yet, as Canales continued on, I realized that his testimony, while
unconventional in some of its trappings, was actually in its most basic structure and experiential essence very similar to canonical stories that have been
told for millennia.[15] The story begins with a troubled, wayward youth—a prodi-
gal son. Canales was coming up strong in the charged social landscape of southern California in the 1960s. But he was doing so in what he says were all the
wrong ways. The son of a resourceful Pentecostal pastor, Canales was using his
own charismatic talents for alternative ends. He was in a band, he did a lot of

drugs, and he got into fights, all before the age of twenty. In the shadow of his immigrant father's meager yet moral accomplishments in founding a fledgling congregation, Canales felt his accomplishments were hollow and actually destructive in comparison. He hit rock bottom at an early age. In fact, Canales admits that he was contemplating suicide late one night, deep in the swirl of an LSD trip. That is when Jesus appeared in a jerry-rigged strobe light that his band built in his garage. By dawn, Canales took his first steps toward following his father's path to become a minister among the poor.

While Canales's story is enmeshed within a very particular social and historical context, resonating in unique ways with his individual biography and incorporating the drug taking that undoubtedly enhanced this encounter, it also follows a very traditional Christian format of being lifted out from the depths through salvation just at the point at which no other option seemed viable.[16] As such one can see the ways in which individual biographical circumstance, theological beliefs, and institutional cultures gel in moments of spiritual epiphany. They mutually reinforce each other in ways that influence the behavior set in motion by this experience—in this case the continuation of the Canales ministry.

Alternatively, an African American's recollection of the Hajj, the Muslim pilgrimage to the holy city of Mecca, at first sounds geographically foreign and religiously and culturally irresolvable with the story of Canales's conversion. However, in many ways this follows a similar pattern of biographical influences on beliefs and behaviors and a communion with the sacred. Whereas Canales's transformation was intimately tied with his local lived realities, Hajj is timeless, reaching back into time-honored traditions and ritual and encompassing a massive scope of global proportions. Yet the outcome for both men is a life of religious social service.

Hajj is one of the five pillars of Islam, along with a delineated daily prayer schedule and charitable contributions, that all Muslims must practice throughout their lives. Hajj is required at least once by any Muslim who is capable—both financially and physically—of making the trip. For many Muslims this is a defining moment in their spiritual journey. Imam Saadiq Saafir is no different.

Inside a storefront masjid on a hot summer afternoon in the Jefferson Park district of Los Angeles, a perceptible change comes across the face of Imam Saadiq Saafir when I asked him to describe his pilgrimages to Mecca. His eyes, typically embracing and engaging, drift off and a broad smile escapes. "I don't think I could—I always say I can only bring back a version. I probably tell somebody something different all the time." And yet without pause he continues, "It is the most imprinting experience of my life." Saadiq has made his Hajj twice, first in 1993 and then the following year in 1994, yet his descriptions are as vivid as if he had just returned. He admits that on his first Hajj he had more passion than knowledge about what the Hajj was really about. But this passion was fulfilled tangibly by the experience. He explained, "[Hajj] brings religion home in such a realistic way. It all makes sense now. You see the universal brotherhood, you see where it's ludicrous for me to look at you and judge you by your skin and not understanding that it's your heart that counts."

Hajj connected Saadiq to this brotherhood physically and geographically. He described the process repeatedly as a struggle in which all pilgrims had to endure their own sets of internal hardships as well as the real risks involved in circumambulating around the Ka'bah, the great black stone structure around which each pilgrim must circle seven times for the proper completion of the ritual. Saadiq warns that falling down while circumambulating could cost you your life, yet walking between a king on one side and a man without legs on the other affirms the significance and the benefits of taking such risks. Saadiq explains, "It's the most phenomenally human experience that you'll ever have that really transcends what is really human . . . . [You] understand that the strongest influence in the world is spiritual rather than what is tangible . . . . When you go there, it's more of a spiritual lesson than anything. Your soul feels satisfied; your soul feels fulfilled." By the end of his story, Saadiq noticed how often he referred to the Hajj as a struggle and, smiling, clarified, "It's not a struggle, it's a pleasure."

Saadiq's story illustrates the transcendent touch of spiritual epiphanies in a very rich, historical, and collective manner. Saadiq's spiritual formation in Mecca was both literally and figuratively far from the intimacies and the known sites, sounds, and smells of his everyday life. Saadiq was lifted from his known physical environment, transported through cultural time and space. This spiritual formation in one way involved a sense of otherness that required ritual far from the mundane elements of American life. It included diverse men of all colors, shapes, and backgrounds, praying in Arabic—for some, like Saadiq, a second language—and performing a collective act of devotion that has existed in a similar form for millennia. Yet on the other hand, this timeless and somewhat exotic practice allowed Saadiq to realize for the first time in such a deeply emotional way the spiritual and social transcendence of differences that can be found in commonly struggling together toward a shared goal.

Whereas Imam Saadiq's experience involved millions of others, Richard Ramos had an equally impacting solitary experience that transformed the direction of his life. Ramos, a reformed gang member who is now a Pentecostal minister struggling with a new ministry in Santa Barbara, remembers that moment in 1990 very clearly. He had just finished preaching for a friend in East Los Angeles. After the service he returned to his hotel room and lay down on the bed. The next thing he knew he was having a vision. He explains, "I knew

I was dreaming, but I also knew that I was very conscious and very awake and very cognizant of what was taking place in this vision." In Ramos's circles this is referred to as an open vision. He continued, "I was in the desert and I saw this preacher friend of mine—he was far away from me—and he points his finger at me and his finger just began to grow out towards me. And he said to me . . . ." Ramos breaks off to reconstruct a biblical image in which one of the Christian apostles, John, is reported to have a vision while on the island of Patmos. The experience is vividly recorded down to the aural experience of God's voice. Ramos explained that in the Bible this voice was like "the sound of a lot of rushing water . . . but yet, nobody else could hear it." Returning to his dream experience Ramos went on in detail.

> And so it's *this* voice that is at the same time thundering. And he says, "Thou man of God." And his finger grows out, but it didn't touch me but it knocked me to the ground. I just began to weep and cry and say "God, are you God, the Holy Spirit?" And he said, "Yes." And I said, "Well, what do you want me to do with my life?" And the next thing I know we're sitting at this cafe-type-place . . . And then he turned to me and said, with a smile and a smirk on his face, and again in a way that I could understand because of my background as a sometimes-violent person, he said with a smile, "I want you to kick the devil's butt. That's what I want."

Ramos's experience was one of the most direct and visually explicit experiences that I encountered. His transformation was undoubtedly linked to his unique biography, incorporating a personal friend in the vision and referencing gang culture. But it is also shaped by his deep scriptural knowledge. More significantly, it was a clear and unequivocal call to action. When interpreting this vision, Ramos utilized the biblical conversion narrative of Saul/Paul on the road to Damascus. Ramos said, "I took [this vision] to mean, through ministry and your life, I'm going to use you as Jesus spoke to the Apostle Paul in a vision, where he got knocked off his horse, and he said: 'I have chosen you to be a minister and to go to the people and turn them from the darkness to light, from the power of Satan to the power of God, that they may receive the inheritance that all those who have faith in me receive.' So that's—I can articulate that now. In my spirit I knew it to mean that at the time."

Although the mandate was unambiguous for Ramos at the time, he had no idea how to implement this call or what action to take. Yet, as the vision continued, Ramos believes that his plan of action was laid out for him. He explained that God directed him to look over at a woman that was being surrounded by gang members. Ramos was crouching behind a bush, waiting for a sign to act. At the right moment, Ramos explains, "as they began to attack her,

I came out and basically saved her from these gang members." Immediately the scene changed again, and Ramos saw himself, a poor Latino from East Los Angeles, "being introduced to all our authority figures in our city and county. I saw me shaking their hands and them recognizing me." That experience was in 1990. By November of that year he was hired by a local Junior High School through which he was able to mentor gang members. In reflection Ramos suggests, "I began to see the fulfillment of this vision, the vision of the future."

Through the success of his initial work with local gang members in his school district, Ramos was approached by community organizations and local foundations to be the director of a Community Based Coalition to Stop Gang Violence. This again served as what Ramos perceived as evidence of "God's providence" in his life. By 1994, students ranked Ramos first in a survey when asked to identify community leaders. Ramos turned this award into a bully pulpit as he gave a keynote address on violence. He explains, "I basically gave a sermon that said the cause of violence is an angry heart and an angry heart is the result of unresolved injustices in the hearts of children that usually take place in the home by their parents or people they know."

By the time of our interview, Ramos had continued to interpret his perceptions of the fulfillment of a vision he experienced over ten years ago. Through his work on gangs and now on affordable housing in Santa Barbara he has been repeatedly in the midst of "authority figures of our city and county," shaking hands and sometimes shaking a fist. Over a decade of committed social involvement stemmed from this significant spiritual turning point, alone on a hotel bed.

Experiencing Change

William James was an American pragmatist philosopher, a pioneering psychologist, and one of the most creative theorists of religious experience at the turn of the twentieth century. In many ways the stories told here are very Jamesian in their experiential quality. William James was no religious purist—all manner of "religious" experience found its way into his analysis. He undoubtedly would be quite comfortable considering a social encounter being described as a Damascus experience and would most likely delight in the story of salvation on LSD. Experience is what counted most. The theological interpretations that are placed upon these direct experiences were, for James, second-order phenomena that could not serve as proper analytical bases from which to determine what is or is not a valid religious experience. Instead, James made the case that rather than doctrinal parameters for distinguishing religious experiences—spiritual experiences for our purposes—experiences should be deemed religious if they produce an entirely different way of seeing the world and one's relationship to it. For these individuals, at least, as their perception of the world changed, so did the way that they engaged that world.

CONVERSION VS. LIBERATION

Each of these stories, from mystical visions to the emergence of an ethical conscience, recounts a moment of significant personal change in relation to their world. But are we to take these moments as evidence of religious conversion or of political awakening? Some accounts, such as Canales's vision of Jesus becoming his own personal savior, might be easily recognized as particularly religious "conversion narratives," while others, such as Dunn's education through liberation theology of the poor, most likely would be categorized as moments of political awakening to the social injustices of the world—a cognitive liberation that opens up one's perspective on social injustices in need of change.[17] Of course, neither of these artificially polarized perspectives fits unequivocally across any of these cases.[18]

Taking religious conversion first, the term conjures up on the one hand notions of bright lights, booming voices, or visions—which sometimes these are—or on the other hand, legalistic processes of lengthy premarital classes at a synagogue or parish church. These definitions imply the adoption of one religious worldview, bounded by a particular institutional affiliation (Mahayana Buddhism or Reform Judaism) and linked to a change in one's perceived salvation or enlightenment, at the very least, or to a change in one's nominal religious identity.[19] Sometimes religious conversions imply changes in behavior, relationships, passions, and even politics.[20] The line between subjective religious conversion and sociopolitical experimentation began to blur in the 1960s, for example, as spiritual experimentation—at times within new religious movements—became political, social, and experiential in very public ways. These instances begin to resemble the transformative moments described here but still do not fully capture this range of experiences.

For the most part, these individuals rarely departed from their religious traditions or their religious families. Instead, in most cases, their traditions were expanded or profoundly enhanced rather than radically changed or displaced with another. Specifying spiritual conversions in which personal identities become closely related to the sacred and more accurately to some spiritual force over religious conversions approximates more of what I heard.[21] Even so, I feel more comfortable using the term "transformation," albeit spiritually powerful and often life-changing, than the term "conversion."

Additionally, the alternative is often true. Cognitive liberation or political awakenings are typically attributed to cognitive processes between social actors and larger movements or activist organizations. While undoubtedly this cognitive aspect is necessary in solidifying a changed perspective on social or political ideas, the feelings and transcendent perceptions of spirituality affect this process as well.[22] Part of the distinction in the transformations of Pastor Ramos or Brother Dunn is that a social component to proactively engage the world was inseparable from their spiritual experiences. What once seemed like permanent elements of the way the world is—from poverty, to crime, to drug addiction and even political oppression—now appear as theirs to shape, manipulate, and effectively change.

While these can slowly evolve over time through interpersonal interactions with others or through powerful speeches or collective actions, they can also be immediate and individually experienced. Certain incidents or accidents in our daily lives may disturb us so intensely that we seek out participation in a movement or around an issue. The death of a child to a gun accident or the closing of a neighborhood elementary school because of lack of funding can produce moral shocks that unquestioningly motivate action.[23] Alice Linsmeier's experience in El Salvador can be attributed to the moral shock of hearing the stories of immigrants fleeing their homeland, motivating her to take part in some way.[24]

Too often the sociopolitical transformation is left out of the conversion literature, just as the spiritual dimension is left out of activism or civic conversations. One misses the social agenda that for these individuals is inseparable from their spiritual life; the other misses the potential that spiritual experiences subjectively generate, and even mandate, for some individuals with broader social agendas. Indeed, it is important to note that with all these examples spirituality and spiritually motivated social commitments for change are not merely echoes or epiphenomena of more fundamental, or more real, social or political philosophies. Put differently, for people like Linsmeier, religion is not window dressing for their politics. In fact, it is quite the opposite. Reverend Hope, for example, explains her view about the work she does by saying, "We're very political people. We always have been. We feel very strongly that our faith impels us to challenge the structures of our society that hurt people and break people or any other part of God's creation for that matter." Political ideals, ethics, and values of equity and justice are very important among the members working in the Tenderloin; however, as Hope clearly stresses, faith is the underlying core of this politics and at times acts as the engine to power political and social action.

So where do we draw the line? If we assign certain experiences exclusively to one category we lose the potency of the other. Instead, the origins of engaged spirituality exist somewhere in the middle between spiritual transformations and cognitive liberations. Spiritual experience or transformation is a medium through which religious morals and doctrinal conscriptions combine with social action and perceptions of justice.[25] Engaged spiritual experience, among people for whom religion and social justice matter, congeals these motivations into a fused whole.

INDIVIDUAL VS. COLLECTIVE

Moments of engaged spiritual experience—spirituality and social action—often straddle the distinction between collective and individual experience. With the exception of the inherited source of spiritual transformation, the other three categories of transformation narratives are at the same time highly individualized and profoundly collective experiences. Ramos may illustrate the most individualized origin for his spiritually informed social action, since in the most literal sense he was lying on his bed, alone in a hotel room, when he had his vivid dream of God's mandate. But beyond the literal individuality of this experience, the dream spoke to him with great specificity about issues that would only resonate with his current set of relationships, his past experiences, and his spiritual understandings. Admittedly, even this most individual experience falls back upon collective meaning systems. Ramos still had to draw on the interpretive schemas of Pentecostalism, itself a particularly individualized theology, in order to identify this as a moment of divinely inspired transcendent communion rather than a psychotic break or a mundane, sleep-induced brain function. Furthermore, Ramos had to identify this man in the vision that sat across from him and spoke in a rushing voice as God and that God had to have the authority to command respect and obedient servitude from Ramos.

On the other hand, one might perceive Hope's collective social encounter as the polar opposite in form to Ramos's vision. Rather than alone in a hotel room, Hope was among a sea of others in a highly publicized and highly public mass spectacle. Thousands were directly taking part in the event alongside Hope, and millions more would take part in this experience through the media and later through collective history. While in form, Hope's experience was as collective as could be conceived, it was also, in very meaningful ways, highly individualized. Hope's own biography and personal history of growing up as an unquestioning participant in southern segregated culture and her active embrace of equal rights later in life were emotionally compounded with this literal homecoming and brought to bear a subjectively unique lens that cast the event in a potent light. The individual salience of this funeral is especially important considering that Hope had to return to San Francisco soon after this communal event. The collective body that congealed during the funeral and generated such a transcendent energy within Hope was, as these effervescent experiences typically are, largely a fleeting and ephemeral one. Undoubtedly, a community feeling formed within the hours of the funeral, and segments of that community would go on as social networks that would sustain in lesser form the motivations, senses, beliefs, and memories of that day. Congregations attended, schools visited, and families marched together. However, Hope and many others would most likely meet few of these participants again.

The civil rights movement had a permeable membership that, while part of its success, fractured among other causes or moved back into the routines of daily life once the goals were met or denied. Unlike congregational communities or family ties that remain flexibly fixed, civic action or social justice communities are, for many participants, temporally bound. Individual transformations, when sustained, are important to consider as potentially long-standing consequences of these otherwise ephemeral gatherings. Hope went her own way following the funeral, and, luckily for the community in the Tenderloin, the internalized, spiritually informed social mandates of that transformation stuck.

What is most revealing is the way in which both of these transforming moments, which are so distinct in form and occurred to individuals from different ends of the Christian theological spectrum, are linked together by the very same biblical interpretations of spiritual experience. Ramos legitimizes his fantastic dream by tying it directly to this scriptural tradition, going so far as to compare the sounds of the voice in his dream with the sounds described in the gospels attributed to John centuries ago and later comparing his call to service to the conversion of Paul on the road to Damascus. In the same way, Hope's collective social encounter invokes Paul's solitary "Damascus experience," admittedly more metaphorically than in Ramos's case but still emphasizing the powerful impact of personal transformation. The symbolic salience of the story lies in the subjective experiential primacy of direct encounters and their consequence on the individual's life more so than the particular form that that experience may take. Ramos and Hope, as well as Saadiq, Linsmeier, Shapiro, and Canales, tell us, "These are the moments when our lives changed. These are the important points of transformation without which we would not be doing what we are doing."

The Evolutionary Change

Born and raised in Iraq, Mudafer al-Tawash has been a practicing Muslim all his life. However, the way he practices and the way he applies this faith to the world around him has changed. Al-Tawash suggests, "When you are born a Muslim and raised within a Muslim family . . . you automatically, you get it from your parents and you don't question things until you are far away from home." Al-Tawash realized this when he moved to Dublin, Ireland, to pursue a Ph.D. in agriculture after completing a master's degree in Iraq. Once removed from the living and breathing Islamic culture that engulfed him at home and left to his own devices, Al-Tawash turned to reading the Koran. He remembers saying to himself, "Ah! This is the thing we used to do as a Muslim and it's wrong. Why [did] we used to do it? Tradition."

As his self-instruction continued, al-Tawash uncovered a deeper passion and purpose for his life. Although he and his wife and children led comfortable lives in Ireland with the job that he secured upon completing his Ph.D., he became fed up. One day he said to his wife as much as to himself, "I have to do something! Because this is not the way." Providing economic and material support for his wife and family, while necessary, was no longer sufficient. Struggling with the decision of what do led to frustration, and al-Tawash turned to prayer. He optimistically believed, "God will not reveal [an] answer to you. But God shows you." Al-Tawash used a specific prayer for consulting God on decisions. Loosely translated, the gist of the prayer, according to al-Tawash, goes like this, "You're going to say 'I am going to go ahead with this [decision]. And if it's good for me and my community . . . make it easy for me and I'll go through it. If it's not good for me, stop me, put some distractions in front of me, let me feel this obstruction and I'll stop.'" Soon after starting the recitation of this prayer, al-Tawash saw an advertisement in the local newspaper seeking a development worker with an agricultural background for a post in a desperately poor, rural region of the Sudan. After just one exploratory visit to the area, al-Tawash packed up his family and moved.

His time in the Sudan proved to be as difficult as he expected. He recalled watching children die from malnutrition and placing the blame on himself for not doing more. Yet along with these emotional costs, al-Tawash explained that the newfound rewards that sustained him during these two years held much greater meaning than merely his salary alone in Ireland. For example, al-Tawash helped organize the first school for the deaf in the region. The school brought together under one roof deaf children who would otherwise sleep on the street, and, because they had no systematic education, they had no standardized form of communication. "And [now] you will see them, they are hugging with you and they could communicate with you through a sign language and that's why we are there. We feel this is our reward . . . That's what makes my days."

Al-Tawash relied upon the Muslim pillar of prayer five times a day during that long trial when he first arrived in the Sudan. He retains that practice today, noting, "It makes your life easier and makes my life easier." At the same time, al-Tawash admits that ongoing prayer challenges him to do more. I asked him to elaborate and he suggested that taking time for the five prayers allows moments to reflect and take stock of the lessons that are laid out in front of you each day. "It's sometimes difficult to describe. You build that personal relation between you and God and you commit yourself to certain things and you stand in front of him, and you [ask] 'Why? Why?' But you have to accept it. I feel it's a lesson for us. It's maybe a push for us to do more. We are not doing our work as well as we used to do. To get involved more in the local community. To get involved more in a lot of things."

Al-Tawash's story sheds light upon the integrated way in which engaged spirituality can unfold as part of a changing biography, deepening beliefs, and social actions. Spiritual autobiographies such as this one reveal changing personal preferences and shifting social contexts that incrementally redirect individual paths over time. In fact, in a few cases, recollecting a lifetime of subtle spiritual nudges and restrained epiphanies produced an acknowledgment of a grander narrative slowly playing out over years of spiritual and social development. Seeing a pattern within this arc can strengthen the resolve and deepen motivations as much as a more dramatic transformative experience. The moment of social awakening, spiritual transformation, or cognitive liberation is immediate for some, while for others it is measured. Indeed, in cases of slow and gradual spiritual development, the social action and the spiritual transformation are often one and the same. For these individuals, as al-Tawash reveals, the spiritual path and the lived reality unfold together; whereas for those who experienced a sudden shift in perspective, a new way of implementing their role in the world had to be sorted out.

In combination, these stories reveal that there is no singular source of engaged spirituality. Years of subtle personal changes over time, familial religious rituals, and volunteering for social organizations, as well as community socialization that constantly shifts as one transitions from youth to adult or from one religious group to another, all lean gently upon the way that spiritual experiences are connected to social action. At the same time, sudden mystical breaks or dramatic moments of existential clarity can snap together a new, or at least newly articulated, framework that demands engagement with the world in direct and ongoing ways. The groupings above speak more to the processes through which these shifts occur, but, even so, they are stuck in somewhat artificial distinctions that do not completely convey the sometimes surreptitious route that these individuals take in developing a fused engaged spirituality of social change. What is common across all these stories is that engaged spirituality introduces, clarifies, or heightens a sense of transcendent exigency that cuts through these differences in origins and perceptually transforms the social world into a space in which divinely inspired change is implemented. Just as there are multiple sources for this new worldview, there are also multiple ways in which this mandate is carried out.

Chapter 3

Acting on Faith

Social Roles in Expressing Spirituality

L<small>EE</small> D<small>ELEON</small>, a Latino social minister in southern California, confesses with a shy smile that he has had "some real supernatural experiences." One of those experiences changed his life. He recalls,

> One night, [my friend] and another fella, we were just sharing what God was doing. Some type of a presence, some powerful presence, like an angel, visited with us, and I remember [my friend] was able to see the angel, I couldn't see the angel. But I remember the angel giving us instructions to lay hands on me. It was then that I received what they call in the church, the Baptism of the Holy Spirit [and I] spoke in other tongues . . . I'll never forget it. It was so powerful—so awesome. I'm always reminded that there's that special touch in my life that needs to be shared with others, and I know that! I know that there's a definite call to my life to reach out to hurting people.

The emotional and intangible weight of this spiritual experience produced a qualitative change in DeLeon's life, crystallizing a new special purpose to spirituality and reaching out to others. The experience alone altered DeLeon's entire outlook on his social world and shook his ideas about what to pursue in life. In his words, it was "a definite call." Yet, DeLeon was relatively young when he received this "baptism," and he was not fully committed to a career of religious service, let alone social service. In fact, while intimately carrying around the emotional remnants of his call to reach out to hurting people, he had no idea just what that would mean, how it would manifest itself, or what ongoing role an encounter with the divine would have in implementing such a plan. He admits, "I wasn't really sure what this was all about. [Speaking in tongues] was a fun thing, if you will."

DeLeon's candid comment gets to the heart of this discussion: how do spiritual experiences get translated from personal fulfillment, or even fun, into specific social action and change? Once the pilgrim returns from Hajj or after the vivid vision evaporates or the sense of clarity and connection recedes into the day-to-day pressures of life, how are these newfound perspectives on the world implemented or turned into strategies for effecting meaningful change? Analyzing spiritual experience as a transforming and mobilizing force in social change, while privileging experience, does not end with experience. Each of the emotionally charged transforming moments and even the slower evolutionary developments of an integrated engaged spirituality are inextricably bound up within social contexts, interpersonal relationships, childhood socialization, or merely coincidental happenstance of modern social life that are all cause and consequence of engaged spirituality. Just as the sources of transformation are affected by a variety of cultural and structural influences, so are the ways in which these new motivations are enacted.[1]

In an attempt to understand the implementation of engaged spiritual motivations, I examined the wide scope of ways that people inserted spiritual frameworks into their everyday activities and found that education, skills, social capital, professional and friendship networks, and status all figured differently into the opportunities for action that made change possible. Spiritual experiences functioned in ways that worked within or sometimes against the externally defined parameters of social positions such as volunteer or imam. At times, spiritual experience amplified motivations to combat burnout or overcome obstacles, while at other times it stimulated creativity for changing tracks along taken-for-granted ways of doing things. For some, an engaged spirituality entailed business as usual with a spiritual overlay, while for others it prompted radical shifts in careers or political action that utilized the resources of social positions to push upon the boundaries of expected social roles. What appears consistent throughout is that social roles and social structural relationships, bound up in personal and professional responsibilities and social expectations, affect the funneling of spiritual motivations into social action. At the same time spiritual motivations transform these very same roles and structural relationships.

There are seven social roles, which will be discussed in detail later, through which engaged spirituality is creatively enacted for social change. Lee DeLeon's story is an example of the ways in which these roles are multiple and shifting throughout a lifetime.

Learning through Life

Lee DeLeon is a fifty-something, second-generation Latino minister at Templo Calvario, a large, vibrant, bilingual Assemblies of God Church in southern California. DeLeon is an exceptionally humble man, although his organizational skills and successes have made him highly sought after as a consultant. Churches and social organizations alike dangle lucrative offers to lure him away. But Templo Calvario is his home, in part because it is a family affair and in part because of the vast array of creative outlets available to him under one community umbrella. Within Templo Calvario, DeLeon is involved with various organizations such as We Care Southland in Los Angeles, City Teams Ministries in Miami, and the Compassion Network, his own consortium of local and global food distribution groups. As a galvanizing figure in these social ministries, DeLeon is part of a relatively new but growing group of socially concerned and socially active Pentecostals who are motivated by their spiritual beliefs and relationships to act responsibly in the world. For DeLeon, acting responsibly in the world builds upon his concerns for personal salvation by adding concerns of others, including poverty, food security, or accessible health care.

From early childhood onward, DeLeon's path was deeply influenced by unique personal relationships and mentors. Both his father and mother were formidable examples for how to lead a spiritually and socially responsible life. DeLeon's father "came to Christ" in California before Lee was born. The senior DeLeon moved to Texas with a newfound "fire in his heart" but found little Pentecostal outlet in the small-town religious communities in the rural plains. Brimming with passion to share his spiritual gifts in constructive ways, the senior DeLeon turned his zeal away from finding a religious home and toward finding an outlet among the social needs of the communities through which he traveled as a salesman.

DeLeon did not have to search far to find social needs. The Bracero Program was in full swing throughout Texas at this time, and the transnational workers who were far from home quickly identified the senior DeLeon as someone they could trust, someone who quite literally spoke their language. At the same time, Lee DeLeon's mother was equally committed to utilizing her spiritual motivation to help those less fortunate. Her service front was the family home. The DeLeons lived across the street from the railroad tracks, and as a child Lee would watch "hobos" eat food off the family's plates and drink out of the family's glasses, his incredulous questions always answered through a gentle discussion of spiritual service to those in need. While DeLeon's parents never held professional positions in social ministry during his early childhood years, these social tableaus burned deeply in DeLeon's memory, fusing together the values and convictions of voluntarily serving neighbors and, more often than not, strangers.[2]

Even with this early influence from his family, DeLeon's trajectory toward adopting a social minister's role had a circuitous path. Although raised in a very dynamic and socially active Pentecostal home, DeLeon did not have a direct transformative encounter until he was nineteen years old. It was then that he understood for the first time, through personal experience, the "fire and passion that my Dad had." As DeLeon described, "It ripped up my heart." Lee's older brother Dan had moved to southern California as a young adult and was incredibly influential as Lee began seeing the choices and paths for his own life during this period. Dan already had the "fire" and was well on his way to establishing the vibrant and growing Pentecostal ministry that would become Templo Calvario.

Lee decided to join his brother, and he saw the drive and social elements within the ministry. "Once again I saw rekindled in [Dan's] life what we had seen in our Dad's life—a real passion to reach out to hurting people." Their close relationship was fused even more tightly as Lee showed a desire to join his brother in developing the church. Their family bond facilitated the manifestation of what they saw as a spiritual mandate through complimentary roles in the ministry. Dan was the natural preacher. Articulate, charismatic, and fiery, he was well suited for the pulpit. Lee, on the other hand, admits, "I had more of an administrative gift, so that's what I did. Took [Dan's] ideas [of serving the community] and put them to work." These reciprocal roles were essential components of the newly formed church ministry that the young brothers were developing following the everyday examples of their parents.

Living in Orange County, California, and serving a growing, often-poor immigrant community in many ways marks the broader social twists and turns of federal policy and the restructured, increasingly informal employment structure between the United States, Mexico, and Central America.[3] While definite similarities in ethos exist between DeLeon's upbringing in rural Texas, the daily activities in southern California are very different. Scrounging up resources is one of the relentless pursuits that span the service work of these two generations of DeLeons, yet there is a significant difference in scale. For instance, Lee recalls strangers and neighbors alike going into a small office his father kept in their modest Texas home. Some needed help translating letters or filling out government documents, but most also needed money to get them through a tough time. DeLeon remembers his dad reaching into his pocket to dole out meager remittances, with his mother later asking, "How are we gonna do it?" Today, at the helm of several growing charitable outreach organizations,

DeLeon understands both of his parents' reactions. He finds it difficult to see more need than he has products and services to fill, but he pushes himself to do so while at the same time asking how they will do it. Whereas the early DeLeons pulled together as a family to sustain their voluntary faith-based commitment to serve their neighbors, Lee DeLeon, as a community leader with an impressive organizational base, pulls together a national and increasingly international family of service providers.

And still, when Lee discusses the rewards that he feels from his ministry, he turns to the intimacy of individual stories rather than the interlocking organizational successes. In fact, many of the people who have joined the DeLeons's congregation and the other churches they have planted are admittedly members because of the individual help or service they received at some point along the way. Lee describes one such story.

> We had one fella, and I remember some years back he was really hungry. Just crossed the border. Was here just a few days, didn't have much to eat. Saw this was a church, came in and said he was hungry, was there anyone who could help him. And our ministry, which is Works of Love, they gave him some food, a little money to get a burger, [since] most of our food is dry goods. That really impacted him. He came back that Sunday, started attending on a regular basis and doing the maintenance and janitorial work, so he took a job here. And later, met one of the secretaries and got married with her. So pretty much [he] found everything he was looking for in life. An incredible religious experience, love, a mate, and I think that's what church should be all about; really ministering to the whole person.

It is precisely these real-world manifestations from congregations, ministers, and community members that sustain and encourage spiritually motivated service. In addition to staying connected through the individual stories that make his work rewarding and reaffirm his affective role in social ministry, DeLeon also draws upon his Pentecostal tradition through prayer, with the gift of tongues and deep reading of the Bible. In fact, it is in reading the Bible that he hears the overwhelming cries of the poor, the needy, or the addicted that, he argues, will not be silenced until some action is taken to alleviate them. Yet these spiritual practices that are bound up in and reinforcing of Pentecostal community tradition simultaneously make DeLeon sharply attuned to the limitations of his community traditions and challenge him to change the institutional structure. DeLeon praises Pentecostal groups such as Teen Challenge and Victory Outreach that are actively pursuing spiritually motivated work among drug addicts and gangbangers, but he admits that

through the years we've not seen a lot of involvement as far as Pentecostal churches and the Assembly of God. . . . What I don't understand is why more people aren't involved in social justice. Living out
their faith in that dimension. I mean, the [biblical] passages are there.
The mandate is there. It hits me, time and again, especially when I
come to passages that speak about the poor, speak about those that are
bound by sin, drugs, alcoholism, you name it. Those things—I think
they really jump out of the Word, jump out of the Bible. They just
speak tons to me and motivate me to do more.

DeLeon suggests that part of the problem with the lack of social engagement is generations of Pentecostals who may have exceptionally devout spiritual lives but who grew up without seeing organized social service outreach
within their own congregations. This remains a particularly American conundrum for the church, since globally—in places like Brazil, Kenya, and the
Philippines—Pentecostal churches are leading the social service ministries
within communities.[4] Fulfilling a similar approach domestically is where
DeLeon sees the greatest potential impact for the work he feels called to do.

I'm determined to be a model. To be different is to say, "I can also
demonstrate some of these principals. I can also live them out!"
There's a constant challenge and motivation in that dimension. . . .
I'm just determined to really see it through, and do what is in my
heart to do. And I believe what's in my heart is to do what scripture
tells me I should be doing.

While DeLeon clearly addresses what he sees as the denominational
missed opportunities for directing spiritual motivations toward social service
and development, he also correctly identifies the social structural barriers to
reconciling this old agenda with a new one. The economic and legal hurdles,
especially those placed upon the largely immigrant Pentecostal communities
in southern California, exclude many who might be otherwise committed to
bringing about change on their own block, in their own neighborhood, or beyond. DeLeon is moved and impressed by the spiritual passions of the immigrant pastors who "set up shop opening churches." However, these churches
do not have the economic resources on hand to adequately provide for their
own congregation, let alone the extended community around them. Yet as these
needs intensify and the populations grow, they become increasingly visible
both socially and politically, sparking hesitant organizational change within
the denomination. In many instances, DeLeon has been leading the way in
reintroducing a compassionate outreach ethos. The models that he has constructed in the field of social services have helped many other congregations

and denominations in the region as well as across the country to work together sharing information, strategies, and even resources. Extending these examples of social ministry programs throughout the extensive network of denominational churches is reshaping the position of the Pentecostal minister and the potential community actions that that role may encompass.

One of these projects that DeLeon has been running for twenty-five years is Obras de Amor, or Works of Love.[5] Open Monday through Friday from eight A.M. to four or sometimes five P.M., Obras de Amor distributes everything, from bananas to cleaning supplies to canned beans. On the day I walked through the large warehouse at one end of Templo Calvario's complex, there was even a dishwasher, still in its box, waiting for delivery to a family in need. Ten to twelve volunteers work each day, unpacking boxes from overstocked grocery stores or distribution centers and repacking boxes for delivery to the fifty churches that provide volunteers and receive goods and services. DeLeon admits with a hopeful rather than frustrated tone, "It could grow into hundreds [of churches] if we just had the food to give them."

Abel Perez is the young and articulate executive director behind Obras de Amor. When asked about his motivation for doing this type of social ministry he unabashedly stated, "The church's sole purpose for being is to serve human needs." In his position at Obras de Amor, Perez attempts to do just this. As he put it, Obras de Amor facilitates the churches that have the spiritual commitment to serve human needs but not the financial or organizational ability to do it. "They have the desire but not the resources. . . . We're putting tangible works to the spiritual convictions the Lord has given us," he said. A worldly manifestation of divine mandates is essential to their definition of who they are as Christians. "You can be social responsible and not spiritual, but you can't be spiritual without being socially responsible."

Perez is a remarkable testament to the burgeoning social ministry within the Pentecostal movement. Still organizationally green, Perez provides an exceptionally clear, fresh institutional ethos of a socially fused, engaged spirituality. Perez agrees with DeLeon that there are more needs than there are resources within this community, but it is his faith that sustains him and the work he does, even when it seems like an insurmountable uphill climb. "We've not been able to help some people who've come to the door asking for help" he said. "There's certain times when we don't have the resources to meet that need . . . But that isn't why I'm here—to just give the resources. What keeps my sanity is I serve my Lord with it and I do my best for my fellow brother. That's the way I balance my spirituality with the work I do. Just being socially responsible. If you want to be spiritual you've got to bear the fruit of responsibility."

DeLeon and Perez successfully face and overcome barriers within their own denomination by others who do not assume this requisite connection between social service and spiritual experience. This first hurdle is in many ways crossed, which leaves the more daunting hurdles of actually effecting change.

DeLeon's story exemplifies the two central arguments of this chapter. First, social relations, positions, roles, and contexts throughout life have an impact on individual actions. As DeLeon and Perez illustrate, spirituality in social action is affected by the real and perceived individual or social networks that can act as either barriers or opportunities within any given social context. At times conventional expectations of a social position such as Pentecostal pastor can be constraining and must be either resisted or creatively worked within in order to carry out a particular agenda, in this case a vibrant social service ministry.[6] At other times or often at the same time, these social positions establish informative networks and confer status and authority that can be enabling and necessary for change.[7]

In this sense, engaged spirituality is always a relational spirituality. Relational does not exclusively refer to a relationship with God or a higher power, although this is clearly the perceived core for DeLeon and Perez—as it was for most people interviewed here—but also to one's position, to their social networks, and to the broader social context. DeLeon's life exemplifies the positive and negative possibilities within this relational nature of spirituality. DeLeon, for example, was indelibly impacted by the positive examples of care that his parents provided to the migrants within the social context of small-town Texas.[8] Once in southern California, the way that DeLeon perceived the social need in a new community as well as the resources that became available there, fueled by spiritual motivation and bolstered by his brother, positively affected the scope of his ministry in ways that it may not have if he and his brother had remained in a small Texas town. Even still, the economic and material realities of the communities' needs in relation to the church's donations, grants, and funding, as well as the original religious institutional culture that DeLeon faced, limited the extent to which socially directed spirituality could be employed.

The second central argument that DeLeon's story conveys—and the central contributing factor in why spirituality must be considered as a consequential social resource—is the way in which spiritual experiences act back upon social context and affect the implementation of social roles. DeLeon's spiritual motivations and spiritual partnership with his brother have significantly impacted the broader social contexts for the individuals and families in the communities surrounding Templo Calvario and increasingly across the country and the world. As these networks and relations of service expand, DeLeon must organize greater numbers of volunteers and paid staff to help implement the vision that he and his brother share, impacting both his personal social position and his social role in carrying out the responsibilities of that position.[9] In doing so, the expected and appropriate actions of a good Pentecostal minister expand based upon differing models and examples of what that position might entail.

Roles for Engaging Spirituality

In the conversations I had with participants during this study, the two sides of a reciprocal relationship between social forces and individual actions played out on different stages, producing multiple ways that people socially engage their spiritual commitments. Some brazenly challenged governmental authorities, while others quietly gave aid to neighbors in need. Stepping back to look at the narratives as a whole, seven different spiritually informed social roles for social action (or inaction, in some cases) emerge. All of these roles can be considered as concentric rings around the pivotal core of the individual; subsequent rings delineate a greater degree of social breadth or scope of potential influence. Individuals closer to the center are often affected by the actions of those in the rings that encompass theirs, whereas those in outer rings are very often dependent upon the activities of those in the inner rings for the implementation of their visions. The range of ministries available through Templo Calvario, for example, requires multiple skills, various networks, and specializations in a wide array of services. As in any organization, roles emerge that serve different parts of the organizational whole. At Templo Calvario, full-time managers, spiritual visionaries, weekly volunteers, and public advocates all contribute to serving the immense needs of the poor communities locally, regionally, nationally, and internationally.

The types of roles required by any complex organization like Templo Calvario parallel necessary roles that fall outside of the microcosm of organized social service, echoing back to DeLeon's parents, who served the community not as social workers, social activists, or visionary leaders, but rather in their day-to-day interactions with those in need around them. Of course these roles, from organizational director to informal volunteer, should not be thought of as static positions that are necessarily fixed, determined, or all encompassing. Some are for some people, but, for the majority, different roles developed at different times in their lives. What is more, others like DeLeon moved in and out of certain roles throughout the day. Each role, whether fixed or highly fluctuating, affects the way spirituality is funneled or employed, while at the same time spirituality acts back upon the composition, expectations, and responsibilities of the roles themselves.

PRIVATE QUEST

The first chapter discussed the caricatured view of spirituality as an internal, private matter devoid of social implications and often derided as overly self-indulgent or retreatist. From this point of view, there seems to be little connection to engaging or changing the social environment. Undoubtedly, introspective journeys for self-help are not only popular but also a very lucrative market for those who can promise individual enlightenment. While many faithful use these spiritual commodities in conjunction with or as an extension of their faith tradition, for others self-help books, videotape guides to meditation, mandala Web sites, and e-prayer allow a new group of faithful who privilege spiritual fulfillment and enlightenment without reference to a religious community or even without reference to one internally consistent religious tradition. This religious bricolage is one end of the spectrum that recombines traditional techniques or creates new practices in ways that suit individual preferences.[10] Admittedly, every participant, to some extent, was engaged in a personal quest of spiritual development, individual fulfillment, or transcendent communion. However, no one held self-fulfillment as the solitary goal without specifically considering the political consequence or social applications of this quest. In fact, more often than not, these women and men viewed such a self-directed spirituality as limited and limiting, both spiritually and socially.

MONASTIC

At the other end of the spectrum, the Monastic, while not participating in direct social engagement, nevertheless embodies in his or her lifestyle the foundation for a perfect society of love, peace, and justice. The term "monastic" here implies, in a very narrow and ideal typical sense, someone who has removed him- or herself from social life so as to emulate the highest ideals, toward which they feel the rest of society should strive. By this definition, or perhaps better put, by current global definitions of familiarity and celebrity, examples of the pure monastic are few and far between. They do not command extensive staffs or convene press conferences to articulate their vision for the world.

The Monastic and the Private Quest teeter tenuously upon each other's borders. While their inner motivations may be quite different—the Private Quest seeks individual personal development, while the Monastic contemplates a new world—their engaged actions converge or are at least indistinguishable from the outside. Monastics without an audience for their vision may have no more affect on the world around them than their counterparts who delve inward for personal gratification. The other five roles engage directly, repeatedly, and spiritually with the social world around them in an attempt to make it a better place.

GOOD NEIGHBOR

The Good Neighbor is one of the broadest social roles and applies to the widest variety of individuals. In many ways, the Good Neighbor as a social role feels nostalgic. It harkens back to an idealized moment in social memory when communities were believed to be mutually supportive, nurturing, and organized around collective betterment rather than individual accomplishments. This collective myth can be a mobilizing ideal in reconsidering social relationships within an increasingly atomized and segmented society; however, if uncritically considered it can mask the strong and real structural issues that defined community differently for different people. In fact, the participants in the Bracero program that the senior DeLeons served so willingly as Good Neighbors required much more powerful allies than simply the random kindness of strangers to rectify the systemic injustices in the federal labor program.[11] Even so, that should not discount these everyday acts that provide moments of sustainability both for the person providing the service and the recipients.

The Good Neighbor's characteristics also correlate with individualized notions of spirituality as well as evangelical motivations to share one's faith with individuals around them. Spirituality for the Good Neighbor implies changing the world one person at a time, either through small acts of kindness or promoting spiritual transformation in others. While focusing on individual acts and interpersonal interactions, the desire to change the world one person at a time by no means requires a primarily Christian or evangelical framework. In fact, in nearly all interviews, spiritual motivations and their religious interpretations were internalized by the Good Neighbor rather than externalized as expressive testimonies intended to change someone else's religious path. Two examples, one Catholic and one Hindu, exemplify the variation in this role.

Sister Dorothy Stoner is a Catholic nun in the progressive Benedictine order. While the activities of the nuns at Mount Saint Benedict in northwestern Pennsylvania can receive international acclaim or consternation depending on one's sociopolitical points of view, Stoner stressed the everyday element of living practice. She admitted that at times the sisters made headlines or attracted news vans, but what really mattered was the day-to-day interactions of the Good Neighbor. Stoner recalled a cold early winter's evening when she had been rushing around trying to complete a series of holiday errands and trying, unsuccessfully, to get out to the "Mother house" for an advent vigil. She and another nun were already behind schedule and neither had eaten, so, she said with a laugh, they stopped at McDonalds for a quick bite. As they sat with their meals in the brightly lit plastic booths, they heard a loud "Merry Christmas" from a twenty-something man standing at the other side of the restaurant.

Both sisters replied with a warm yet subdued "Merry Christmas." The young man immediately made his way across the restaurant, chatting continuously about the soup kitchen that the nuns support and rattling off the other mission services in the area. As Stoner herself suggested, the nuns' roles as volunteers at the soup kitchen must have indicated their social positions and most likely instigated this particular exchange.

As the man approached, Stoner guessed that he was "struggling with his own mental health," since his conversation wandered at times into the obscure. Still, he accepted their invitation to join them at their table. As the conversation unfolded, Stoner thought, "Isn't this interesting. We were trying to get out to pray [at the Mount]. The sister and I were going to have a conversation on something, I'm sure a reading or whatever, and here we are engaged in conversation with this young man—certainly a different conversation than we would have had. We were certainly late for prayer out here. And yet isn't that what we were supposed to be doing? To hear him talk about his life; for us to be kind and respectful." They could have been curt and cut off the conversation with the man, something Stoner has done in the past. "I guess we were being at our best," Stoner says, laughing. In reflection she suggested that nurturing the conversation with the man, "that is the voice of God. And I learned from that." In this example, spirituality was very mundane in its implementation, but it provided profound introspection and connection for Stoner. Spirituality does not require institutional resources, particular social/political status, or deep theological acrobatics. Stoner, as the Good Neighbor, interprets spiritual opportunities for action in the smallest, sometimes accidental, and typically most intimate interactions of everyday life.

Across the country, and drawing on a different set of theological doctrine, Sara Desh Arpana tells of her experiences in a similar sense. First she explained her literal and spiritual journey to becoming a monastic at the Hindu Vedanta in Hollywood. Later she spoke about her personal understanding of karma and how it might affect the way she encounters the homeless and drug addicted people in her immediate surroundings. "First of all, I accept the circumstance of my own life as my karma. But karma is not a static thing . . . just as you've got here you also have the same power . . . to transform those circumstances."

One way to transform one's circumstances is through serving others. However, serving others, she explained, is different than changing their life for them. Sara Desh Arpana used as an example the rampant drug addiction evident is some nearby Hollywood neighborhoods. The role of the Good Neighbor from Sara Desh Arpana's perspective is clear and distinct. "I am probably not going to be able to transform that person's life. I can serve them. I can see they're given food, I can see they're given shelter. I can make educational and employment opportunities available. But the choice to pick those [opportunities] up is up to that person." Service in this sense helps the neighbor in need if they so choose, but it more directly transforms the person who serves.

The vast majority, like Sara Desh Arpana and Sister Stoner, merely try to serve those around them without forcing a particular religious perspective or assuming what is best for that person by asserting a direct line of action. Rather, having a warm conversation with a man who most likely does not have that opportunity often allows the other person to dictate what they need even if this is just a moment of time. Transformation might take root in the other, yet it might also occur within the Good Neighbor, keeping alive an ethos and sustaining a spiritual perspective through these actions. There were variations in the degree to which religious preaching helped someone down on his or her luck, but service was never rescinded because of a theological or religious difference.

VOLUNTEER

As these roles move out from the social core of the individual, they become increasingly reliant upon greater degrees of organization. In some ways, the Volunteer is a more controlled embodiment of the Good Neighbor. Volunteers work within their community, providing direct services or aid as part of an organized form of social service and, although spiritually motivated, may or may not express this as part of their service. The conventional modern American image of the Volunteer is in the soup kitchen, which became prevalent among Protestant churches throughout the twentieth century and for many was their first introduction to social service work.[12]

Many of the people I spoke with had been volunteers at one point in their life, although most now held more formal roles in social change organizations. Brother Dunn, for example, discussed volunteering during his summers at college in the Appalachian Mountains. A former Catholic nun explained her volunteer role in the antinuclear movement. Another woman toured public schools, discussing various misconceptions of Islam and, in particular, Muslim women. A Jewish attorney who attributes his secular Jewish identity to the social service work that his family routinely engaged in while he was growing up now volunteers his evenings as a legal aid director at the Gay and Lesbian Center of Los Angeles. As these examples illustrate, the Volunteer is crucial for the successful implementation of complex projects that are notoriously underfunded and marginalized either politically or socially or both. Volunteers engage their spirituality for social change in flexible ways. They often are constrained by various social responsibilities such as work, school, or family that dictate the degree to which they may participate in direct social service or full-time advocacy. The Volunteer has more scheduled blocks of time to relegate to social service (or creates more blocks of time) than does the Good Neighbor but has not been able to or has little desire to build an entire career around these motivations and actions.

PROFESSIONAL

The Professional holds a paid leadership role in a religious, political, or non-profit organization and administratively organizes their spiritual motivations and the spiritual or often secular motivations of others in ways that increase service distribution or program efficacy. A vast majority of the people I spoke with were Professionals. While some had to create professional roles for themselves outside of conventional religious or secular organizations that could not or would not accommodate their particular vision, most worked within mainstream institutions where they pushed at the boundaries, sometimes gently and sometimes with force.

Father Michael Kennedy is a Catholic priest who organizes a series of social ministries in East Los Angeles. Programs such as child care for working parents, mother-operated afternoon street patrols launched by Comunidad en Movimiento, and a night shelter for recent immigrants each reflect the socioeconomic and ethnic demographics of the immediate neighborhoods surrounding the parish church. However, the community is not only reflected in these projects, it is fully incorporated in the holistic vision of Kennedy's ministry. While holding an authoritative position in a notoriously hierarchical religious tradition, Kennedy uses the status and resources of his position in ways that relinquish or delegate as much authority as possible to the community members themselves. Kennedy's reinterpretation of traditional Catholic organizational structure is based not on the way things have been done in the past but rather on the political shifts in the Catholic church over the past generation and Kennedy's own ongoing Ignatian spiritual practices. Kennedy uses his role in ways that redefine the Catholic congregation as a congregation of the streets. According to him, "there's not a kind of dualistic thing . . . this is people's lives. So, to have a divorce between life that's inside this church and life on the streets—isn't that what Jesus was about? He didn't spend all days sitting in the synagogue reciting the psalms."

Kennedy suggests the motor of all social ministries at his parish is the Christian Base Community program that has been in effect for nearly twenty years. "The dynamic is [small groups] reflect on the word of God and put it into action." He continued, "Basically it's kind of a place where people can have a spiritual uplift, but also it's just not left there like a prayer group. A prayer group has its own purpose, but it pretty much stays right there. But this is to always have some type of action that's connected to the reflection on the word of God." From these small group spiritual gatherings, community members organize. Meetings provide both a physical location and an open forum in which to raise the concerns of neighbors and work collectively on strategies to rectify them. At the time of the interview the pressing issue was community policing. Kennedy explained, "We're going to try to develop a pilot program where there's a different model for police relationship with the community." And, in fact, organizing around this issue had recently produced a telling example of the synergy between spiritual motivation and action.

Inspired by a Gospel reading about bringing good news to others, base community members went door to door collecting signatures in support of new community policing regulations. The very next Saturday a formal action was planned in which Kennedy successfully connected community members and their initiatives with prominent civic leaders. In the parking lot of the church, five hundred members met with the chief of police, representatives from the mayor's office, and a local city councilman. In the second phase of their action, Martin Sheen joined the participants, and along with police officers and parishioners a three-hundred-strong group marched through the streets, ending back within the walls of the church. This entire action included a liturgy, a public civic meeting, and a community policing action in a seamless afternoon.

When asked about the Christian liturgy being a core element of the events that integrate police officials, local politicians, and civic leaders, Kennedy answered in a way that unearthed his own interpretations of what his social role as a pastor should be by drawing directly from his understanding of Jesus. He said, "Well, big deal. That's what church is . . . I don't think Jesus was that selective of people he hung around with. Always a nice mix." This nice mix illustrates the relationship between social roles and social change, from spiritually motivated community base leaders through the office of the mayor. One role that a Professional such as Kennedy takes, far from an aloof authoritative model, is to organize, inspire, and orchestrate this nice mix by employing the networks and resources at his disposal and mobilizing his constituency on the ground.

Naim Shah also maintains this mix of people in a football summer camp that he organizes, blending rich and poor, religious and secular, famous and not so famous, and Muslim and non-Muslim. Shah was an up-and-coming football rookie, scouted for college with his eyes on the NFL and their eyes on him. Unfortunately, a knee injury ended any dreams of going pro. Shah always balanced his football with education, and, armed with an accounting degree, he set up shop with one of the nation's leading accounting firms. In his free time Shah traveled a circuit of schools to challenge students to focus on education and any athletic aspirations they might have. Following one of Shah's speeches, a man asked Shah to take his message to a local masjid as a personal favor to him. Coincidentally, Shah happened to be struggling over what to do with his future. His athletic career crumbled and, while making a substantial income with the accounting firm, he somehow felt hollow and unfulfilled. Immediately upon setting foot in the masjid and meeting the head imam, Shah knew that this was the place where he could passionately devote his talents.

Shah has been at the masjid for nine years as masjid administrator, and he is now taking on greater spiritual leadership as assistant imam. This position has been eye-opening and has afforded him a whirlwind education that his college years could not approximate. He admits, "Not having any experience in terms of Islamic affairs and community affairs and affairs of humanity in general, I've met the homeless but I've sat with kings. I've sat in meetings with millionaires and then been right downtown."

The variety of experiences that Shah has accumulated as assistant imam has sparked creative ventures and provided networking outlets. One of the most innovative ways Shah has utilized his new professional role is by working through the Ilm Foundation, a nonprofit organization affiliated with the masjid. The Ilm Foundation's main focus has been on Islamic education both for Muslims and the community at large. Shah argues that a greater knowledge of Islam for followers as well as for others is crucial to dispel the misconceptions of the religion in the United States. However, this core of education is only the starting point for action. The Ilm Foundation has partnered with other nonprofits to focus on community education, health care, and other service provisions such as food and clothing.

Working within this nonprofit service wing of the masjid, Shah has integrated his own interests and professional expertise both in sports and accounting to create a new summer program called Go Beyond the GAME. The program recruits recent Muslim college graduates who, as Shah says, are "trying to find their way, just like I was trying to find my way." Shah wants to create conduits that connect these young adults with their community in productive and creative ways beyond simply religious or spiritual connection. Shaw says, "They need to see themselves as a part of the community more than just through prayer. That's your main link, but for them, they also need to see additional links." The football summer camp, headlined by an NFL sports hero who also happened to be Muslim, provided lessons and skills and even medical service and physicals for participating children. As the program develops it will include year-round participation and training of young adults, bringing in additional skill sets such as conflict resolution, entrepreneurial training, and college and corporate tours to expose the youth to alternative hopes and dreams beyond sports. In all, Shah's vision is to provide "nurturing to fatherless children in the community, then we can see new products in being able to improve the communities in which we live."

The initial program was a success, with sixty children participating, ranging in age from eight to eighteen, 80 percent of whom were non-Muslim. Islam played a subtle but open role in the event. Shah reported, "We didn't say anything about Islam. But they knew when they heard Naim, Haaqim, Hasaam, you know, that these are different than the names I have." Shah believed that serving as an example was their strength. He explained, "[The parents] were ecstatic that everything was free and that people actually took the time out to serve them." When I asked why he thought 80 percent of the children who participated were non-Muslims, he replied, "We are targeting our children. So, you don't need to get too caught up in this percentage of Muslim versus the percentage of non-Muslims. We're concerned about what you're giving us in time to share what you, what we've been blessed with, and trying to mold some good character into your life."

Shah's response, like that of Kennedy's, illustrates that for some professionals, serving the community as a model of how to live life morally, ethically, and holistically was more important than espousing dichotomous terminology or divisive labels about the sacred. An unconditional spiritual motivation drove each of these men in their professional roles to create new forms of lived religion within their communities. Shah commented, "To put together programs, it really is from the scripture. . . . It talks about neighborly needs and different services in the Koran. It really obligates you. If you were sincere and you were reading [the Koran] this reaffirmation does not stay within yourself. It will actually at some point in time register for you to really share this with others. Now, how that's translated is up to your level of expertise and knowledge to make it compatible in your society." And herein lies the unique capability of the Professional. While all of these roles could translate this desire to share in particular ways, the Professional has at his or her disposal a variety of resources, including financial pools, perceived authority, social networks, trained and experienced staff, and oftentimes a preestablished constituency, not to mention the allotted time that may be devoted to such endeavors.[13] Of course holding a professional position does not ensure an activist stance by any means. In other words, the social position alone does not determine the specific way in which the role will be acted out. In fact, religious institutions may hamper radical change and perpetuate the status quo through their central leadership. Working within these parameters can be empowering but can also result in bureaucratization or even marginalization.

Some of the most ardent activist Professionals that I spoke with, even if they had religious credentials, operated outside of the institutional boundaries of the religious orders—sometimes because of institutional, social, or political constraints. Rabbi Shapiro, for example, was very much working at re-creating the institutional culture of Jewish congregational leadership and worship practices, but he was doing so from an independently founded institution for spiritual growth. For some Professionals, stepping outside of the institutional boundaries allowed the freedom with which to articulate the connections between spirituality and social activism.

ADVOCATE

The Advocate focuses his or her spiritual motivations on public education of particular issues and/or attempts to initiate changes in social policy or community development. Advocates are the instigators, the educators, and the mouthpieces for particular platforms or social causes. Advocates can work within or outside of institutional channels. They may be professionals who as part of their daily responsibilities must act as watchdogs for government systems and corporate responsibility or they may be weekend activists who devote their free time to raising issues in the public consciousness.

Javier Stauring does both. As Catholic youth chaplain in the Los Angeles Juvenile Hall, he provides direct ministry to children incarcerated by the state, organizes volunteers, and advocates for the children. While Stauring identifies the direct ministry as the core of what he does both spiritually and practically on a daily basis, he aggressively pursues his advocacy role for his charges. He says, "I think a lot of it falls on us that are behind the walls—the chaplains, the volunteers—that actually get to meet the kids, get to know what really is going on, that they're not monsters, and how the system is working against them. . . . We have a bigger responsibility to speak out and to educate. And a lot of the educating has to be done in the pews, in the churches."

When I asked to what extent his advocacy is wielded to express the inmates' humanity to the outside world—a social justice goal—and to what extent it is expressing a transcendent moral mandate—a religious or spiritual goal—Stauring replied, "I think it's both things. I don't think you can put religion in one little box and say, okay, we're just going to deal with religion on this aspect. I think religion is everything we do in our lives. Spirituality is everything we do in our lives. And if there is injustice being done, I think that's immoral. I think that's wrong in God's eyes in that it goes hand-in-hand." This moral resonance between injustice and faith is palpable for Stauring, who is theologically trained and intimately exposed to the struggles of incarcerated youth. "It's clear in the Bible that we should be childlike to enter the kingdom of God. I think it's shameful what we do to children here—in that aspect of relating one to another."

Stauring uses an unambiguous moral vocabulary when speaking publicly about the treatment of children in the juvenile justice system. His words do not always fall on receptive ears, but those are often the ears that Stauring believes must listen. Stauring reconstructed a recent talk he gave at a prominent religious community sympathetic to progressive social causes. He unabashedly said, "I called the system evil, because I don't think you can sugarcoat it. It's sinful what we do. You send a fourteen-year-old to prison for the rest of his life, that's evil. That's sinful and there's no other way of looking at it." At the time of his speech, Stauring did not realize that there were several judges in the audience that night along with district attorneys, none of whom responded well to this accusation.

At the end of the talk, Stauring said, "One of the judges got up and he said, 'You know, this presentation might work over there in your area, but here you're in a very affluent area and I would suggest you look into changing your presentation if you want to effect change.'" To Stauring, this judge was only reinforcing the underlying message of the presentation. He explained, "Yeah, you treat us differently. And that's what the system does. And the poor ones, and the 'ones over there,' they might go along with what you're saying, but we're different." Stauring unflaggingly tries to make juvenile justice an issue of common humanity rather than an issue that can be subdivided and categorized and ultimately neutralized as something that happens elsewhere to others. By using terms such as sin and evil, Stauring is drawing classes, ethnicities, races, and neighborhoods together under a different authority that he feels does not answer to rules of status propriety and social appropriateness. In doing so, Stauring says there is no way to say "right now, I'm the activist and right now I'm seen as the spiritual guide. No," he specifies, "I think it goes together."

Stauring's speeches may not always have the impact that he intends or would hope for, but as an Advocate he tries, at the very least, to get people to pay attention. As he put it, "The biggest benefit is just to get them thinking about it." Although Stauring does not divide the spiritual from the advocacy in his own life, at times he will admit that the vocabulary of sin and evil is more effective than at other times. In a recent opinion piece in the *Los Angeles Times*, for example, Stauring coauthored a forceful indictment of the current state of affairs in juvenile detention centers in California. Reading this opinion, there is no denying his passion. The essay details the "Kafka-esque" system that keeps children in cages during classes, an overuse of isolation cells for the inmates deemed disruptive, and "excessive rates of violence" among the youth. Stauring pulls no punches, suggesting that if these incarcerated youth in the California system came from "white, middle-class neighborhoods, the public would never stand for its failures and abuses."

Although I only know Stauring from our one conversation, it is not difficult to hear the words "evil" and "sin" between the lines of this excoriation. However, neither word is included, nor are any references to a spiritual mandate, save the nominal description of Stauring in his byline as "director of the Office of Restorative Justice/Detention Ministry for the Archdiocese of Los Angeles." Still, Stauring did not separate his spiritual mandate from the civic responsibility of shining light on these conditions. Quite the contrary, his spiritual meanings, like those of others, infuse attempts at social transformation in ways that are not necessarily evident on the surface. Instead, they can be turned up for certain audiences, such as when Stauring is recruiting potential volunteers following a church liturgy, or turned down when engaging in the social politics of the public square. By rekeying moral advocacy in social terms for some occasions and spiritual ones for others, public figures like Stauring may not always be perceived by outsiders as particularly motivated by spiritual mandates.[14] Often missed by social analysts and social activists alike, these subterranean or backstage spiritual energies across the political and theological spectrum serve as deep emotional and social reservoirs for action.

VISIONARY

The Visionary sees the world not only as it is but also as it could be. Often the Visionary acts in ways that disregard seemingly insurmountable odds. Visionaries may have dramatic eschatological images in mind of the violent destruction of the world in the rapture, but more often, and just as subjectively profound, other visionaries may have images of a society with less poverty and injustice. Pastor Cecil "Chip" Murray is undoubtedly one of the most recognized visionaries among the Los Angeles religious community for the sprawling network of services provided throughout South Central Los Angeles. This vibrant, charismatic African American preacher of the First AME Church has inspired an activist congregation, which has grown to more than eighteen thousand members under his watch, to go beyond the walls of the church. This charge challenges each and every member to get involved in at least one of the various service programs that the church and its nonprofit wing offer. The church now has under its auspices a free legal clinic on Sundays, as well as housing loans; an elementary and middle school (named for Murray); a family resource center; environmental protection services that counsel on energy efficiency, recycling, and hazardous waste disposal; a welfare-to-wealth program; a business incubator for launching entrepreneurial interests, particularly in the high-tech industries; and multiple training courses for various populations. Considering the abundance of services provided, Murray's primary function is as a Visionary. He is unable to actively participate in the micromanagement of each project, but he perpetually rallies the troops to see the world, or at least the expansive community surrounding the First AME Church, in new, successful, and sustainable ways—a vision that has transformed the local neighborhoods through health care systems, schools, and affordable housing.

One of the institutional strengths that Pastor Murray has at his disposal is the resounding network of black churches and the long history of social ministry between the church and the African American community. Other visionaries must work against the grain of institutional cultures that may not have supported such integration of social platforms in the past. This was the case for Lee DeLeon, too, as he began developing a Pentecostal social service and development ministry. The same is true for other visionaries as well. For example, I visited the core of South Central Los Angeles where a free health clinic schedules appointments for twenty-five to thirty-five patients a day. Such a scenario may not appear remarkable in many poor, urban areas across the United States. However this clinic, the University Muslim Medical Association, or UMMA Free Clinic, for short, is unique in its formation and operation.

In 1990 several young medical students at the University of California at Los Angeles were searching for a socially responsible outlet for their health care skills. Some had volunteered in tutoring programs in California prisons while in college and were eager to continue giving back through some similar form of public service. Perhaps more important, this original group of motivated medical students was composed predominantly of second-generation Americans and, more specifically, a decisively new generation of American Muslims. Founding member Dr. Mansur Khan recalled, "We had come out of the Islamic Centers and the mosques where we had been affiliated and gotten religious training, but we saw a lack of social activism, of people going out into the community." He continued, "Whereas a lot of Islamic charities had been focused on causes abroad, given that there's a lot of third world countries in the Muslim world, we decided that, 'Hey, there's a need here. And why not take our expertise and put it towards serving the community *here?*'"

Based in their religious upbringing, these young adults expressed that social service in the name of Allah is not just an option; it is an obligation. However, from its inception, the clinic has been ardently nondenominational, interfaith, multiethnic, and nonproselytizing in its mission, which is reflected in its diverse staff of volunteers and array of clients. By all accounts, UMMA is achieving its twofold objective of impacting the availability and quality of health care in the immediate community as well as radically transforming the broader definition of Muslim service in the United States. At the dedication ceremony six years ago, a former professor pulled aside one volunteer and confessed, "I didn't know Muslims cared." Clearly the actions of this handful of

committed students prove they do, and changing minds is one positive consequence of the visionary move by these young adults to put their faith into action. Unlike other long-established social ministries in the United States,
these young second-generation Muslim Americans had little institutional en-
trée and had to ferret out substantial funds from institutes and individuals who
had no understanding of what Muslim social service might entail. However,
these cross-cutting ties that UMMA was able to establish between the local
community of South Central Los Angeles, city and state political leaders, charitable foundations, and UCLA have started a ball rolling that is transforming
the idea of what charitable Islam means and the way that Muslim Americans
are employing their spirituality to affect local neighborhoods in need.

Spirituality, Changing Roles, and Sense of Identity

Social roles reveal the expectations and responsibilities of social positions that
affect the implementation of subjective spiritual motivations. At the same time,
individual action, influenced by spirituality, alters expectations and changes
the responsibilities of roles. The seven categorical, spiritually informed social
roles outlined in this chapter may appear clunky and overly functional. However, these categories by no means universally determine action due to preestablished, socially agreed-upon role parameters. Family, community, religious
institutions, occupational position, educational training, and friendship networks, just to name a few, can all influence the way in which roles are enacted
or the way that spiritual mandates to make a better world are implemented. In
fact, most of the individuals I spoke with continually challenged their roles in
life. Both formal and informal roles were pushed, pulled, stretched, and manip-
ulated in ways that more closely correlated with their newfound, continually developing subjective spirituality.

Conventional social role theory acknowledges that each and every time a
role is carried out there is an ongoing creative process that conforms, to greater
or lesser degrees, with these social expectations. In other words, positions and
roles are continually being redefined because of changes in the social ways in
which they are enacted. Women religious, to take just one vivid example, are
very different today then they were prior to the sweeping changes of Vatican II that altered the social structural expectations of what nuns should and,
indeed, could do. In part, these changes can be attributed to macrolevel changes
such as technological advances, mass media influences, economic turns, or
even major sociopolitical upheavals such as the civil rights movement or the
women's movement. On the interpersonal level, these changes in the way roles
are enacted can also be attributed to changes in socialization, such as particu-

larities of parental influence or, later in life, the biographical accidents that reshape one's ideas and motivations.[15] All of these changes in society and in social positions affect individuals' sense of who they are, their motivations, their choices of individual actions, and the way they act collectively to reproduce and reconfigure society itself.

Even though most participants in this study attribute the way they negotiated roles and their actions to a profound spiritual experience, little analytic attention has been paid to these moments as consequential to their sense of self and their actions and, more significantly, the incremental impact that spiritual reinterpretation of roles might have for society as a whole. Take, for example, Lee DeLeon. Clearly parental influence, presently and as memory, and the ongoing influence of his brother shapes the way that he pushes the expected boundaries of social ministry within the Pentecostal church community. Yet if one takes DeLeon's own words on the matter, it was the "fire and passion" that "ripped up my heart" and therefore definitively altered the direction of his life and his ministry.

Sister Stoner's example of taking the time to talk to a poor man "struggling with his own mental health" even when she was late for another appointment illustrates that the taken-for-granted—although perhaps not publicly admitted—way to act would be to disregard the man and diffuse the situation quickly. There was little direct accountability except for the other nun accompanying her, and Stoner even admits that, at times, she has been less generous with her time. The deciding factor at the moment in the sister's choice to have a conversation with this man was discerned spiritually.

For the Volunteer, in a time when apathy and individualism in American civic culture appears rampant,[16] organized participation and civic responsibility are enhanced by a transcendent mandate. The Professional redirects resources or reconceptualizes her job description. The Advocate finds passion, the Visionary creativity—none of which might be experienced or, more important, acted upon similarly otherwise. As such, these categorical roles should not be considered fixed but rather socially and spiritually negotiated categories that are affected by the world, by patterns of interaction, and by the agreed-upon social definitions of appropriate actions as well as the profoundly spiritual experiences that produce innovative ways of action. In short, spirituality, as evidenced in these peoples' lived experiences, has the potential to rearrange previously constructed patterns of action and identity—both because of one's social position and in spite of it.[17]

At the beginning of this chapter these seven roles were explained using a visual metaphor of concentric circles, which allows for the role switching or "traveling" that occurs over a lifetime or even within the course of a day. The

Advocate becomes a Good Neighbor when she leaves the press conference and, on her way home, takes groceries to a single mother in her mosque who is struggling to make ends meet. The concentric ring model also captures the progressive, embedded dependence on social positions. Not only do individuals possess their own set of tools or resources that got them into a certain social position or that were acquired as part of that position, but they also have a symbolically conferred status (either positively or negatively applied) that derives from a patterned interaction. The Professional, for example, has opportunities for employing her spiritual motivations in ways that the Volunteer may not. She typically has a staff; a set of material resources, such as computers, office space, and a budget with salary; and a symbolically significant title for her actions. Conversely, the Visionary may have such significant access to the media and such a competent staff of organizers and volunteers that she is constrained from face-to-face interactions with the people that the Good Neighbor serves on a regular basis.

Finally, these roles should also be considered as fundamental elements of personal identity that resonate much more deeply than their actions alone may imply. Social roles, whether they be doctor, teacher, rabbi, computer programmer, sister, or activist, each represent an expected set of behaviors to others but simultaneously constitute part of an individual's personal identity. Individuals do not assume that a mother does certain tasks simply operationally, but rather because it is intrinsically rewarding to her as a mother; in fact, people often disregard the real effort that goes into certain roles because of the social value expectations of what that identity should mean reflexively. In the previous chapter I pushed the assumption of social service work as what religious folk unquestioningly do. Here I lend credence to this assumption from a very conscious, subjective position. For many who are religious and socially engaged, what they do is what makes them religious or spiritually in tune. Recall Abel Perez. Social service, or what he called "the fruit of responsibility," was essential if one is truly to call oneself a spiritual person. Social action substantiates a spiritual identity. Perhaps nowhere is this clearer than in the case of the students at UMMA Free Clinic. The ramifications of the health clinic include not only the tangible results of providing health care to some of the poorest of the poor in Los Angeles but also a rearticulation of Islamic compassion and ethno-religious identity of who individuals are and what they do. For all of these people, spiritually informed action was more than merely civic participation and much more than just a job. Instead, the closer the spiritually informed action was to their notion of who they were as Jews, as Christians, as Muslims, or as Buddhists, the more passionately it was pursued.[18]

Chapter 4

Keeping the Faith in Action

Cultivating Spiritual Practice

Those who wish to sincerely serve society must be spiritually pure and only those who are spiritually pure can sincerely serve society." Doctor Pujya Swami of the Swaminarayan Santhsa, a Hindu service society, voiced their motto straightforwardly and, refreshingly, without irony or any tinge of skepticism that is often directed at the integrity of public servants today. Yet his advice—or admonition—is obviously much more complex and difficult to sustain than what these simple words suggest. How does one become spiritually pure and how does one stay that way in the world of social service? Among spiritually motivated activists, the answers are varied but repeatedly include a strong footing in ongoing spiritual practice.

While the catchall term "spirituality" can be vague and abstract in everyday conversation, trying to label the acts people use to bring about spiritual connection can add even more complexities and, unless specified, more confusion. Terms like "spiritual disciplines," "prayer," "meditation," "communion," "spiritual practice," "salat," "finding time for God," or "centering" swirl around in ways that convey a general sense of a particular kind of communication. But at the same time as they relay such connections, these terms can also divide the spiritual experience into doctrinal segments that can obscure the common links that are highlighted here.[1]

Admittedly individual practices are always bound up in social and theological apparatuses—passed along by family, peers, and religious institutions—that teach a particular way to structure and experience communication. I suggest,

73

however, considering the theological component, perhaps better defined as the doctrinal differences between faith traditions, as part of the broader socio-historical influences that color and redirect practitioners' understandings, choices, and experiences of spiritual practice. By focusing on the common experiences across contemporary faith traditions in the United States as well as across the diverse individuals for whom spirituality and social transformation are inseparably fused, it is possible to uncover the underlying social traits that make spiritual practice a significant variable in social change. In other words, what does meditation do and how does this overlap with what prayer does? What effects does *puja*—the Hindu daily prayer rituals—subjectively produce that are similar to the effects of centering practices? How might one begin to understand the social and subjective process behind spiritual practices? And how do any of these connect to commitments and motivations for creating a better world?

The answers to these questions are highly textured and sometimes even idiosyncratic. Even looking within one religious tradition—or, more specifically, one denominational family—does little to sharpen one's understanding of what the act of spiritual practice means. Its meanings, functions, forms, and feelings slip around from experience to experience. Consider Lee DeLeon once again. While Lee admits that personal spiritual practice drives, directs, and sustains the personal commitments of all those involved in social ministries at Templo Calvario, his individual practice differs significantly from others around him who similarly ascribe to the more global denominational directives of the Pentecostal church. Lee's brother, Dan, the charismatic preacher, for example, enjoys being outside and takes prayer walks each morning as part of his regular repertoire of spiritual practice. During his walk, Dan explains, "I lay out the day to [God]. I say, 'Here's my life, spirit and body. You take it. I am your child. Do with me what you want.'" While this is followed by a scheduled hour of reading scripture, this first practice is unscripted and incorporates an activity that Dan DeLeon already enjoys. There are very few doctrinal steps to this practice and any order is a combination of Dan's interests and his daily habits. This is, for Dan, an unscripted conversation and an experience of the senses.

In contrast, other people in the congregation, Lee realizes, have vividly impacting visions and dreams that are intensely personal and variable yet still fall within the acceptable parameters of Pentecostal practice. Lee says he neither judges nor envies either of those alternative practices but simply understands that other peoples' paths and their connections will inevitably differ from his own. Lee, for example, finds reading the scriptures to be one of his most meaningful practices of choice, particularly tailored for his temperament and personality. He admits, "I guess [that's] the way I'm made. I can't think of anything else that really sustains my walk; that keeps me motivated."

Reading sacred texts is one fairly common and straightforward practice that spans faith traditions. However, even this seemingly standard practice, as performed, is not rote and cannot be easily replicated outside of one's own experience. For Lee, reading scripture and praying are not passive acts that imply simply reading or reciting words. Both are interactive and therefore very individually particular experiences. He explains, "I find a command or a question that's rather strong and really communicates a powerful message. I take time to highlight those types of things. So it's more of a study than just a casual reading of the Bible." This interactive reading is intellectual, emotional, and even physical, requiring a close reading, interpretive skills, and the actual marking of the text in ways that redirect his practice at the moment, as well as reshaping his experience in the future, if he should return to this same passage.

This is also true for prayer with DeLeon. One technique that he has slowly learned to cultivate over the years, and one he advises others to try, is focusing on listening as much as talking while in prayer. Since, in DeLeon's experience, responses are not immediate or verbally articulated in prayer the way they are in face-to-face interactions with others, the listening side of prayer life, DeLeon suggests, is often missed or not even considered by many people. He smiles as he says, "If you were to walk in my little office at home you wouldn't hear me talking much. I do spend a little bit of time just really bringing some things before the Lord [but] most of the time I just listen. I listen to what I just read. I listen to what He has to say. A whole lot of listening and just kinda being open to what the Spirit would say to me during that moment, that time."

DeLeon highlights the differences that individualize spiritual practice even within religious denominations. While doing so he also notes the variability of practice over time by referencing what the Spirit would say at a particular moment, reinforcing the fluid and changeable nature of spirituality. Prayer, even when specified in form, involves subjective interpretation, moods, shifts in personal experiences, or particularly troubling issues that may be weighing heavily at some times but not others. Throughout these interviews, individual resonance, interactive practice, flexibility of interpretations, and experience over time result in sets of spiritual practices that appear to have as many possible directions as they have forms of implementation for action within society.

What I ultimately came away with was a rich mosaic of personally tailored practices and subjectively interpreted experiences from which three categorical processes of spiritual practice could be distilled: spiritual benefits, or the *function* of spiritual practice; spiritual repertoires, or the *forms* that this practice takes; and spiritual meanings, which directly involve the *feelings* produced through practice. This chapter focuses specifically upon the functions that spiritual practice provides to practitioners as well as the various forms that this practice takes in people's lives.[2]

The Significance of Practice

On a blustery winter's night, locked deep within the lavish confines of his London home, Ebenezer Scrooge had a "spiritual" experience. Three times through the night he was visited by three different ghosts—transcendent other-worldly figures—whose visions radically transformed his sense of place in the world. Charles Dickens's A Christmas Carol is well known. Whether it is considered a redemptive tale of holiday goodwill or a cautionary tale of the perils of capitalism, it is not explicitly a spiritual tale. Yet much like the epiphany that Ebenezer Scrooge had upon awakening on Christmas morning, profound spiritual experiences reconfigure one's place in the world and clarify one's responsibility and sense of generativity or lasting legacy for family, friends, and community. Scrooge's purchase of the biggest goose and the warmth with which he eventually reached out to his employee's struggling family were newly awakened attempts at changing the way he would be thought of in this world and remembered when he passed into the next.

The evidence of Scrooge's overwhelming change in disposition came directly on the heels of the ghostly spirits' revelations. However, putting these new feelings into action consistently over time can be much more difficult than showing holiday cheer the day after a spectral dream or radical vision. What will never be known about the life of Ebenezer is what happened on that following Monday morning after the holiday, when Bob Cratchit was back hunched over the ledger books. What happened three months later when the business took an unpredictable slump, and what happened two years after those first powerful premonitions visited upon Ebenezer on that long cold winter's night? Dickens assures us that Scrooge lived according to "the Total Abstinence Principle ever afterwards," and if readers take that one line to heart then they might be content with this happily ever after. But just how was that complete transformation sustained? Might the reader quite easily imagine a less happily ever after considering the personality of the previsitation Scrooge, particularly given contemporary examples of fleeting promises to change and short-lived resolutions.

One of the most significant hurdles in maintaining a new or "converted" identity is the influence of one's lived environment in which family and friends may not fully understand the new worldview.[3] Sometimes surprisingly to the person who has just gone through a transformative moment, the rest of the world, including friends and family, do not change. Of course, Ebenezer pleas-antly shocked the neighborhood as he shouted out his newfound sympathies on Christmas morning and then spent the day carrying them out in generous deeds. While Ebenezer met a receptive audience among his previously belittled worker and fellow citizens, people for whom spiritual experiences are profoundly impacting may not always receive such a warm welcome from family, friends, or society at large and therefore must find other sources of affirmation for their transformation.

Literary allusions aside, these interviews revealed precisely this hesitation and, at times, reluctance. Pastor Canales, who found Jesus while he was on an acid trip, admitted that he had to put distance between himself and his previ-ous network of friends, including his bandmates. He remembers that for weeks after he had gone through his transformative moment the guys would park outside of his house, pot smoke oozing from the cracks in the car windows, taunting him to come back out. When he refused, they would laugh and call back, "Oh, did you see the light?" To which Canales had to respond, "I sure did. You know what? God is good, man." Not succumbing to the peer pressure and alluring taunts of a decadent past is hard, especially for a teenager, al-though Canales notes that for him the bottom line was a newfound strength through God. Practice helps fill this gap, reinforcing new commitments when peers and social networks do not.

As time passes, the trials and responsibilities of everyday life roll out much like they always have, and maintaining a spark or motivation requires some-thing more, something ongoing.[4] For some, that something more comes in the form of new networks established through volunteering or social service work, such as in DeLeon's case or in the case of the Benedictine nuns. However, even for those who did have a new or supportive social network through which to bolster their spirits and commitments, maintaining a vividly profound passion—not to mention maintaining an arduous social service work—still required some form of consistent spiritual connection.[5] Reliance on individual practice is particularly useful in the diversity of contemporary life in the United States, where, unless cloistered, it is increasingly difficult to be surrounded exclusively or even primarily with others who maintain similar spiritual ways of compre-hending the world.[6] Of course, individuals all similarly share many common cultural ideas, such as traffic laws or manners of speech, that reinforce ways of thinking and allow society to function. However, part of a shared set of cultural understandings includes an unspoken sensitivity to public statements about strongly felt spiritual motivations or experiences.

Indeed, in many situations—unlike Canales standing up to his friends about his new relationship with God—the individuals interviewed here did not always feel comfortable articulating their spiritual motivations in secular settings, and at times they turned completely to highly individualized spiritual practice for connection and motivational maintenance. Whether surrounded by a tight network of people who thought similarly or left to their own devices, the participants' individual work was required through some form of spiritual practice in order to keep alive both the transcendent motivations for making a change as well as the strength and support to continue acting upon the motivations. Spiritual practice reaffirmed the social and spiritual commitments forged through transformative experiences and provided useful cultural tools that turned these profound and emotional moments of connection into guiding principles and actions that directed and redirected their everyday lives.

Cultivating Spirituality

Approximately twenty miles east of downtown Los Angeles is a predominantly Chinese American suburb that over the years has slowly shifted demographically away from its Latino-inspired name, Hacienda Heights. Banks and real estate signs beckon in English, Spanish, and Chinese along the main road that leads off the freeway and up into a small, rounded ridge of foothills. After passing fast-food chains and strip malls, the boulevard begins to climb and before long the stunning gold-tiled roof of the Hsi Lai Buddhist Temple emerges from eucalyptus trees, chaparral, and California Oaks. Built in 1988, Hsi Lai—literally translated as "coming to the West"—is a major spiritual and cultural center for the dispersed Chinese and Taiwanese community across southern California, as well as for the thousands of tourists and students who visit each year.

The traditional Chinese architecture of the temple complex, designed and constructed by Taiwanese craftsmen, transports visitors from the surrounding commercial landscape—replete with exhaust fumes, neon advertising, and honking horns—to a gentler environment marked by chimes and wafts of incense. A vast open courtyard leads to a structurally dominant main temple and provides visual relief from the ornate detail and Buddhist sculptures that surround the perimeter. Shaved-headed monks, mostly women, in saffron-colored robes, walk in and out of the warren of temple rooms that circle the courtyard—including various classrooms and a cluster of rooms set aside as a museum. Most of the monks at Hsi Lai are from Taiwan and many do not speak English conversationally. However, flyers for English dharma classes dot the bulletin boards throughout the temple, and while most visitors appear to be of Chinese or Taiwanese descent, it is not unusual to see many more diverse faces from Los Angeles. In the far corner of the temple grounds, a tearoom is open for those who need a break from the oppressive heat or for those who have just come from chanting mantras in the incense-shrouded main temple.

Hsi Lai and the community service-oriented Buddha's Light International Association serve the spiritual and social needs of the region through a variety of services, including interpersonal and family counseling, daycare, senior housing services, and educational donations to local schools. Hsi Lai representatives stay active in a variety of interfaith partnerships throughout Los Angeles and southern California, creating bridges not only with community service work but also with the greater religious community around them. The Reverend Man Yee Shih is one of the most civically active resident monks at the temple and maintains extensive connections with the greater Los Angeles community. Originally from Taiwan, Man Yee moved to Hsi Lai after giving up a highly profitable real estate career in Toronto. Her organizational skills, personal charisma, and command of the English language have contributed to her prominence in the interfaith community across southern California.

During several conversations that I had with Man Yee over two years, she described the different forms of contact the nuns have with the community on a daily basis at the temple. The nuns mostly serve specific needs, such as generational conflicts and cultural transmission within Buddhist families or guiding school groups and a constant stream of Asian tourists through the multiple representations of the Buddha and Bodhisattvas that fill the temple grounds. But service is not only institutionally planned. It can also be intimate and unexpected. Man Yee explained one particular interaction that encapsulates in a very personal and embodied way the functions of spiritual practice in her life.

One afternoon, as Man Yee described, "a seriously mentally ill gentleman came in and you could see by his eyes that he was very sick." Once inside the inner courtyard of the lavish temple grounds, the nuns at the information table were concerned that the man might hurt himself or others and called for Man Yee to intervene. Man Yee, who is no taller than five foot two inches, arrived quickly. She knew that if she had called the police or the fire departments that they would most likely send him away for hospital treatment, if they did anything at all besides escorting him off the premises. Man Yee instead countered by saying, "[This] is a moment for us to reflect our spiritual practice [toward others]. . . . As a Buddhist monastic it is a time for us to practice what we have been taught: compassion." Rather than calling for police intervention, Man Yee ushered the man to a private sitting room just off the courtyard. In the few yards between the information booth where she met him and the door of the sitting room, Man Yee needed to draw upon her years of spiritual practice in a very deliberate way. She recalled, "At that moment I tried to recite and contemplate the name of Kuan Yin Bodhisattva because Kuan Yin Bodhisattva symbolized great compassion. I needed the energy of compassion at that moment in order to be able to help this particular individual." Her contemplation time was brief and highly charged with the instability of the moment. Yet Man Yee admitted with a broad smile, "It works! The energy was in me at that time." Once inside the sitting room, Man Yee explained that she was able to calm the man and explore what types of services might be needed to deal with his problem. An earlier stint as a social worker unquestionably contributed to the resources that Man Yee had at her disposal in offering service to this man, yet chanting the name of the compassionate Bodhisattva benefited Man Yee in an additional, value-added way.

While practices differ greatly from Man Yee's recitation of the name of the Bodhisattva of compassion, the benefits or functions appear relatively consistent across traditions as well as the individual appropriations or application of practices. Ongoing spiritual practice hones skills and develops spiritual resources or reservoirs that can be tapped in times of specific need. In this way, spiritual practice can be understood as both a routine practice—as defined earlier—as well as a directed tool for responding to acute or emerging concerns.

Benefits of Practice

Man Yee's story provides a nice backdrop for pulling apart four functions or benefits of spiritual practice. While these benefits might occur simultaneously, they may also be sequential and additive stages of a particular spiritual practice. One way to read through these different personal contributions is to do so very broadly, as outcomes of spiritual practice in general. For example, the spiritual benefits outlined through this specific case at the temple would also play out similarly for purely long-term religious ends such as being a "good Muslim" or assuring salvation. However, the focus here, of course, is on the role of spiritual practice on the actions individuals take in their communities in an attempt to make a better world locally or globally. Still, spiritual practice for transcendent or applied results need not be an either/or option. For the individuals interviewed here, spiritually informed social action is intrinsically wrapped up in the inner-worldly ascetic concept of what it means to be a good Muslim or what it means to achieve future salvation.[7]

EGO ADJUSTMENT

Nearly everyone described leaving behind his or her everyday concerns, worries, individual drives, and agendas. While not always successfully achieved, this *ego adjustment* is typically a first step in spiritual practice. Man Yee, a lifelong expert at meditation practice, was able to clear her mind of self-interest—in this case, the fear and anxiety of physical harm to herself or others—by drawing upon the mantra of the compassionate Buddha. Man Yee, referencing Buddhist philosophy, calls this "detachment" and suggests that when it is achieved through meditation or contemplation there are no longer individual feelings of fear, worry, competition, or anxiety. This detachment is what enabled Man Yee to put aside her own initial anxiety, compounded by that of the nuns at the information booth, and respond to this man without fear. Detachment allowed Man Yee to refocus her thoughts on the role of the contemplative Buddhist: compassion. This compassion extended not only to the mentally ill man in the courtyard but redirected Man Yee to consider the anxieties of the nuns who were waiting cautiously with the man.

While Man Yee provides a direct example of the way in which her practice effect immediate action, across disciplines this feeling of selflessness is one of the most commonly mentioned direct effects of individual spiritual practice as a routine part of everyday life. Self-motivations such as material considerations, status, or the stress of modern living dissolve and on a regular basis nudge the individual to reconsider the world beyond these individual desires. Of course, even though ego-driven perspectives may shift, this does not imply that worldly concerns completely disappear or that the sense of self dissolves entirely—although in extreme situations this may be the case. In fact, most people explained that their spiritual practice was often engaged for a specifically directed everyday purpose such as gaining clarity on a particular policy decision. The change that practice brings is that these concerns shift from questions of "What do I want" to "What would the Bodhisattva instruct" or "What does God want for me?"

This spillover effect from practice to everyday life is perceived by various practitioners to keep egos in check throughout the day as well as reinforce nonmaterialist or other-centered views about the world and the individual's role in it. Man Yee's direct and practical application illustrates the spillover of spiritual practice in action; however, dissolution of the ego is often less surgical. It is also realized as a diffuse part of life that requires practice and attention. Man Yee, for example, in her everyday life practices spirituality through regularly scheduled meditation routines and communal temple services at Hsi Lai that seem much more mundane than her example of directly applied practice for calming her nerves and generating compassion. It is through these everyday practices that these benefits such as detachment are cultivated and understood as resources that can be utilized when, as in this case, selfless compassion is needed.

The perceptual shift of ego adjustment involves both practical time and space considerations as well as more cognitive elements of concentration. First, spiritual practice often requires carving out a set time and place from a busy work life. Incorporating times and spaces into a somewhat regular pattern integrates the formal or physical element of spiritual practice. Sitting quietly in a particular position, lighting a candle, turning on music, or turning off the computer all entail symbolic codes that signal a change from the immediacy of ego-driven concerns. Rabbi Shapiro says that spiritual practice shuts down the ego-driven level of daily life and allows for the opening up of another level of consciousness or perspective simply by creating the time to practice. He explains, "As soon as I sit down—because I've been doing it so long, it's Pavlovian—but as soon as I sit down [on a meditation cushion], all the anxiety and stress and the impact it has on my body . . . all that just stops."

Slowing the body through practice was a common way of trying to slow the mind. Some practitioners even suggest that these physical or environmental changes must preface authentic spiritual practice or at least spiritual communion. Rabbi Shapiro believes so strongly in this conscious decision to make time for contemplation that at Metivta a prayer/meditation room was constructed in the office space, and each day, during scheduled periods, employees were encouraged to stop working for ten or fifteen minute intervals. The same was true at the United Religions Initiative in San Francisco, where all work paused for brief periods throughout the day. In each case, no one was bound to one particular form of worship or contemplation or any at all, for that matter, but all were expected to physically stop working and, if nothing else, take some time to refocus and reset the tempo of their day. These organizationally structured downtimes—enabled through both time and space—encouraged individuals to alter the consuming pace of office work, deadlines, and callbacks and reconsider the reasons for their work beyond the paycheck or the secular accomplishments of status or productivity.[8] This organizational structure provides outlets for what most individual practitioners must otherwise find on their own.

However, many of the participants I spoke with had less scheduled or at least less explicit parameters for a perceptual shift away from their egos, and they typically had to create these moments themselves. Instead of carving out specific times, finding allotted spaces for practice, or physically manipulating an environment in ways that redirected their thoughts, they felt that a perceptual shift, wherever and whenever possible, can act like flipping a switch in their outlook. In other words, each person might consciously or reactively decide to shift onto a transcendent plane or universal authority, reducing their human motivations or orientations. Turning things over to God on the fly, so to speak, or calming one's mind while driving on the freeway, similarly repositions the ego-centered perspective that is to some degree necessary for certain tasks in everyday life. Man Yee did not stop on her way to the temple reception area to sit in meditation but instead spoke the mantra internally as she escorted the man to the sitting room. This spontaneous capability integrates spiritual practice into everyday life and, while sounding very conscious and concerted, is often reflexive or situational.

It is instructive to take these two influences together, the temporal, spatial, and physical structure of practice—the external element—and the perceptual or intentional shifts—the internal element. The first influence patterns the time and space for practice that could easily get put off until later. However, the intentional shift of being in the moment requires focus and concentration. Without keeping spiritual practice a fairly regular part of one's lifestyle and paying close attention to the feelings of this practice, the first function of reorienting one's ego and motivations can be easily undermined, limiting the additional benefits of practice. For example, regularly structured practices are especially susceptible to a routinization of rote movements or recitations, and many people suggested prohibitions about an easy slide into an auto-pilot mode of spiritual practice.

The time and space for prayer plays a significant role in Islam. Prayer schedules are set throughout the day for five specific times during which prayer is actively embodied. Facing Mecca and bowing down in prayer require external capabilities, such as an appropriate space, as well as internal reorientations that make the ritual meaningful. Imam Saadiq lyrically describes his experience of salat this way, "When you're praying, even though you're bowing down, you're actually ascending; your soul ascends even though your body stays." Assistant Imam Shah echoes, "according to tradition, at the lowest point in prayer, you're actually the closest to God." The physical prostration and bowing down structures the day in ways that conversational prayer in the car or at one's desk cannot. Both men admit that it is the physical time and space demands of this schedule, from which they cannot widely deviate, that puts their priorities in order and calls them back to a spiritual mindset even when they are organizing a downtown food drive, administering to their masjid, or rushing between speaking engagements across the city.

At the same time, Shah underscores the importance of concentration and this conscious switch-flipping when he cautions, "Prayer is an institution. You have some who pray, and it may become a habit. So there's more than just formal movements. But Islam, when it talks about prayer, it talks about the establishment of salat. It's really a prayer that consists of a whole entire concentration. It consists of you being in a state of humility, you being in a state of consciousness. You have knowledge of what you are saying. You're aware that you are within the presence of God." Humility and awareness of transcendence beyond oneself constitutes authenticity for Shah and illustrates well this ego adjustment.

In very similarly ways, Benedictine Sister Dorothy Stoner warns that among Catholics as well routinely scheduled prayer can "almost become an idol."[9] Stoner uses the term "authentic" in ways that are quite similar to Shah as she describes her evolution to finding a spiritual practice that works for her. She admits that "if I spend a lot of hours in prayer it can become inauthentic." In contrast, authentic prayer is prayer that "makes one sensitive to all creation. It cannot be an escape from the world." And yet this can be the seductive quality of setting aside time and space for spiritual practice. By this definition, prayer becomes inauthentic when it emphasizes the individual's piety, which is ego directed, rather than the sense of service and connection, which is other directed.[10] As Stoner's Benedictine sister agrees, "It's so easy to be irreligiously religious. And religiously irreligious. Somebody said once, if you want to sin, it is not necessary to break the law. Just keep it to the letter."

VESSEL

In the experiences of those interviewed here, spiritual practice empties the self or dissolves the ego in order for the practitioner to become a receptacle or vehicle for spiritual intervention and direction. Returning to the mentally ill man in the temple, Man Yee described clearing her mind of ego-driven thoughts even in this brief span of time and subsequently physically feeling the energy and power of the compassionate Bodhisattva filling her body. "The energy," she said, "was within me at that time." Being filled as a vessel is often described across interviews as spiritual energy or power that can be redirected in real ways with real consequences. While Man Yee found this through the Bodhisattva of compassion, others described this benefit in equally vivid and physically experienced ways, such as speaking in tongues or seeing visions. This connection to the spiritual energy or direction is often the apex of spiritual experience. This is the communion with the divine that may be experienced directly or subtly or only recognized later in reflection.

Yet while seemingly the goal of spiritual practice, this is not always the end result of sitting in meditation or bowing to Mecca and the manifest examples of feeling energy or a presence are not often the reason for engaging in practice in the first place. Man Yee's daily meditation practices, as mentioned above, for example, do not require that she feel that energy within her each and every time she meditates. Rather, mediation allows her to accumulate skills and experiences and cultivates the confidence in detachment that she can then draw upon later when she needs to find compassion for an immediate problem.

Pujya Doctor Swami of the Hindu Swaminarayan Temple combined these first benefits concisely when he pointed out, "When the mind is at peace, the power of God can work through us and we can serve people in a better way." Nearly everyone mentioned turning themselves over in prayer or contemplation to the spiritual direction of a divine will, discernment, or guidance, even if the sensation is not as vividly embodied as Man Yee describes it. Allowing God or some divine voice or, most abstractly, love or compassion to reach them once they have shut down the self-motivations and stresses of the day was, for many, the reason they engaged in practice. And, as Pujya Doctor Swami illustrates, direction was universally tied to some form of service or active change in the world that can only be accessed once the individual drive slows down and a transcendent energy replaces those drives.

The first two functional benefits of spiritual practice occur during the practice itself. However, if left in practice these benefits can easily lead to immobility or satisfaction with the communion itself as a form of self-fulfillment or self-exploration—spirituality for spirituality's sake, so to speak. Among this group, practice created a clear and unambiguous roadmap for action. As such, these practices have consequences that extend beyond the experiential immediacy of the ego shifts and transcendent connections of spiritual practice. And, indeed, spiritual practice produces residues that are carried out in work, volunteerism, or time with family. Spiritual reserves get replenished through practice and help people find a sense of purpose for their actions and uncover the strength to maintain their commitments and actions over time. By providing purpose and sustainability, practice keeps motivations, commitments, and values closer to a conscious level throughout the day when, following the half hour of meditation or the hour-long scripture reading or the ten minutes of prayer, the afternoon shift begins, the phone again gets answered, a homeless man approaches, or the funds for the new women's shelter dry up.

PURPOSE

The third functional benefit, and the first that extends throughout the mundane elements of spiritually informed social commitment, is the ongoing sense of *purpose* or meaning behind the work. Rick Warren's runaway bestseller, *The Purpose-Driven Life*, much in line with other positive-thinking promoters such as Norman Vincent Peale, encapsulates, in explicitly Christian and evangelical terms, the notion that each person is here on Earth for a reason. This purpose, for Warren at least, involves all the expected elements of evangelical commitments—serve God, serve each other, and share your faith, to name a few.[11] While a similar sense of divine or transcendent purpose in life was common throughout these interviews, most discussed this purpose in much more diffuse ways that emphasized social service work equally if not more than sal-vation. In fact, purpose was rarely couched in terms of direct personal benefits but rather seen as a moral and sacred responsibility in communion with others.

John Woods, introduced in the first chapter, spent all of his adult life, since World War II, in various forms of Christian social service. When asked why he had devoted himself to social change throughout his life, he put it this way, "I think the essence of it, the heart of it, the taproot of it is [spiritual]." This sense of spiritual purpose, for Woods, had its origin in a Christian up-bringing but was crystallized through his participation in the MRA. Obviously, these men and women who gathered for the expressed purpose of rebuilding Europe through personal, social, and national reconciliation had an over-riding social influence upon their interpretations of spiritual experience as having a social purpose. Yet Woods puts the spiritual element first, nominat-ing this as the taproot of all else that was to emerge. He described, "out of the quiet time, out of your change of heart and so on, flows, naturally flows, issues into the social, political, and economic transformation. And we saw that hap-pen again and again."

"Power, incredible power," explains Pastor Isaac Canales about the way his spiritual practice feels when he becomes a vessel for God through practice. The power he feels is directly connected to the work and struggles he faces each day. He clarifies how this power connects: "Not to go out and be arrogant, but incredible power to change the world, to make a difference. To encourage somebody. To reach out to someone. To go a little bit beyond what I could nor-mally go in a challenge in life. Or a problem. To look at a problem as an op-portunity for Christ to be glorified. So that it sets the tone for my life." Practice sets the tone for Canales in many ways, but it revolves around a deeply per-sonal relationship with God that informs his interpersonal ministry and his vision for the broader social service ministries of his congregation.

For Canales, and for others who resonate with Woods's idea of a motivat-ing taproot, practice has the ability to reconnect and keep present the original moment when an engaged spirituality of social commitments was first felt and understood. Pastor Canales vividly explains that his daily spiritual practice of reading the scriptures connects him to the original moment in his garage as a teenager when he gave his life to Jesus and saw a new reason for bringing about change in the world. Now sitting in an expansive office in the campus of warehouse-style buildings that make up his urban ministry, Canales is sur-rounded by shelves of theological manuscripts and Bibles in English, Spanish, and Latin—a far cry from his religious upbringing in a makeshift church. Yet these books constitute a potent part of his daily practice that positions him in a long lineage of change agents. His sense of responsibility and spiritual purpose is heightened by the transcendent connection he makes with these texts, linking past, present, and future into a unified, purposeful life. He explains, "Drinking deeply from the wells of scripture keeps the fire going of the day when I gave my heart to Him. And I hope to keep it going until the day I die."

For others an ongoing practice must continually re-create and reshape personal motivations and understandings of why they do the work they do. Motivations and understandings slowly mutate over time or might even dramatically swing because of an unforeseen event or a turn in public policy. Spiritual practice provides a sense of purpose for individuals caught up in these changes but can also be used to galvanize communities to take a stand. I asked Julie Weill of the Jewish Fund for Justice what kinds of strategies or connections work best when she speaks at synagogues or temples about social justice issues. Hands down, Weill replied, "Jewish sacred texts always play a role in motivating a community." Weill not only points out the mandate for social justice in these texts but also the significance for adhering to this mandate by the Jewish people. In this way, the sense of purpose may have to be reinvigorated for each new generation and, in doing so, rearticulated to fit new social issues and concerns.

A sense of purpose answers the question, why must I continue to do this or, if mobilizing others, as in Weill's case, why should I begin to do this in the first place? A sense of purpose is flexible enough to incorporate shifts in policy by tapping into something out there. The mandate becomes not simply political or social but transcendent and extends beyond individuals' day-to-day victories and losses. The cumulative stages of spiritual practice help maintain purpose and perspective.

Reverend Man Yee invoked the name of the Bodhisattva of compassion in order to be filled with compassionate energy that would hopefully allow her to serve according to ancient Buddhist moral principles and to what she believed was the purpose of a Buddhist monastic. Her phrase "as a Buddhist monastic" connotes the centrality of this type of action not only to her sense of spirituality but also to a sense of duty and a moral identity. The energy that filled Man Yee was not hers alone to squander as an internal spiritual experience. It had to be deployed for a social purpose in line with who she was as a monastic and how her spiritual progenitors would expect her to act.

SUSTAINABILITY

Finally, whereas receiving a sense of transcendent purpose is important in understanding the subjective motivations for why certain actions are taken, the function of spiritual practice for *sustainability* sheds light on how this is possible over extended periods of time or in the face of repeated failures and seemingly insurmountable odds. Practice, as seen through this fourth benefit, is a form of renewing the energy needed to continue.

Cultivating a meaningful practice provides confidence and a personal spiritual strength required to participate in social commitments on a daily basis or over time. Man Yee attributes this to being mindful, a direct benefit that she sees of her meditation practice, if practiced dutifully and with concentration. She explains, "When we are mindful [there are] a lot of things that we can handle." But this sustainability in handling a lot of things comes with practice. "When we have a moment of our own time," Man Yee describes, "like when we're walking, or sitting, or eating, we always recite the name of the Buddha in our mind because it reminds us of [his] teachings." However, this mindfulness transcends the moment of contemplation or chanting, extending into situations such as the incident with the mentally ill man. Man Yee continues, "Once we try to memorize what we learn, and practice it in our daily lives, when a difficult situation comes, we will be able to handle it." This confidence can easily translate into the sustained motivations that enable these individuals to forge ahead, sometimes even in the face of seemingly helpless situations and against overwhelming odds.

The day-to-day social service provided in the Tenderloin is incredibly trying on the workers and volunteers that come in and out of the variety of ministries Reverend Hope oversees. Drug abuse, HIV/AIDS prevention, poverty, prostitution, and violence are systemic structural problems that plague many inner cities in the United States and increasingly worldwide. Nevertheless, Hope perceives her spiritual practices and deep sense of faith as responsible for her ability to sustain her commitments and rigorous work pace. The sustainability of spirituality is reflected in her workers as well.

Having witnessed voluntary thankless service among countless participants, from the struggles of the civil rights movement through decades in the Tenderloin, Hope suggests, "In general, not exclusively, the people who stay and whose hearts are kept tender are the religious people. You have to have a transcendent faith and a transcendent view of life to keep doing this. . . . And in general, it's the religious people, and the Marxists, interestingly; the people who clearly know why they are there and have a larger view of human history than just the immediate." Hope's words give powerful testimony to the experiences of many of these individuals who have spent years if not lifetimes in the service of others. The spiritual benefits of ongoing practice are, by definition, based within and focused upon a larger view that sustains social action in ways that other resources and practices—with Hope's noted exception of Marxism—would not. Practice connects the individual with the transcendent and, for these people, holds the social world up as the arena in which to con-firm this sacred purpose through an active, engaged sense of self.

Categories of Practice

The four functional benefits of spiritual practice sustain, enliven, and develop the spiritual traditions they follow as well as the social commitments they mandate. Cultivating a personally meaningful set of spiritual practices enables individuals to perceive the benefits. Through practice, individuals regularly—although not always routinely—create the time and the space to reorient their everyday modern practical realities. Yet as these examples have so far indi-cated, practice is not always enacted in scripted patterns. Spiritual practice varies greatly, to include the stereotypical notion of praying a rosary, sitting in an incense-filled temple room, bowing toward Mecca, incorporating Tai Chi into a Christian discipline, or simply striking up a conversation. Indeed, for some people spiritual practice is much more fluid than conventional ideas of prayer.

Again, rather than focusing on specific doctrinal forms, such as chanting meditation versus reading sacred texts, one should focus on the ways in which practice fits into the lives and social action of the people who practice. In this study, categories of practice clustered around the different ways individuals meshed their various repertoires of spiritual practice with their lifestyles and the texture of their everyday lives. There are five broad categories of spiritual practice that typify the way individuals experience or live their practice: daily practice, eclectic improvisation, habitual worship, communal connection, and spontaneous connection. While these categories are separated in ways that give some structure to the discussion, individual collections of practices rarely conformed purely to one category but rather were composites of several differ-ent strategies or forms of practice. Moreover, some may connect directly to social action while others do so only tangentially through shared community networks or implicitly through moral reasoning.

DAILY PRACTICE

For nearly everyone in this sample, spiritual practices or spiritual disciplines are regimented parts of everyday life and often occur at scheduled times or in patterned ways. One of the clearest examples, already briefly considered earlier for its functional benefits, is the five daily prayers at the core of Islamic reli-gious life. There, Assistant Imam Shah referred to a repetitious daily prayer schedule as an institution that might easily produce rote adherence if not consciously and thoughtfully enacted. But it is precisely the structured regularity of daily schedules that Shah enjoys the most and finds most rewarding, saying that "as long as I'm consistent, [my prayer schedule] is one of the main mechanisms for restraint. [The Koran] says, 'How can dirt stay on you if you dip a person that's dirty into water five times a day?' Well, how can sin stay on you if you pray to God five times a day?"

Regularly scheduled daily practice was central to the lives of monastics from Hsi Lai Buddhist Temple to the Anglican Mount Calvary Monastery. The daily regimen of selected mantras, passages, and prayers orders the day temporally and requires attention to meditation and prayer even in the midst of busy office work or hectic family schedules. As mentioned, organizations such as Metivta and the United Religions Initiative have built in daily times for practice. On a more individual level, Pastor Lee DeLeon and Pastor Isaac Canales described beginning each day reading scripture as a way to set the pace or tone of the day. These strictly scheduled practices revive the mindfulness— broadly used—that connects each day with an otherworldly agenda.

Other rituals that take on daily significance through repetition have been recovered or appropriated. Rabbi Beerman, for example, pays particular attention to his morning ablutions, which for many are merely private bodily functions that are performed unconsciously. However, Rabbi Beerman notes that there are specific prayers for the human needs and bodily functions. Reviving these prayers for his morning habits, Beerman draws his attention to the mysteries and miracles of the human body that in the literal sense of the word are often thought of as mundane but when considered in their biological complexity are quite remarkable. Acknowledging the sacred in even the most seemingly profane activities continues the mindfulness that others experience through regular prayer schedules.

ECLECTIC IMPROVISATION

Whereas the daily practitioner typically follows fairly structured patterns of practice, the eclectic improviser experiences spiritual practice sporadically or experimentally, when the opportunity arises, and therefore follows few organized schedules, recognizable patterns, or traditional formats. Informal conversations with the divine, praying on the freeway, and "trying out" different practices from different traditions at different times are all examples of the way innovation adds ingenuity to spiritual connections, either out of creative impulse or necessity. While through daily practice someone may incorporate mundane elements into their routines in ways that order everyday life according to traditional sacred patterns or rhythms, innovation cobbles together new practices that sacralize everyday modern life as it happens. In other words, the

emphasis for the daily practitioner is on traditional forms while for the improviser it follows adaptation and novelty.

Take, for instance, two similar forms of spiritual connection that had two
very different points of connection for two rabbis. Rabbi Beerman eloquently
describes the sacred and scriptural precedent for acknowledging the mysteries
of the body through a much-patterned practice that has been consistently integrated into everyday life for millennia. Rabbi Steven Jacobs similarly draws
spiritual connection from his bathroom moments, although he his inspiration
comes from a very different source, which evokes a generational difference
between these men. Jacobs recalls hearing a speech by the beat poet Allen
Ginsberg during the Vietnam War protests. Ginsberg was vilified by many conservative Jewish congregations and, at this particular poetry reading at such a
temple, one member chastised Ginsberg by asking, "How can we respect you?
You're wearing jeans and a T-shirt." According to Jacobs, Ginsberg responded
calmly: "Every morning I get up, I have two pairs of jeans, I have two T-shirts,
and I wash each one every day, and I go into the bathroom and I take care of
myself the way I need to . . . I do my alms." From this, Jacobs recalled, "He gave
me a great religious insight, that the bathroom isn't just a place to look pretty,
the bathroom was a way in which you got in touch with your own bodily functions." By linking bodily functions with spirituality, spiritual connection takes
on an everyday veneer that is regulated by physical cycles rather than prayer
schedules or meeting times.

Jacobs's merging of Allen Ginsberg, bodily functions, and spiritual insight
involves some creative thinking and some deft improvisation, whereas Rabbi
Beerman's similar insight draws upon time-honored patterns for everyday life
provided through scripture. While the source of these forms of practice differs,
they are not the decisive factor in establishing the two categories of the daily
practitioner and eclectic improvisation. Instead, it is the piecing together of
two parts of life—spiritual practice and a poetry reading, a bodily function, a
sunny day—that otherwise would not be connected in expected ways that
defines this improvisation. Jacobs, for example, carries this insight into other
bodily intimacies such as sensuous touch and sexual intimacy. He regrets, "We
don't talk about sex as love. It's always something dirty to talk about from the
pulpit. But when we begin to talk about some of the great love poetry that
comes out of the Song of Songs and you get by this punishing God, then there's
so much of value." While sexual spirituality has gained some popularity through
common examples of Tantric sex or the Kama Sutra, these are often pitched as
commodities for improved sex lives rather than as embedded parts of one's spiritual life. In other words, as Jacobs suggests, spiritual sexuality is not coming
from the synagogue or church but rather from the bookstore or the Internet.

Forging these connections, although they are changing among religious communities throughout the country, still involves some improvisation, at least for now.

Other improvisation stems from the practical realities of everyday life. The Reverend Altagracia Perez is an Episcopal pastor whose relatively young career features a remarkable record of public service for HIV/AIDS advocacy, immigration reform, and worker rights. Juggling the demands of a family and most recently an ethnically diverse parish, Reverend Perez argues that improvisation is not an option; it is a necessity. The gym is one place for such improvisation. Here the reverend can appropriate a spiritual space for connection. She explains, "I work out five days a week. And that's very spiritual for me. To take that half hour to an hour—to be about another thing—just to be lost on a different level—my mind free to wander, to listen to music. That nourishes my soul." In the era of multitasking, Perez has found a time and space that works for her. The gym becomes the space in which she is not expected to return e-mails or phone calls or solve parishioners' problems—although clarity and insight about these problems, she assures, can come on the treadmill. The gym, through Perez's improvisation, is transformed into a space in which she can physically and consciously reorient herself to the spiritual purposes in her life and the spiritual commitments that sustain her actions. The gym works for Perez in ways that it may not work for others, which is the point of eclectic improvisation. It allows spirituality to flow into the crevices of everyday life in ways that tailor-fit the diversities of individual experience. Perez elaborated that, for her, exercise as an integral part of her spiritual practice is crucial to "balance the energy so that it's not all mental and God. So there's something functioning in my body."

Still other improvisers were spiritual bricoleurs, combining a variety of faith traditions picked up from friends, lectures, retreats, or even online and stringing them together into a newly eclectic and personally assembled repertoire of practices. Reverend Hope, for example, practices Tai Chi, slowly moving herself in controlled movements that fuse the connection between mind and body. Once a week, Hope also takes part in a Taize group, which holds a service involving chanting, spoken and silent prayer, and scripture reading, connecting Hope to a very different form of collective, participatory, and audible worship. Years ago Hope also picked up meditation practice from a Buddhist master in San Francisco, long before meditation reappeared across Christian traditions and seminaries. Finally, Hope performs nondenominational services within her community, often using street performances to highlight neighborhood social issues such as homelessness. Ultimately, Hope is fulfilled by various practices that foster a spiritual connection and often, as with performing street services, a connection to social action.

These improvisations are not the superfluous or unconnected personal indulgences often derided as consumerist spirituality or individualism. Rather, they integrate practice more fully into their lives than traditional means. In fact, when experiments with new forms of spiritual engagement fit or work, they may become part of an individual's scheduled routine of practices, supplementing other routines and work schedules. In this way, improvisations may become part of a daily practice or organized worship routine.

ORGANIZED WORSHIP

While the first two categories of practice draw upon personal and sometimes private practices, communal and organized forms of worship offer spiritual connection that might typically conjure religious services. For those who find organized worship fulfilling, spiritual practice includes periodically organized or institutional forms of practice. Weekly mass or scheduled meetings with a spiritual adviser fit this category well. In the last category, for example, Reverend Hope pieced together various practices into a uniquely improvised repertoire. Since she finds it difficult worshipping in a formal way when she is officiating a service, she explains that "[Taize] is really my Sabbath. . . . So Wednesday night is really my communal worship time."

Spiritual retreats comprise a similar form of organized worship for many people. This was especially true of professionals who devote all their working hours and sometimes all their waking hours to their spiritually informed commitments. Pastor DeLeon, Reverend Hope, Rabbi Shapiro, and Reverend Man Yee were just a few of the professionals who found the organized worship of retreats to be particularly refreshing and insightful, not only for their spirituality but also for their commitments to service. Brother Dunn said retreats are important for him, especially since his spiritual adviser chides him for having a "spirituality of special events." Not an avid daily practitioner beyond the daily group petitions with other Franciscan Brothers in his order, or perhaps readings of Gandhi, Thomas Merton, and the novels of Graham Greene, Dunn finds his greatest spiritual contemplative connection on the retreats he joins four or five times a year. During the concentrated time and space of the retreat, Dunn says, "I gain a bit of perspective on why I do what I do and . . . checking out your motives, you know? Do I do this or that for my own ego or for some recognition or is this what actually needs to be done?"

While retreats or services are one way of practicing organizational worship, so are informal gatherings. Brother Dunn, for example, sits down once a week with a community member or immigrant rights organizer he works with, usually someone different each time, and seeks spiritual inspiration through their words, their experiences, and, most important, their faith in action. For Dunn, hearing the stories of faith and hope from the communities is more beneficial than conventional spiritual disciplines. Although now scheduled as a regular and community-based form of organized worship, this type of lived, collective practice also merges into communal connection.

COMMUNAL CONNECTION

Spiritual connections powerfully emerge from interactions with members of one's own community or, more specifically, members of the community being served. However, more often than not the distinction between who is being served and who is serving is intentionally blurred in ways that reveal the spirituality of communal connection. Epitomized by liberation theologies of the 1960s and 1970s, Catholic reformers throughout Central America challenged those who were faithfully acting through service to recognize the face of God in the poor, the politically oppressed, and the disenfranchised.[12] Using a now widely dispersed sentiment, Bill Doulos of All Saint's Episcopal Church says that he sees the "eyes of Christ" in the homeless as he creates relationships with them as they venture down the path of economic and sometimes substance rehabilitation. Pastor Canales aptly summarizes the sentiment of mutual or reciprocal benefits through service::

> Joy and glory and power and divine presence is when you bow your knee to help someone up. . . . You never stand as tall as when you take a break from your office and go out to the pantry when they feed the homeless and you go out there and you touch the people. You say "God bless you" without judging whether they came up in a Cadillac or a bike. That's my vision. That's what I believe is true. We encounter the glory of God when we step out of ourselves like Christ did. Where was Jesus the most glorious? He was most glorious when He came down from the hilltop. And He ministered to prostitutes and drunks and hungry people and chubby little boys with a filet-o-fish sandwich. When He ministered to people that needed Him.[13]

Those who see the divine in the struggles of their communities feel as if they are the ones actually being served through the work they do. Examples of this public theology permeate these interviews and reflect the cultural influence of a global, service-oriented theology across traditions and across types of struggle. In fact, most of the people I spoke with fit neatly within this category, even though they also fit other categories.

Brother Dunn, for example, spans the categories of organized worship and communal connection through his regularly scheduled meetings with people in the community. Dunn recalls the first time the connection between the faith in the community and his own spiritual path really hit home. Dunn was on retreat in the United States reflecting upon experiences that he had had in El Salvador years earlier. This retreat was for spiritual reflection but had a practical purpose as well. Dunn was asked to contribute to a collection of essays on spirituality and service work. While working on his piece, he realized that the true strength he gained while in El Salvador was from the people in the community. He gave one example in particular that captured this moment. Villagers were returning to their community after it had been bombed by the government. There was a huge crater in the middle of the town, and members of the community laboriously dug for water at its bottom. Dunn asked them what they thought about the aftermath of the bombing, and he was taken aback when they replied, "God gave us this crater so that we could be seven feet closer to the water."

Dunn was shocked. "I thought, man, where does that faith come from? And of course I realized that's what sustained them. And [in reflection] I realized in many ways that their faith was what sustained me." Years later, Dunn now continually listens for this faith. "Part of the practice that I have now is to make sure that at least once a week I'm having a conversation with somebody who is usually from an immigrant community, who is poor but whose faith is very strong and asking them what is it that keeps you going? And having them remind me—it's almost like a rabbinical practice—reminding me about who the real teachers are."

Alice Linsmeier, of Jesuit Refugee Services, learned similar lessons about her own spirituality while working within a Catholic service group helping Salvadorians return to their homes. Linsmeier notes, "There's something really amazing about someone who's been forcibly displaced and—the whole idea of accompaniment and walking with that person or with that community, really helps to clarify so much, because they have taught me so much about how to see the world, how to have faith in adversity, what kind of things need to be changed." Linsmeier articulately captures the social commitment that is inseparable from this form of practice. Communal connection attempts to understand in deeply profound ways the lived experience and lived spirituality that accompanies commitments to change. The separation between spirituality and practice evaporates more in this category of practice than in any other.

The Reverend Altagracia Perez, who neatly illustrated eclectic innovation through her gym spirituality, also reveals the transforming function of ego adjustment that can emerge through communal connection. Perez is in high demand in Los Angeles for demonstrations, protests, public speaking, and spiritual guidance. Her presence has power. But along with her public charisma and leadership comes the constant struggle for balance, not only within activist commitments but also with her parish and her family. Such a schedule can take its toll. Perez remembered when janitorial union workers started a fast to raise awareness of a strike against a large local university. It was graduation weekend and the employees had been working without a contract for four years. They invited Perez to join them. "I was just in a very bad place. So I was coming off like, 'Oh I can only do three days because I'm a very busy person and I've got kids to take care of. And I can only do a couple days on juice and one day on water,'" she said.

On the first day of the fast, however, Perez arrived to lead a devotional the organizers had planned for each morning of the strike. When she arrived, "the people were so touched. It meant so much to them [that I was there]. I was embarrassed by my callousness." On that morning, Perez met a cafeteria worker with five young children who was fasting for five days on water alone. Her children came to the demonstration area after school to do their homework, and the older children looked after their younger siblings. Perez recalls, "I was just put to shame. Like, 'Hey, see, this is the gospel! It's happening! It's at work!'" By the debriefing session at the end of the fast, Perez was deeply moved. When discussing the fast as part of the strike tactics, several of the organizers made the point that fasting was not simply a gimmick to get attention. Perez's eyes began to tear as she elaborated, "They really did feel that—that God was present with them. That God was moving on their behalf. That, that this struggle was right in the eyes of God. And that they knew that God was gonna be with them because of it. And—it just broke me down. It was the kind of ministry I always envisioned myself being a part of. It was the way I wanted to be in my community." The spiritual energy that Perez almost unwittingly helped frame during morning devotionals returned to her in full force when she realized that when public struggles are seen as sacred struggles for justice, the community can reveal what Perez interpreted as the real and lived gospel. It was this community in action that embodied spirituality.

Sister Stoner brings communal connection to a much more mundane level than global relief or union politics while not discounting or ruling out either of those effects. However, she notes that finding this connection is possible in each life and in each community no matter how large or small or domestic. She discounts, for herself, contemplation or prayer that is segmented from the vicissitudes of the mundane. Contemplation is not about meditating in one's bedroom and then going off to work and not seeing that as prayer as

well. "That's what I mean by inauthentic. Because it's isolating. It can be helping me escape the demands of life, the world. It can help me miss the face of
God in you or in whoever is around." Instead, authentic prayer for Stoner does
entail a time and a space to be alone and "hear the voice of God," but at the
same time, it impels her "to go out and hear the voice of God in others. To be
very much sensitive to what's happening in the world and to feel that pain,
that joy, that hope, that despair, deep within me."

Post–Vatican II Catholics such as Stoner, Dunn, and Linsmeier have made
a concerted effort to engage the world through a social ministry.[14] Spiritual
practice involves the social pains and social joys of local and global communities. However, the shift in social politics and social gospels seemed pervasive
among this generation of activists in other religious traditions as well. For
example, one of the elements of Hinduism that first attracted Sara Desh Arpana was the diffusion of spirituality into the community and among the people
being served. Integrating practice through service, or seeing service as a form
of spiritual practice and worship, drives Sara Desh Arpana's work . "The goal
of this [form of Hinduism] is to go out and see and treat each person as just as
you serve the image of the shrine," she said. "The divine presence in the
image—that divine presence exists in all people. That each occupation we do
is sacred. That each thing that we use for our occupations are in a sense the
same as a sacred vessel. And so in a sense the whole of life is like a ritual."

Experiences such as these reinforce the spiritual nature of social service
and become practice when they are reflexively understood as fitting in to a
larger framework or interpretive grid of spiritually informed social action. Some
form of devotional acknowledgment—for example, Sara Desh Arpana's imagining the shrine in others—at moments when the spiritual is profoundly perceived in the service of others brings moments of individual satisfaction into a
much larger understanding of purpose and the energy to sustain what one is
doing. Often it was moments such as these that indelibly imprinted social action with spiritual power and revealed the potential of social action as a form
of practice in itself.

SPONTANEOUS CONNECTION

Finally, similar to eclectic improvisation, spontaneous connections produce
spiritual experiences in a variety of settings and through a variety of unexpected or nontraditional spiritual activities. Whereas the person who impro-
vises is the active agent in making the spiritual links, through spontaneous
connections the individual interprets his or her experience as induced by the
in-breaking of a transcendent force. This is fairly evident in Pentecostal Christian communities, but others experience these moments as well.

When Lee DeLeon first developed his gift of tongues, he said it was almost fun but not really constructive or outwardly directed through action. Over time, he developed his gift and incorporated it into his daily practice in ways that grew along with and contributed to his commitments to social action. According to DeLeon, the true strength of this gift appears when his own words or actions are insufficient. He explains, "There are sometimes points in my time of prayer where I no longer know what to say and I maybe don't listen and I need to express what's in my heart, and when we run short of words, that's when the gift kicks in." His spiritual connection is spontaneous. Practice does not follow form, it is not organized or scheduled, it is intimately personal and nonrational in its experience. DeLeon admits, "I don't really understand it, but there's something going on, and I know it's very pure worship. That's probably the purest worship you can ever experience. Because then it's just you and God and it's your soul and your spirit and God just really communicating."

While glossolalia can be part of DeLeon's regularly scheduled daily practice, along with reading the scriptures each morning, it can arise at other times as well. "Sometimes I'm driving and I've sung a couple of songs on the radio and they move me, but I want to continue to worship God, so there, once again I use that gift of tongues. Sometimes I just, for five minutes, fifteen, whatever, I'm just in tongues worshipping my God." While this form of practice is a form of communication, it also produces very clearly the types of functional benefits discussed above, perhaps most directly the sustainability needed to maintain commitments. DeLeon explains, "Very honestly I can feel myself being built up. . . . [It's] very uplifting. Boy, you can really feel the power."

What's more, DeLeon's spontaneous connection can provide insights for his spiritually informed actions. Earlier, DeLeon suggested that these social commitments "really jump out of the Word." Yet at times insight comes later, through the unexpected in-breaking of the spirit. "All of a sudden, [the gift] impacts me in a powerful way. An insight that I had not considered as I read the Word becomes very clear, it comes to light. So that baptism of the Holy Spirit is a dimension that I would never ignore. It's a part of my daily walk." There is a particular dynamism in what DeLeon discusses that parallels repeated references in these interviews to the mystical and nonrational elements of spiritual practice. This dynamic component, as DeLeon so successfully captures, was one of the most significant aspects of a rich, rewarding, and meaningful experience.

Rabbi Jacobs, whose improvisation with the morning ablutions culled from Allen Ginsberg became a form of daily practice, also acknowledges the improbable or unanticipated moments at which he might feel a spiritual communion or experience a spontaneous connection. According to Jacobs, "Prayer isn't restricted to me just in the synagogue or at a designated time. It can be anytime, any place. I can be on the freeway, upset that I'm not moving and it's like a parking lot that you can't move, and yet I can listen to something on the radio or some song and be moved and transform myself even in the car. Not to be entertained, but to put in perspective what I'm doing."

Individuality through Spiritual Practice

Understanding engaged spirituality conceptually or even practically means acknowledging that variations in practice are essential for connecting spirituality to social service and participation. These variations depend upon institutional interpretive frameworks that might privilege one form of practice over another (indeed, as one rabbi at Hebrew Union College suggested, "Jewish spirituality is most often found in community rather than in individual practice"). Yet while the institutional imprints are noticeable, the individual negotiations of these are as important for many of the people interviewed. Perhaps individual negotiation is best perceived in the functions of spiritual practice.

The functions of spiritual practice should not be considered without acknowledging the vast variations in form. Religious institutions and faith-based social service organizations know the benefits of practice well. They understand that taking time and creating space for practice can calm the mind and reorient the perspectives of the day. They also know that sustained practice can sustain action. However, if doled out as a clinical prescription without emphasizing the personal relevancies of practice, this advice may flounder for those who hear spiritual practice and imagine one static form that may be alienating or unfamiliar.

Each of the virtuosi of engaged spirituality that I spoke with personalized their spiritual practice according to their own lived experiences, some in subtle ways and others more profoundly. When I asked Sister Stoner about her own selection process she acknowledged the relationships between spiritual functions and personal meaningful forms and, in doing so, pointed out that particular forms are not universally fulfilling but rather are differently effective. "There are prayer forms that I don't find helpful at all. You may. So if I wait for you to come to mine because then you'll be at a better state of prayer, then I need to look at that, I think. Again I'm just creating a hierarchy and I'm not sure prayer is about that."

The above categories of practice differentiate ways that people incorporate spiritual practice into their own lives in creatively resonant ways that connect them to their perceived spiritual core, or taproot, as well as to the social commitments and actions that propel changes in the world. Daily practices structure routines and provide stability, improvisation fosters flexible appropriations and creativity, organized worship generates community bonds, while communal connection fuses compassionate commitments and spontaneous connections allow for the unpredictability of the transcendent and the indescribable. Countless combinations result as individuals assemble different varieties of routines, disciplines, practices, and spontaneous experiences that provide more than thoughtless ritual or habitualized motions. As Stoner alludes to, these categories should not be read as a hierarchical typology, with one category being better or more authentic than the others. Instead, individuals pragmatically select what works best for them based on past experiences and the experience at hand.

Of course, this variation does not ignore the external factors that affect practice. Most of the time and for most of the people, directly engaging in spiritual practice involved decisions about when, how, and why, all of which require more than simply personal interests or schedules. First, people decide when to engage in spiritual practice and must make room for it in their lives or even create disciplines that protect their spirituality from the overwhelming routines of modern life. While not always formal, making time for spiritual practice is up to the individual. Second, each person decides how to engage in spiritual practice. Sets of practices are obviously passed down within traditions and faith communities or made possible through theological explanation, but personal imprints are meaningfully if not always conspicuously applied. Finally, at times people decide why they want to engage in spiritual practice. Spiritual practice can be engaged intentionally for specific results. "Discernment" is one common theological term for seeking guidance when making a difficult decision or actively seeking strength, courage, sympathy, consolation, or even radical innovation.

When looking at the perceived costs and benefits of spiritual practice, spiritual connection, communion, or transcendence were never predictable or uniform outcomes of a specific repertoire of practice, making it much less rational than would be expected. Spiritual experience, unlike spiritual functions, is mercurial at best. Of course, expected experiences do occur as the result of scripted spiritual practice, as some of these interviews suggest, but at times they occur through unexpected experiences that bubble up as well. Some, such as Lee DeLeon, describe that "the gift kicks in," almost independent of volition and with different consequences. Sometimes DeLeon revels in the joy of the experience, while at other times he cries , and at still other times he feels an overwhelming sense of physical and existential power. But these feelings are not always the outcome of concerted prayer or devotional singing. There are times when no spiritual connection is elicited from engaging in a personally tailored practice.

Sister Stoner echoes the slipperiness of spiritual practice. While sometimes she feels the presence of God, there are also days when "I just don't feel anything—and that's okay, too." Rabbi Beerman concurs: "I can feel [spiritual connection] anywhere. I don't always feel it in the synagogue and I don't always feel it in prayer. Sometimes I feel alienated in the synagogue. And I can't call it up at will. It isn't a constant in my life . . . I can't make it happen." Engaged spiritual practice and spiritual payout, for lack of a better term, is not a consistent outcome or predetermined end. Much like attempts at social change, spirituality is unpredictable, elusive, and enigmatic as much as it is directed, pragmatic, and intentional.

Engaged spirituality seems unmanageable, impractical, and slippery because it is. However, when one looks closer at the similar functions of spiritual practice and the categorical variation in forms that individuals create, one can better understand the way in which this seemingly chaotic, personal, experiential element is also social, interactive, and constrained by individual preferences, actions, and interpretations. In fact, it is the consistency of spiritual practice and ongoing social action that give shape and continuity to these experiences.

So what can be said about spiritual practice in form and function? First, profound spiritual experiences are energizing, grounding, consoling, and inspiring, but they are not the determined outcome—nor necessarily the desired outcome—of all spiritual practice. Second, beyond these otherworldly communions that everyone admitted experiencing, the functions of spiritual practice for engaged social action are often more mundane or subtle but are the essential building blocks that provide consistency and structure to everyday life and sustain motivations or commitments over time. Third, these uniquely transcendent moments instill a fundamentally different quality to personal experience and social engagement. As such they create a deep reserve of emotional energy that can be drawn upon throughout practitioners' lives, sustaining commitments as political administrations cycle through or philanthropic donations rise and fall. Finally, individuals have agency in the types of spiritual repertoires they construct. Of course, while individuals make decisions on when, how, and why to practice, their agency is contextually affected by life experiences, practice formats within their faith traditions, interpretative networks, and structural opportunity. While spiritual practice and experience might require narrow adherence for some practitioners, for others the flexibility, dynamism, and even inconsistency of spiritual connection can allow for or even spark creative innovation that redirects the way that social action unfolds. As one pastor laughingly said about his spiritual pathway, "Sometimes I feel orthodox in the extreme in terms of Christian theology and other times I'm out there flirting with heresy."

Chapter 5   Experience and Emotion

The Influence of
Spiritual Feelings

Pastor Jim Ortiz, a fit, straight-talking, no-nonsense man in his fifties, was born to Puerto Rican parents and spent the early part of his life in the New York barrio of Spanish Harlem. Ortiz, in thinking back to that time, recalls the powerful influence that his mother's religious passions had upon him. Although born and raised Catholic, Ortiz's mother later had a born-again conversion experience and became what Ortiz calls "a faithful prayer-warrior and church attendee." Ortiz now carries that moniker proudly in ways that more closely reflect the battlefield that the term "prayer-warrior" connotes. He is the current and founding pastor of My Friend's House Assemblies of God Church in West Whittier, California, a predominantly poor Latino urban neighborhood southeast of downtown Los Angeles. Since its founding, his ministry has always been part of the streets. Ortiz tells of the early days, now over thirty years ago, when he and his wife walked door to door sharing their faith with community members. Today, his ministry still reflects the streets, although in the intervening years the streets have taken on a harsher quality. The church's name, My Friend's House, indicates one of the primary goals of the ministry: to provide a safe, embracing alternative to the streets for the many latchkey kids attending the two schools that flank the church within several blocks. Even though most of the newly immigrated families retain strong Roman Catholic roots, Ortiz's Pentecostal ministry welcomes all children regardless of faith tradition, and, in fact, the vast majority who drop in after school are not members of his congregation.

When speaking about his own spiritual practice, Ortiz first and foremost discusses relationships. "Relationship with God is like relationship with anyone else. God is a person. And as a person He engages us on personal levels." Ortiz speaks with God throughout the day, much like he would with a friend or a significant other. While he admits that much of his conversation with God takes the form of an internal and sometimes vocalized discussion, there are other times when silence communicates as well. "You don't always have to talk. You just have to be present. And involved. Sometimes it's just walking down the street and holding hands. Or putting an arm around somebody and just expressing through that contact that there's a relationship. That's the kind of thing that goes on with me and God."

Ortiz's intimate and personified connection with God represents many of the feelings others said fueled or gave meaningful essence to the form and functions of their spiritual practice. As Ortiz said, if spirituality is going to have an effect in communities such as his, "it has to move from the head to the heart." Emotions are more than buzzwords in contemporary society; they are requirements for authenticity and action.[1] Feelings are highly personal and deeply intimate, and words often cannot adequately describe them. But feelings are what motivate, sustain, and sometimes transform engaged spirituality. As Ortiz said, "[God] does engage us at levels that you're not able to articulate. But you know it's real. Because it has become a personal experience . . . an experiential communication."

The Social Shape of Feelings

Feelings connect individuals with social institutions, and spirituality is a particularly powerful carrier of feelings. Spiritual passions, for example, may make someone feel empowered to change the institutional definitions of their social role as a professional. Or, alternatively, the social context of a particular demonstration may produce feelings of insecurity or alienation that constrain the spiritual drive and an explicit articulation of a spiritual mandate. Social norms and structural patterns affect how people feel. Arlie Hochschild, a scholar of the social influences on emotion, suggests that humans have internalized, through early socialization as well as the ongoing socialization throughout their lives, the ways to determine which emotions are appropriate for which events, as well as the degree of emotion that is permissible during those events. These "feeling rules" guide individuals' social, affective life in times of great emotion, such as funerals or weddings as well as, and perhaps more important, during everyday social interactions at work and with family or friends.[2]

However, while feeling rules are culturally shared in ways that dictate emotions in certain situations, this uniformity should be taken lightly when applied to the dynamic nature of spirituality. Rather than adhering to explicit feeling rules, emotions, and especially spiritual emotions, slip away and are much less conforming to preestablished rules, making them difficult to manage in uniform or predictable ways in everyday life. Feeling rules are more like guidelines that are always shifting and being reassessed and negotiated.[3] They emerge out of what people do and out of the changing circumstances in which they find themselves. This is especially pertinent for those changes that occur in the margins, tweaking the taken-for-granted structures of feeling, as Raymond Williams put it.[4] From this more dynamic perspective, ways of interpreting feelings are often implicit, picked up through ongoing interactions with others as well as changing interactions with social institutions such as religion.[5] To these various influences on feelings should be added spirituality.

Ortiz's move from his head to his heart, for example, is shaped by his intrinsic knowing—from living in this area for years and knowing the hearts and minds of his neighbors—that this move from ideas to feelings is not only possible but required if he is to sincerely connect with the members of his community. While this shift in feeling is shaped by his Pentecostal framework and would differ from many Buddhist notions of feelings, his feelings are not solely determined by institutional differences alone but simultaneously by a variety of influences from intimate, individual experiences in prayer through the large social structures that affect his community.[6] Clearly, Ortiz's mother's passion had a significant impact, as did his ethnic identity, his desire to work in an immigrant community, the economic conditions of the area, the gang affiliations of the youth, and the constant battle against street drugs as a threatening alternative for after-school recreation. Ortiz must negotiate all of these influences at the very least as he adjusts his emotional response for engaging these kids. What's more, he must imagine the response that his degree of emotion will have upon the children and parents of his neighborhood. This emotional management acts upon his spiritual life and social action as well, affecting the types of feelings that spiritual practice generates in ways that provide courage, strength, empathy, and comfort to deal with the particular circumstances that he must face daily.[7]

In fact, many times these felt connections with everyday life and community are purposefully imagined in order to conjure a greater emotional connection to the spiritual.[8] Emotional responses and connections are produced in institutional religious ritual through rhetoric, images, statues, music, or incense. While at face value these may appear to be managed stage props, the emotions produced by ritual and imagery are often what sustains religious participation and vitality.[9] Similarly, within spiritual practice the imagined or perceived realities of the transcendent have direct consequence for social action and outcomes.[10] Emotions and felt experiences are precisely what produce the connections that fuse institutional realities with individually felt motivations, zeal, and passions, resulting in engaged spirituality and action.[11] Alluded to in doctrine or religious institutions, engaged spirituality is often, in practice, constituted by subjective experiences such as the perceived presence of otherness, the imagined community—both present and past—of which one is part, or the very physical charge, of energy cascading through one's body. There are three broad families of feeling—feelings of community, feelings of empowerment, and feelings of transcendence—that may be read as shorthand for a more nuanced typology of overlapping felt experiences and the internalization of meaning as a system for understanding, and often changing, everyday life.

Feelings of Community

Most of the time, when the word "community" is used in religious scholarship, people think of the local and extended interpersonal networks that organize in relation to a common form of worship, beliefs, and a shared religious identity. In the United States, this tends to take the congregational form.[12] Of course, beyond the physical location of worship and the face-to-face interactions with other members, religious community refers to a perceived group of others who similarly worship, believe, and share religious identities across the world and even across time. These two types of community, the face-to-face and the extended—or what one might think of as the *lived* and the *imagined* communities—were not usually differentiated between by the people I interviewed. Instead, the lived communities of today were simply one manifestation of the imagined communities around the world, in the past, or even in the future.

Religious communities are not only organized identities; they are also the source and shape of profound feelings. Feelings of belonging, feelings of solidarity, and feelings of moral responsibility emerge from these real or imagined connections. Spirituality becomes the carrier of these feelings, allowing access to experience and interpretation. Perhaps not surprisingly, community for these individuals was not only a religious community. Just as often, or perhaps more often, the community that produced spiritual feelings, and toward which these feelings were directed, were local neighborhoods, economic classes, the politically oppressed, or a global human community.

SOLIDARITY

Resonance with community and the unique feelings that are produced in communal religious activity has long been a presumed key to understanding the origins and unique qualities of religious transcendence. Emile Durkheim, in one of the most creative and theoretically lasting contributions to the understanding of religion, argued in *The Elementary Forms of Religious Life* that when humans gather together in groups a particular feeling bubbles up inside of them that is unique to the collective experience.[13] As mentioned earlier, this effervescence, this affective product of tribe or society in Durkheim's mind, was the true origin or source of all religious belief, behavior, and, important to this discussion, emotion. These early totemic tribes, according to Durkheim, used religious experience in ways that projected their "real" community bonds and relation to the lived environment onto an eschatological framework of universal, sacred meaning. Somewhere along the way, society forgot this early link between society and the sacred, now mistaking the real or most fundamental essence of what they worship.

While few contemporary scholars of religion would agree with such sweeping normative and reductionistic evaluations, there are insights to be pulled from this suggestion, not the least of which is that emotion matters.[14] Community and community feelings, produced together in both real and imagined ways, facilitate individual spiritual life. It is probably not surprising that those who have devoted themselves to communal monastic life experience these feelings of community most directly and concretely. Sister Stoner of the Benedictine order notes that the routine communal order has a noticeable if sometimes ambiguous effect on how she experiences her faith. She says, "I think there's something that happens to us in being faithful to [community practice of the divine office]. Even though I may go there and sometimes I don't realize a word I'm saying—I'm just saying the words—there's an authenticity there I think because I'm coming together in that routine and I think that routine has a transforming effect."

Rather than being duped into a false adoration of communities that members project onto a transcendent realm, practitioners such as Stoner are explicit and reflexive about the role that a sense of community has upon producing a deeper, more powerful, and intensely meaningful connection with the divine. A feeling of community extends inseparably in the case of the Benedictine order, for example, from the collective experience of the divine to the struggles for social justice and fighting for social change, a potentially disruptive consequence that Durkheim's model of social cohesion did not fully expect. Yet for these Benedictine sisters, it is precisely the supportive joint actions among the homeless or directed against nuclear arms that result in greater degrees of solidarity, loyalty, and moral responsibility.

Admittedly, the monastic lifestyle is not a path chosen by many today,[15] and as the social universe gets exponentially more complex and fragmented, religious individuals and institutions must create novel ways that appropriate meaningful face-to-face community experiences. The astronomical rise of non-denominational Christian parachurches is one particularly noticeable manifestation of this trend in American Christian organizational restructuring. Yet, packing larger numbers of participants into expansively massive "warehouse churches" seems counterintuitive to the notion of intimacy or feelings of connection, solidarity, and unity. This idea is not lost on organizers of religious behemoths. While thousands of adults undulating to high-tech Christian rock under a canopy of projected digital images can affectively pull together communities on one level,[16] generating feelings of intimate community connection is simultaneously farmed out to family groups or cell groups. These micro-communities, comprising ten or so members, meet regularly during the week—often on Wednesdays—to hold Bible studies and share with each other their personal struggles and successes.[17] The intimacy of the groups requires greater individual participation of each member and, since the success of such small groups depends upon the input of its members, feelings of ownership, acknowledgment, and responsibility are byproducts by definition that increase the participants' sense of personal responsibility and participation.[18] Small group organizing extends beyond weekly gatherings and personalizes individual spiritual practice throughout the week by including prayers of intercession for others in the group or simply through imagining the other small group members who are doing the same.

Small group subdivisions are not only beneficial for generating and sustaining feelings of community; they also become places in which solidarities are struck around personal local issues that confront a smaller and manageable community. . Each of the base communities in East Los Angeles discussed earlier provided a time and place for face-to-face reflection on sermon topics and Bible readings, but they also, under the spiritual guidance of Father Kennedy, functioned as spots where common concerns were raised, support was found in numbers, and creative action was dreamed up. These intimate, interpersonal communities are, as lived communities, one space in which feelings of solidarity are fostered. But for many participants I spoke with, the conventional sense of religious community was only one aspect of their perceived spiritual community of social action.

Spiritual practice and experience are also bound up in rich and changing cultural webs beyond face-to-face, lived communities. Part of this web is the imagined community of which practitioners feel a part.[19] Daniele Hervieu-Leger suggests that one of the reasons why religion persists in the modern world is that the embedded historical and traditional authority, found within practices and texts and manifested through experiences, provides a sense of grounding and plausibility, even though these texts and practices may have been picked up and strung together independent of their original communities.[20] In other words, texts and practices, when fit together in new ways for new circumstances, provide a sense of place in the world.

These imagined communities are more accurately real, in terms of friends, family, or religious congregation, and imagined, in terms of the historical lineage of others who have engaged in similar endeavors for millennia or of the greater communal body of the faithful around the globe. Each form creates a connection to a tradition that provides feelings of rooted stability, affirmation, and validity for socially enacting one's spirituality and in doing so generates additional feelings of solidarity, love, trust, respect, unity, and belonging. Lived communities, such as the base communities in East Los Angeles or the Benedictine sisters, facilitate these imagined communities by providing the space and framework through which to connect a spiritual past with a spiritual present.

For others, these moments of interpersonal connection and community have to be re-created in ways that are less centralized and more self-generated. Rev. Glenda Hope provided one such example earlier as she described in detail the mosaic of practices, both Christian and other, which make up her spiritual repertoire. Each practice, including meditation, Tai Chi, and prayer, allows different levels of affective communion and belonging that reinvigorates her spiritual core. Much of Hope's practice is contemplative, and while the practice itself may appear internal and private—often performed alone in the small meditation garden in one building of San Francisco Ministries—even these moments are infused with imagining the women currently in her centers, as well as those who have not found their way there yet, the immigrant families huddling their children to school past corner drug deals, or of the city organizers who must steer there way through allocating budgets and making the decisions that are ultimately life-and-death decisions for many of the residents around Hope's home.

Hope's private practice is very much a practice of imagined community through which she is aligning herself not only with other practitioners but also with those who constitute the social fabric of the geographic community in which she lives and works. In this sense, feelings of community and feelings of solidarity that embrace the prostitutes and drug dealers can be as comforting, reaffirming, motivating, and vitalizing as imagined religious predecessors or a worldwide body of the faithful. Community bonds based in justice and the struggle for a better lived environment can be quite strong and quite resilient, especially when coupled with spiritual feelings that, through solitary practice, keep these community bonds intact, in mind, and infused with sacred importance.

Hope, however, strikes a balance when attending to her spiritual feelings of community and by no means discounts the communal power of worship. Hope noted that weekly Wednesday night Taize gatherings functioned as her Sabbath to a large degree because she found it difficult to truly worship when she was leading a religious service, as she usually does each Sunday. Taize allowed the time for her to gather with others in a regularly scheduled and patterned way and concertedly devote her time to communal worship. However, while feelings of community connection and solidarity could easily be fulfilled through such group or congregational settings, Hope amplified these with feelings of loyalty by specifically noting that each week she attends "with a friend—the same friend." Hope makes the point that they both go to dinner together first to spend time catching up with each other before the service. They have been doing this for years and have been friends as couples throughout each other's marriages. In fact, Hope performed her friend's wedding. This lifelong friendship and the shared tie to Taize increases the way in which Hope experiences a sense of community connection, extending it beyond time spent chanting, singing, and praying to make it part of a defining communal web of practice.

For others, cultivating a sense of community simultaneously entails a slew of historical, cultural, and socially directed connections between spiritual practice and social action that stretches back across a long history of people that have come before and paved the way. For these engaged spiritual activists, adopting traditional rituals or texts produces a sense of a historical, corporate body of the faithful and the socially committed. Sacred texts, scripture, or traditional styles of prayer or meditation were common ways individuals connected with their moral histories and communities, while texts, biographies, and oral cultures connected individuals with the social change sparked by earlier members.

Reverend Canales, although he had already experienced a vivid, physical, and visual encounter with Jesus that dramatically changed the course of his life and his day-to-day actions, said he also had a "second conversion" when he entered graduate school and earnestly began a deep and critical engagement with others involved in a similar historical dialogue of spiritual discovery and social action. For Canales, the feeling of belonging was critical. As Canales described his early life hanging around the projects, "I drink on the way to school then smoke dope on the way to school ever since I was twelve." School did not hold significant relevance and neither did the humble church that his father and mother built from scratch. It was smoking and drinking that established a close network of friends who reinforced each other. But when Canales saw Jesus in the strobe light and gave up smoking and drinking, his friends left him and he sought out a new feeling of belonging. The morning after his conversion, Canales went to a small shop blocks from his home and bought his mother a bunch of flowers. He recalls being very contrite with his offer, saying, "Mom, those are for you. Thank you. Thank you for always keeping a plate of beans and tortillas in the oven when I came home late as a bad kid. Thanks for getting me out of jail." These feelings led to a new understanding of his upbringing, connecting him differently to the immigrant struggles of his parents and the economic hardships that made sustaining their small church a sacrifice for the entire family.

At the founding of Mission Ebenezer—"Ebenezer" means "stone of help"—in 1962, Canales's father consolidated his savings from Social Security benefits and bought a small rundown house, which he gutted for the meeting hall. Inside, he built two rows of pews and a makeshift platform out of two old but newly shellacked orange crates. The church moved several times—always upward, but only slightly—during Canales's adolescence. Having decided to follow in the footsteps of his father, Canales now sees himself as part of the church's history.

Canales put himself through Vanguard University—a local Pentecostal school and the oldest in Orange County—by waxing hospital floors and immediately surrendering his paycheck to his father. Ultimately, Canales attended Harvard on a full ride. Upon entering the halls of one of the most prestigious universities in the world, Canales admits that he felt a newfound sense of real but, perhaps more profoundly, imagined community. "I entered into the conversation of all the great thinkers in our Christian heritage." Canales developed a feeling of newfound solidarity as he embarked down this path with some of the most respected theologians of Western thought. Now Canales is part of that heritage, thinking through and struggling with the same concerns, under different times and different circumstances. Canales brings a new set of life experiences as well as a new array of social concerns to the conversation, and he feels the lineage intimately as he reads scripture each morning and bats around the ideas of historical scholars as if they were sitting alongside him.

Canales also feels solidarity with his community through the spiritual practice of engaging the texts of theologians. One of his favorites is Henri Nouwen, a contemporary advocate of spiritual social justice. Nouwen's words have helped Canales feel a new sense of relationship with the people his ministry serves. Paraphrasing Nouwen, Canales says, "When we're helping the poor, we're saying 'thank you' to God. Although the poor can't say thank you to us, because they have no [spiritual] overflow—and we shouldn't expect it from them because they have no overflow—we have overflow. And it is out of our overflow, our overflow in Christ, that we can say thank you to God by helping the poor. And I had that initial personal experience of thankfulness. It's [derived] out of that initial spiritual experience."

Rabbi Rami Shapiro similarly took his emotional connections to theological predecessors in establishing a reading guide for his intensive study series on Jewish mysticism. Shapiro, a longtime contemplative, found that introducing meditation as an outside practice, for example as a Buddhist exercise, would produce mixed, although ultimately limited, reactions from long-standing Jewish congregations. However, linking a meditative spiritual practice to a historical community of Jewish contemplatives conferred a greater feeling of legitimacy and connection to the practices for participating Rabbis. Interpreting the practices as part of Jewish identity and Jewish community led rabbis to take them back to their congregations, a step that Rabbi Shapiro believes could have extensive consequences. He suggests, "If [understanding spirituality and Judaism] is just an intellectual thing, it doesn't go too far. If you can tie it into a meditative practice, chanting practice, some kind of ongoing daily spiritual work, then I think you really transform the individual and the individual can go out and transform the world."

Not everyone interviewed was a Harvard-trained theologian or a re-educator of Jewish rabbis, nor, as mentioned, did everyone experience feelings of community through a real corporate body or formally institutionalized congregation of others. By critically reading scripture or rigorously abiding by the individually enacted communal practices, such as the daily office or the scheduled prayers in Islam, others felt connection from a collective yet dispersed imagined community engaged in similar practices around the world and across time. Praying the Divine Office, for example, a set of scheduled prayers originally established for the priesthood and now prayed by many members of the laity, provided a feeling of community for a graduate student involved in community development work. He felt connection even when alone in a study cubicle or in the middle of a bustling Starbucks. Rather than a lived community, his connection was simply a deep realization that others around the world—or at least in his own time zone—were engaging in the exact same practice as he at the very same time. Even when no one else is around, spiritual practice is not necessarily experienced alone; the individual practitioner feels part of a larger whole.[21]

The sense of imagined community stretches through time as well, imputing connection, respect, and a sense responsibility. Naim Shah Jr. eloquently reflects upon the five prayers in Islam that make up one of the central pillars of faith: "You're aware that this prayer is how the prophets have prayed. You know that God answers prayers. You know that this is the greatest currency you have here on Earth. You know that your Islam cannot stand without prayer."

Imam Saafir Saadiq adds on to this historical lineage by describing his Hajj experience: "You really realize that that's where Abraham was tempted to sacrifice his . . . son. You're drinking this water, and as you're going around and understanding this circumambulation of the Ka'bah, and where Hagar ran, it brings religion home in such a realistic way. It all makes sense now. You see the universal brotherhood, you see where it's ludicrous for me to look at you and judge you by your skin and not understanding that it's your heart that counts." For Shah and Saadiq, these historical resonances are not merely intellectual footnotes for religious historians; they are the emotional connective tissues that make contemporary spiritual practice and social action meaningful and vibrantly alive.

Sister Joan Chittister, of the same Benedictine order as Sister Stoner, agrees with Stoner's assessment of the face-to-face community but also notes that there are lived and imagined connections—geographic, spiritual, and historical—that she feels by following a lifestyle of a Benedictine monastic that is laid down through sacred texts—what she calls being "steeped in the scriptures." The scriptures not only speak to her through individualized communication but also through an understanding of the collective and dispersed audience. For Chittister, the scriptures are "for us as a people, as a group. And a very high level consciousness also that the order is international. You know? We're not American Benedictines. We're Benedictines who are Americans. If the Roman Catholic Church has any strong witness whatsoever in the world it surely is that it's a universal church. And that it simply leaps over national boundaries, accepts all of them, but sees something above and beyond any national boundary. So that's a contemplative edge. To see beyond yourself. To see from above, in essence."

With a few brief words, Chittister taps many of the internalized feelings of connection that imagined communities foster. When she mentions the universality of the Roman Catholic Church, she also raises issues of power that are cultural, religious, economic, and political. Such power relations are not lost on Chittister, as anyone who has read her sharply honed critical essays well knows.[22] Power and structural influence clearly have an impact on the legacies available to communities and individuals to draw upon for feelings of community. The losers of the power struggles in the religious and political skirmishes of the past centuries are not prevalent cultural actors that hold influence over broad constituencies and therefore do not have the same imprints upon interpretations. Even so, practitioners are not completely determined, as Rabbi Shapiro's work illustrates. Current patterns of spiritual experience and social action that shape the boundaries of community are always changing. Older practices are renewed, new connections are made between communities, and unknown texts resurface. Furthermore, the lived communities in which people also take part are always shifting and changing in ways that affect the imagined communities as well.

The breadth and historical scope of spiritual practice allows individuals, in their solitude or in their communities, to transcend the immediate, lived communities to access a sense of solidarity with a broader imagined community or to deepen the connection they feel with the people sitting next to them. Through spiritual practice and the internalized knowledge that others, living similarly in other communities, past and present, are reading the same passages, reciting the same words, and engaging in similar struggles to promote justice locally as well as universally, they feel connected, which is especially crucial for those battling against the odds. A connection to a collective identity that transcends the self can motivate and sustain social action even when so-called cost-benefit analyses would suggest otherwise.[23]

MORAL MANDATES

Social responsibility, sympathy, and connection to those in need were implicit elements within each of the stories of emotional community connection across time and space. But as Chittister and Canales point out, the connections are not bound up in spiritual or religious similarities alone. Most of the people interviewed felt intimately tied to their predecessors in engaged spirituality, those who actively struggled for social change and paved the historical way, as well as set expectations, for current spiritually mandated action. Sister Chittister summed it up best as she recalled the fifteen-hundred-year lineage of Benedictine monasticism, which she draws heavily upon in her daily reflection:

The monastic were the first, for instance, to set up toll roads through their farms. You had to pay to drive your horses and carriages through their farms. Why? Because they took that money and used it for alms for the poor. The monastic were the first people to take dying people out of ditches in a period when sickness was still considered—still after the time of Jesus—considered punishment for sin. And to take them in to their own hospices so they could die a dignified death. The monastic were the first groups who gathered the peasants of the area to teach them farming so they could earn their own living so they could sustain their own family. These were the people who drained the swamps of Europe, who wouldn't take good land, who went in and took the worst land that was there, drained it all, cleared it, replanted it, so that it flourished. That's ecology from the thirteenth century! This—the whole monastic notion of taking care of things—those are all manifestations of the way we should be socially present in the world.

Chittister's emotional appeal connects feelings of community with a sense of responsibility for continued action. Her use of the word "should" when referring to the way monastics must take care of things indicates the type of directive that Chittister feels has been laid down for her as an ongoing part of this long lineage of caretakers. Purpose can be felt in various ways, although for those who take an engaged spirituality to heart, purpose is felt through some form of transcendent moral mandate. Chittister did not pull out thirteenth-century ecology in order to spruce up her interview with rich historical detail. She used the example as a wake-up call for how life should be lived daily.

Compassion, sympathy, outrage, and indignation are just some of the feelings that emerged as participants connected their predecessors, their scriptural texts, and their current global service communities to the issues surrounding their own current cause. For Julie Weill, who works for the Jewish Fund for Justice, "repairing the world and making it the way God wants it" is intricately bound up in both Jewish lived tradition and in Jewish scripture. Weill admits that reading great Jewish thinkers such as Martin Buber and Abraham Joshua Herschel, in part, help shape and redirect her own personal perspective. But part of her work is to go out into the trenches, so to speak, to the synagogues and congregations, and invigorate a spiritually informed social conscience within lived communities. In this role, the ideas of Buber and Herschel come in handy for articulating the message intellectually, but the strong feelings of community, compassion, and responsibility to go out and do something, Weill explains, resonate much more emotionally if taken directly from Jewish scriptural texts. There is not a lot of framing work that needs to be done in making these connections. Weill argues that social action and community service have always been part of a Jewish identity, and the sacred texts connect congregations in intimate ways to that historical mandate.

She also feels that that active members of synagogues are truly yearning for a deeper sense of community, although "they may not know it," she adds with a laugh. Fusing feelings of community with moral mandates and social issues extends the Jewish sense of community and makes members feel more connected to the world around them. According to Weill, this combination of moral mandates, ethics, and community feelings stirs Jewish communities for social justice.

The Reverend Sandie Richards is the current pastor at the Church in Ocean Park, a quiet and affluent community that is liberal with its theological interpretations. Pastor Richards is active in several social justice organizations focused on labor rights for immigrants in the service industries surrounding the highly touristy beach communities of Los Angeles. While Richards's substantial networks and organizational skills contribute to the logistics of the group's public demonstrations as much as to their moral tenor, she confesses that her connections to the spiritual work of social activism are sometimes more emotionally reactive than they are theologically or academically studied. She admits that she often struggles to control her morally stoked temper when dealing with corporate hotel chains that deny union organizing, health care benefits, and job security to their often underpaid and overworked immigrant staff. She laughingly says that the last thing she wants is to start having phone calls circulating about this "minister who was calling people a bunch of names" at a demonstration. Even so, she maintains strong words are not off the table when talking about gross inequities. "I don't think God minds harsh words," she says, adding, "there are certainly plenty of harsh words in the Bible, but you've got to be careful and maintain humanity with a person, which is always a challenge—especially if you feel like the underdog."

Richards's passions come from the combined feelings of compassion for the disenfranchised workers and indignation about the resistant and noncompliant stance of certain corporate bureaucracies. These moral mandates, for Richards, are unambiguously evident in her interpretation of the Old Testament. The Ten Commandments, Richards explains, are not about archaic tribal sacrifices, bogged down in quaint ritual form. Instead, "The Ten Commandments are don't kill each other, don't lie to each other, don't steal from each other. And, of course, take a day off and rest, and of course don't have any other gods before me, that's important too." But the punch line for Richards is that these commandments are "really about allegiance to one another in God's name. God's saying I'm your God and there's no other god and what I, your God, am telling you is you better take care of each other. That's basically the Ten Commandments." When Richards does not see this being enacted—even once it is made clear to those who are violating what she sees as basic codes of moral conduct—it is infuriating. The moral feelings, culled from a deep, interpretive reading of scripture, wield an undeniable emotional authority. Emotions such as these, while they require a social filter to remain civil to others, are by no means something that must be tamped down. They are the fuel for acting on spiritual insight and convictions.

Myra Marx Ferree, an analyst of contemporary social movements, makes the point that emotions should be understood for collective action so that the unpredictability of too much emotion can be adequately assessed ahead of time.[24] Feelings of fear, outrage, humiliation, and even pain must be thought through, both in light of individual participants and the people or social control agents that they might encounter. This is particularly useful in civil disobedience training, playing a role in the civil rights movement and many contemporary new forms of street protest. But just as emotion must be managed in demonstrations, it can also be a salient source of motivation and sustainability. James M. Jasper adds that gut instincts, such as moral outrage, can be very functional as immediate impetuses for action, opening people up for participation.[25] Gut instincts are even more important when they can be tied to subjectively powerful meaning systems such as religion. Moral outrage is not simply an irrational reaction of the body but rather a transcendently mandated call to action.[26]

Finding the appropriate language to act on these emotional convictions can be difficult and require a close reading of the "feelings rules" of each situation. But the degree to which these feelings rules work in practice are more determined by the particulars of the situation than the prescribed ideas of what is appropriate. Hearing a desperate story of an undocumented single mother after September 11 who, due to loss of revenue in the tourist industry, lost her job without recourse, ratchets up the passion. Of course, Richards is very cautious with the way she incorporates religious rhetoric and passion into her public role as an advocate for immigrant rights. Although she may wear a collar to a rally or demonstration to symbolically represent the participation of religious institutions in civic actions, she admits that, more often than she would like, she hears from other participants that in her speeches and dialogues she just does not sound like a religious leader. Wary of sounding like a religious zealot, but more likely trying not to alienate other faith traditions from participating, Richards laughingly laments, "If only they knew it was my love of Jesus that brought me here in the first place!"

Feelings of Empowerment

Rabbi Steven Jacobs, who is sixty years old, got involved with the Inner-Faith Coalition United for Peace and Justice when he was nine. Now a Reform Jew, Jacobs grew up in Boston as part of a very religiously observant Orthodox home, which he admits was frustrating at times as a child and adolescent. His shift from Orthodoxy, however, had little to do with doctrinal frustrations and ritual proscriptions. Instead, it had "everything to do with justice and spirituality" and began at a very early age with the social realities of his childhood in midcentury, urban America.

One day at his grandparents' house, Jacobs was playing with "what was known as a colored boy" from the neighborhood when a stranger passed by and angrily spit out "Nigger!" Having never heard the term before, but picking up on the tone with which it was said, Jacobs ran into his grandparents' home. He tugged on his father's sleeve and asked what the word meant. His father became livid and "took off after this guy." Jacobs has no idea what his father did when he caught up with the man and never asked. While the specifics of the consequences always remained vague, the emotional reaction of his father stuck as an early lesson about issues of justice or, more correctly, the vehement indignation of injustice and discrimination.

Years later, when Jacobs was thirteen, he had another experience that shook his faith to its core. During a family vacation on the beaches of Maine, a nine-year-old child at an adjacent beach was pulled from the water and was not breathing. The beach was unguarded and Jacobs and a lifeguard from another beach were the first responders. Both teenagers took turns administering artificial respiration. The scene was chaotic. When the ambulance finally arrived, they rushed the boy to the hospital, but even though they "shot him full of all kinds of stuff," the boy was pronounced dead. Jacobs recalls, "My world was shattered, because I believed in a God that was omniscient, knew everything, was all powerful. How could this happen to a child?" Someone answered that "God wanted another young one up there." This response was intolerable to Jacobs at the time, and the entire experience deeply affected his sense of identity and his relationship with God. He could no longer believe in the God that he had grown up believing in.

When Jacobs found his way back to believing in God, an experience that grew out of the shared music used in the civil rights movement, it was no longer the same God. "I've moved away from that traditional kind of God which I pray to, that God is actually going to make changes [in this world]." Jacobs no longer relies upon a personified God to pluck him up out of his troubles, even if that means he can no longer blame God for not saving the child on the beach or preventing the stranger from using a racial slur against his friend. Instead, Jacobs intuits a diffuse and ever-present reality of God that empowers him in ways that are not based in dependence or subservience but on interdependence and empowerment.[27] This reimagined God requires, demands, and inspires Jacobs to be an active participant—a "cocreator," in Jacobs's terms—in the social work of an unfinished world. It might have been easy and understandable for this emotional, sensitive teenager to turn his back completely on an all-knowing, all-powerful God when that personification failed him. Instead, although taking a lifetime of finding spiritual fulfillment through music and social activism, Jacobs was able to reconceptualize God in a deconstructed way that fit and actually enhanced his feelings of spiritual empowerment.

Emotions have always played a large role in Jacobs's spirituality. "I spend an incredible amount of time with my own emotions because I react to the sense of the miraculous," he explained. Yet, while he identifies his emotions spiritually, at times they have few perceptible elements of what most might consider spirituality. "There are times when I'm moved to tears, sometimes by somebody just saying hello. . . . I can emote about things like that, so those are spiritual moments." Spirituality and emotional connection are inextricably tied for Jacobs and, in turn, affect the way he sees the world. Most important, he feels responsibility and a sense of empowerment. Feeling empowered creates a sense of agency, a respected role, and a sense of authority to take up the moral mandates of engaged spirituality.

SPIRIT AS ACTION

Deconstructing the Abrahamic god from the bearded, typically white male god who held back the seas and thrust lightning bolts has experienced a groundswell of support within pockets of the progressive religious community over the past generation. This trend parallels the rise of identity politics in the 1960s and 1970s, as well as the decline in membership of certain mainstream Christian denominations and a shift from hierarchical traditions in the Roman Catholic Church. Personally resonant forms of spirituality have morphed and appropriated previously rigid religious interpretations of the divine.[28] Feminist theologies in particular, but also postcolonial theologies from the "southern hemisphere," challenged outdated, culturally biased, anthropomorphic ideals, giving rise to highly contentious debates that continue today. If God could be a white male, why could God not also be black? Or female? Or lesbian, for that matter?

As these questions began to loosen the transcendent human figurehead of the Abrahamic faiths, God, for some adherents, came closer to the essences of Eastern traditions and spiritual philosophies. God permeated everything and everything constituted God. The sacred instead is experienced and interpreted directly as emotion and the spirit as action. God, in other words, appears more as a metaphor for the guiding emotional power of religion and spirituality. For those who felt constrained by the traditional hegemonic representations of religion, this diffuse interpretation is empowering, or at least allows for a more meaningful, effective connection than other potentially alienating images of God.[29]

World renowned for her writings, lectures, and institutional challenges within the Catholic church, Sister Joan Chittister described her view of the sacred: "Well, God is not male. God is not white. And God is not snooping around waiting for human beings to fail so they can be forever punished." With this positional opening to her answer, Chittister articulates a response that emerged not only from feminist responses to religious patriarchy but also from racial, ethnic, and class-based sentiments that dismantled an angry father figure that women, ethnic and racial minorities, the poor, and other marginalized groups thought they could never please or even identify with by nature of their social identities.[30] But much like Rabbi Jacobs, Chittister did not dispose of all the spiritual qualities that even an older and angrier God had. Instead, she sought new ways to understand or to imagine and experience God. She continued, "God is that initiating energy beckoning all of us to fullness of life, but not just for ourselves, for all life. God is that impulse, that living impulse that gives life and seeks life and wants life. God is the energy of all that is and more than we know."

Such descriptions of God weave together feelings of personal empowerment, representation, and belonging. Women, African Americans, gays and lesbians, and, indeed, many white men, such as Jacobs, can feel a greater sense of inclusion and acceptance from a spiritual God that is understood through one's feelings than by a personified image. As Chittister pointedly quips, "God has become more real as God became less real." She explains this transition in terms of her own growing feelings of empowerment. As she explored and pushed upon the boundaries of what she was taught to believe God was, she could find God potently in each and every element of the universe. As she said, "Everything began to speak differently."

These feelings of empowerment are socially transforming by their articulation alone. As disenfranchised voices turned up their volume and found receptive institutional ears, the constitution of religious theologies of all stripes began to change. The recent flap concerning the ordination of a gay bishop of the American Episcopal Church is only the latest example of the remarkable change that can be wrought by shifting spiritual understandings and feelings of empowerment within formerly outsider constituencies. Of course, the vehement resistance to this ordination worldwide indicates that Christian spirituality, not to mention other traditions, are culturally shaped organisms that are highly contested terrain.

But beyond reshaping theologies, deconstructed spirituality translates into much broader social mandates for action and change. Spirituality is not only or primarily experienced through traditionally conceived practices such as contemplation, prayer, or communal services, although, as strongly expressed by many people, these are powerful and useful tools in accessing different emotional elements of connection to this spiritual base. Yet as this new perspective suggests, in addition to religious practice, spirituality is everywhere and always; it is felt in every act, including change. "I don't see change as threat," Chittister continues. Rather, she argues, change is facilitated by a feeling of the divine, a dynamic energy rather than a notion of a static, tradition-bound, and institutional God. If God can be found in the energy produced by change, Chittister suggests, people would be more embracing of making the changes necessary to live more compassionate lives. That power for change has been spiritually invested within each of us. In fact, Chittister echoes Jacobs by using the same notion that humans are active cocreators with God on earth. She concludes, "I believe God left the work unfinished and seeded in us the right and the responsibility to finish it. So when I say God is presence, God is energy, God is word, that's all the same to me."

PHYSICAL FORCE

Feeling this energy within can manifest itself in many ways. For Jacobs, Richards, and Chittister, these feelings were emotional and resonated at the core of their understanding of universal belonging and connectivity to others suffering the injustices of the world. Others felt these feelings more directly and literally as an embodied manifestation of a real and palpable physical force. This physical force might be articulated through feelings of courage, strength, or energy, but it is typically experienced first physically. When Reverend Man Yee Shih's encountered the mentally ill man on the temple grounds, she specifically identified this form of feeling after reciting the name of the Bodhisattva of compassion. She said, "The energy was in me at that time." When Man Yee recounted this feeling, she swept her hands across the front of her body, and I could not help but imagine that physical feeling myself, that charge or wave that consumed her at that moment. Emotions such as these are the embodied connections between the self and the environment, whether a homeless man or global poverty.[31] Engaged spirituality facilitates the connection between self and structure as both a medium and an outcome of actions and changing environments.

Others felt this physical force in very explicit and mystically compelling ways. The suggestive metaphor of the self as a vessel that was illustrated as one of the benefits of spiritual practice is literally experienced among some practitioners. Pentecostal social activists like Richard Ramos said, "Without prayer there's no power." Spiritual power is emotionally and physically felt, and typically it is experienced through spiritual practices such as speaking in tongues. Ramos explained, "Prayer, to use a metaphor, it's the way you turn on a faucet. The faucet in this park is connected to a lake. So that lake [is] the Holy Spirit, God . . . and I'm the faucet. And if I want that source, I got to pray." For Ramos and even Man Yee, these gifts of energy or power are directly related to their spiritual practices. While attribution of these feelings of empowerment are more theologically bounded—energy comes from the Bodhisattva and it flows from the in-breaking of the Holy Spirit—the feelings of courage, power, strength, assuredness, and empowerment can emotionally connect across very different theological paths.

Feelings of Transcendence

Through all of these stories runs a common thread of otherworldliness or the sacred. Admittedly, while this otherworldliness can be experienced through face-to-face lived communities and networks of social action in this world, it is also felt in ways that perceptibly transcend the day-to-day plane of mundane reality. Although active members of a highly rationalized and technological society—even the cloistered monastic now receive emails—many of these individuals continually refer to moments that cannot be rationally explained, quantified, or calculated. And they do so without paradox or disjuncture from other realities. The power of these moments lies in their felt transcendence. This underanalyzed subjective element of human experience, where spirituality most clearly carries the emotional experience, is central to understanding the connections between spirituality and social action and, in both its explicit and extended form, is the crux of engaged spirituality.

SUPERNATURAL SENSATION

While one strain of emotion derived from deconstructing vivid iconic and ideological personifications of God, supernatural sensations in terms of dreams, visions, and voices provide others with some of the most conventional and vividly illustrative components of spiritual meaning and emotion. Religious art is the main conduit of the visual representations of these visions and voices and, in their own right, were often created to reproduce the pronounced emotion of the spiritual experience or to anthropomorphize abstract entities and represent transcendent principles.[32] Whether experienced directly in prayer or meditation or mediated through stained glass, statues, candles, or mandalas, vivid representations of the sights and sounds of the transcendent are, arguably, the emotionally resonant, embodied, and/or material forms of spiritual focus. Supernatural sensations produce powerful feelings of ecstasy and fear in the short term and awe, wonder, and devotion over time.

Sara Desh Arpana notes that spiritual experience is a crucial addition to learning the sacred texts and leading a spiritual life. Among Hindus at the Vedanta Society in Hollywood, spiritual practice or spiritual disciplines must be individually tailored following the advice of a teacher or mentor. A good teacher takes into consideration various aspects of each individual, including personal temperament, daily schedules, and even a person's stage in life. An energetic, retired widower might require different disciplines than a student who works two part-time jobs to support a new family. For Sara Desh Arpana, part of this calculus involves the ongoing work that she does as an advocate against domestic violence throughout southern California. She is reluctant to share her own spiritual experiences but agrees to talk hypothetically about what a mystical experience might entail. She thinks judiciously for a moment then responds, "Visions of divine forms, spontaneous hearings of mantras, dreams. They can be many, many things, and they will be very different for different people."

Sharing such mystical encounters with a personal spiritual leader is expected. Understanding the path it took to get there, unpacking the emotions that were produced, and planning how to further that spiritual path rely upon an open communication about the intimate details of the experience. These meetings detail the interactive components of the spiritual experience between mentor and disciple, between lived experiences and spiritual paths, and even between social action and spiritual connection. Developing these connections involves emotion work on different levels as well. Through her spiritual leader, Sara Desh Arpana maintains a sense of lived community that is intimately linked to her spiritual development and includes a reinforcement of the moral mandate and empowerment that sustains her advocacy work within an interfaith civic community. Moments of supernatural sensations through visions or sounds provide a transcendent validation that all of these elements are developing properly together.

Others also actively fostered the feeling of spiritual awe and wonder in very intimate and personally resonant ways through guided meditation. Father Kennedy finds supernatural sensations very useful in making ancient sacred texts emotionally relevant to the twenty-first-century reality of life in the Los Angeles Juvenile Hall. Kennedy constructed an entire series of lessons that he arranged into a meditative study series. When we spoke, he had just completed a round of lessons with a group of seventh graders with whom it had worked quite successfully. Kennedy's lessons are based closely upon Saint Ignatius's Spiritual Exercises. In the original book of exercises from the sixteenth century, Ignatius introduces a new form of contemplative prayer practices now known as the application of the senses. Kennedy describes that, consistent with dominant trends in philosophy and conceptions of rationality during Ignatius's life, imagining oneself into Gospel stories was believed to have profound effects upon behavior and action. If one enters a Gospel scene through meditation or contemplation, Kennedy further explained, "[the Gospel] would become real and the movements of the spirit would be realized or actualized at that moment and there would be a deepening of knowing a person of Jesus, simple as that."

Kennedy's contemporary version is embedded in this long-standing Christian tradition. He guides his young participants slowly into meditation, suggesting the Ignatian premise: for the duration of this exercise they are no longer charges of Juvenile Hall but actual followers of Jesus in the first century.

He steers them toward feeling the desert heat on their faces, hearing the sounds of the ancient markets or bazaars, smelling the stone ovens, seeing Jesus and his other disciples, all of their clothes billowing in the occasional breeze. By applying the human senses to these Gospel scenes, Kennedy suggests that the values that Jesus had or the morals found within the Gospel stories begin to enter emotionally and sensually through the imagination. Gospel lessons are no longer just moral cautionary tales but rather are incorporated into a lived and emotionally felt experience.

Through his own experience of the Spiritual Exercises, Kennedy finds that "there's a reality that's just as real as me talking to you." Although he once debated the nature of reality and perception, he no longer has time for such debates. Kennedy is experiential and pragmatic; what he knows is what he feels and what he sees work. He says simply of his own experiences with this technique, "It sustains me and it's personal and it's life-giving and it's relational."

And it is just these kinds of feelings of intimate relationships with a perceptible Jesus that Kennedy wants to pass along to others. His mission is one of democratizing this very emotive practice that brings the Gospels to life for everyday folks rather than theologians, seminary students, or monastic orders. According to Kennedy, "People have no idea what the Spiritual Exercises are; never will. Never heard of St. Ignatius; never will. And all that's irrelevant. All that's theology." Simple accessible language and basic techniques allow the laity to incorporate this contemplative practice outside of the cloistered halls. It is on this level of emotions that Kennedy believes people will actually understand the biblical principles that are not established by a priest on Sunday or even a visiting pastor who regularly ministers at Juvenile Hall. For Kennedy, it must be felt to become real, and moving into these scenes through physical and supernatural sensations of sight, sound, and touch makes this real.

By going into the Gospel scenes with his new series of exercises, Kennedy is reaching young people. "Somehow, something happens," he said. While feelings of empowerment and supernatural sensations motivate and sustain other activists, these feelings typically are managed—returning to the notion of feelings rules—in ways that connect to the social issues or problems that are being addressed. Kennedy, in contrast, successfully reaches adolescents in ways that produce an alternative reality, a transcendent space that transports them away from their cells and their pasts, even if only momentarily. Kennedy hopes that feeling liberated from present constraints will encourage these teens to pursue deeper changes in their lives.

Several miles from Juvenile Hall, Pastor Jim Ortiz explains that supernatural sensations clearly transcend the day-to-day emotions of everyday life.

In his church, "encounters can take on unusual kinds of experiences. People see visions. People engage in dialogue with God. They hear God speak to them. They have encounters with angels. They may experience a miracle. They may have a physical response to God. They may speak in tongues. They may have prophesied and engage in some of the gifts of the spirit that the New Testament teaches. And all of these are a part of an experiential encounter with God that is not always rational, not always intellectual. And that's what we try to communicate with our people."

Angels, visions, and tongues transcend the mundane and signal to those engaged in practice that some otherworldly element is touching their lives. These supernatural feelings and imagery can be appropriated for social outreach. Along the brick wall that runs the length of My Friend's House, ornate spray-paint art depicts a cartoonish devil in boxing gloves doing battle for the neighborhood's soul. The names of the deceased teens within the community who have fallen to gang violence or drugs are scrawled in spray paint at various points, providing important reminders of the tangible carnage of this otherworldly battle. But Ortiz's scenario is redemptive. The devil is bloodied and back against the ropes, his boxing gloves are Neverlast rather than Everlast, and the final bell of the bout is about to ring. This representational imagery through spray-can storytelling, while somewhat comical, resonates through the local vernacular of tagging culture.

A similar metaphor of a cosmic battle lends transcendent authority and awe to the daily struggles that Assistant Imam Shah faces in his walk of faith. As with other faith traditions, the Koran and the Hadiths describe angels who sit to the right and left of Muslims, recording all of their deeds. At the beginning of every Islamic prayer service, Shah turns to his right and left, saying the Muslim greeting, "A salaam a lakum." As Shah puts it, "It's like they're our greatest companions here in this struggle for good." By keeping the angels' presence in mind, Shah no longer has to rely as strongly upon others to physically look out for him and encourage right or moral decisions. More than just an imagined community, these angels represent the supernatural sensations of another realm that call Shah to what he calls "a higher level of consciousness." However, he laughingly cautions, "There's always inspiration coming from the angels; there's always inspiration coming from Satan."[33]

While feelings of community and empowerment link the everyday world of social action to spiritual communities and moral authorities, supernatural sensations, according to those who experience them, render these connections in unambiguous ways. Jack Barbalet argues that emotions are the bridges at the junctures between a variety of separations or dualisms in contemporary life, separations such as mind/body, nature/culture, public/private.[34] The experiences described here, in particular those of supernatural sensations, make the case that the sacred/secular dualism should be added to the list. The sacred is not merely metaphorical, nor is it set apart as separate; it is real and accessible in felt everyday ways that heighten and are even found within the other forms of connection and the mandates for change.

EXISTENTIAL CLARITY

Supernatural imagery can be visually and even aurally dramatic, transmitting feelings of awe and wonder. However, similar feelings can emerge in the quietest of contemplation when overwhelming feelings of calm, certitude, and assuredness envelop the practitioner. These moments of existential clarity emerge when people struggle with decisions, and they can be preceded by a great deal of internal conflict. At other times they may be moments of novel inspiration and revelation. This calming presence is experienced or interpreted as transcendent nudges or authorizations of one action over another.

Presbyterian Pastor Frank Alton lyrically personified moments of existential clarity. One particularly poignant moment resulted from reading a Bible passage with his wife. Guidance and direction for his ministry were the practical outcomes of this experience, but I asked more specifically, "How did that *feel?*" He laughed and admitted, "It was clear, but if I analyzed it enough I could muddy it up quite well." Alton tried to put words to this ineffable moment of calm, pausing between each descriptor. He said, "It was a moment of clarity. And no doubt. And relief." Silence hung between us, then he looked at me and said, "It was a gift."

Reverend Hope has also experienced the revelatory aspects of transcendent clarity and its connection to inspiration for social action. Each year, twice a year, Hope embarks on spiritual retreats away from the sirens of the Tenderloin and the constant ringing of her office phone. She goes into nature—in the fall to the ocean and in the spring to the mountains—in order to listen for God's voice. She admits one direct benefit is that these retreats are restful and silent. However, this silence is by no means inactive. She laughingly confesses that there is a time-honored saying that rumbles through the offices of San Francisco Network Ministries: "Don't let Glenda go on retreats or she'll come back with something else for us to do." Although she laughs at her own predictability, she admits that is true. And these revelations or inspirations are no small orders.

While on retreat not long ago, she inexplicably felt very clearly that the ministry was going to build an apartment building, "which was a totally ridiculous idea. What do we know about construction? We had nothing for collateral. We didn't know anything, but here it is," she said. And with a sweep of her arm she motioned to the recently opened, award winning, multipurpose facility, complete with an outdoor meditation garden, in which we were sitting. "It's astonishing. You just decide, 'Do you really believe this is what God is calling?' And, right. You just don't wait to get all your ducks in a row. You just start. You just start and say, 'This is what we're going to do.'"

Existential clarity from a transcendent source, as Hope points out, is by no means merely a mode of solace or comfort. Clarity, calm, and sound, sacred assurance inspires radical and even seemingly irrational creativity. Opening oneself fully and completely to spiritual guidance, either through routine practices such as reading the Bible or more singular moments such as nature retreats, can trump secular practicality. Through these sensuous emotional connections, Reverend Hope and Pastor Alton were no longer deterred by material or organizational limitations or nagging insecurities. After intuiting a spiritual direction, all other concerns become secondary issues that unquestionably and faithfully fell into place. This appears to be the case across all feelings of engaged spirituality. Emotional spiritual communion, through community, empowerment, and transcendence, impacts spiritual commitments, particularly spiritual commitments for social action and change.

Emile Durkheim argued that the social origins of religion bubbled up through community participation in ritual. Ultimately, these moments of collective emotion were codified through sacred rituals and spaces, developing into what is currently recognized as religion. But Durkheim also acknowledged that these emotions were dynamic and never solely contained within the bounds of one institution or used only for social order. The surplus of emotion, for example, might find its expression in art or intellectual development.[35] This energy helps strengthen individuals in other endeavors and sparks new collective action. Following this line of thought, it is not surprising that the overflow of spiritual experience produced through communities, through practice, and through visions spills into (and even bubbles up from) social action.

Extended Experiences

As the functions of spiritual practice provide extended benefits, such as sense of purpose and sustainability, the feelings of spiritual practice color and illuminate those functions, often extending beyond the specific moment of connection. Reverend Hope is a perfect transitional example of the way in which a spiritual feeling of clarity while on retreat extends into the practical decision-making processes that necessarily must follow the initiating moment of connection.

EFFICACY

Spiritual feelings can provide an enabling and inseparable sense of efficacy or confidence that one's efforts in social action will have worthwhile results, as was the case with Reverend Hope. Even though the notion of building an apartment building was, in her own words, "ridiculous," once it was clear that this was what she felt God wanted done, everything else fell into place. Not only did Hope feel certitude in bringing her own staff on board, finding donors to fund the venture, and orchestrating the contract work of actually erecting the structure, she also felt fiercely confident in forging ahead before tying up loose ends. She half-jokingly claimed that one of the mottoes of her ministry is "It's better to ask for forgiveness than to ask for permission."

In many ways this attitude is all Hope. Understandably, some would argue that this is purely personality talking, but she is strikingly similar to many of the other activist leaders interviewed for this project. Engaged spiritual feelings, born out of practice and experience, do not override the influence of Hope's infectious personal ambition, nor do they completely obliterate the social structural influences that have nudged the twists and turns throughout her career. These are still dominant players in the way that her ministry has developed over the years. However, these spiritual feelings can work in the intersections of personality traits, social structures, and religious denominational influence to produce novel consequences that surprise even the strongest of personalities.

If Hope illustrates the combination of efficacy and an ambitious personality, Assistant Imam Shah reveals the institutional efficacy of an all-encompassing religious philosophy that seeps into the marrow of adherents in undeniably motivating ways. When asked about the creation of his innovative summer program for inner-city youth, Go Beyond the GAME, Shah told me that when it comes time to establish the parameters of a new program, "You can't help but recall all of this that you're reading [in the Koran], and you just want to make sure that, even though it's dated fourteen hundred years ago, it's compatible with the same essence for today." By appropriating elements of contemporary culture, such as Web site advertising and professional football incentives, Shah still follows Islamic principles in the planning stages of this project. He suggests, "It's a formula that worked in the past because it's pretty much some guidance from God, and the actions of the prophet. We've seen it work here in the present."

According to Shah, sticking to faith and adhering to Islamic codes has proven effective not only through millennia but also across contemporary projects. Time and again, new programs have sprung up within his storefront masjid even without the required financial or material resources. Shah insists with a broad, assuring smile, "This currency is prayer." These sequential suc-cesses heighten Shah's sense of efficacy for the future. "We're confident that when the resources do come into our midst, we are able to serve more people. That's the greatest incentive. We see it as the opportunity to instead of serv-ing thirty or forty, we might be able to go to four thousand. . . . That's really what separates one who's maybe active versus one that's inactive," Shah sug-gests. "There's something that's dictating to them 'Get up! Go out there and remove this, the ills of society.' [Prayer and practice] must be as repetitious as possible, because you have those other insinuations and whispers that are trying to keep you from tapping that potential. Islam constantly invigorates you to go to your highest level for the service of yourself, family, and humanity."

Sense of worth or value in one's actions and the belief that one's actions might produce a real change often emerges as part of the participation itself. In other words, as people spend more time with other participants or service providers, learn about the issues, and feel the solidarity and strength in col-lective action, their sense of efficacy increases. It is out of personal and inter-personal experience that individuals interpret a sense of efficacy, confidence, or internal control of external circumstances.[36] More than just lived examples of success, a perceived sense of efficacy is significantly reinforced or even sparked by spiritual experience and deep spiritual feelings.

ONTOLOGICAL SECURITY

Perhaps somewhat paradoxically related to a sense of efficacy for radical change is the feeling of ontological security, which provides an effective base from which to explore opportunities to change.[37] Spiritual connections to religious worldviews often supply the unquestionably solid and transcendently secure base from which new definitions of the world, or even of individual selves, can be explored.[38] In *God's Daughters,* R. Marie Griffith notes that prayer and rit-ual activity among evangelical women created a symbolically meaningful and safe world where they could redefine themselves. Through their redefinition these women, who were often chastised as apologists for traditional patriarchal hierarchies, instead found "possibilities for new worlds to be imagined and lived and thus may open the way for vital transformations of another, more concrete, and potentially radical, order."[39] In very similar ways, spiritual expe-rience and staying close to this transcendent otherworldly base, often through community but sometimes simply through individual practice, allows for ex-ploration and vital transformations.

Sister Stoner teaches religion at a private liberal arts college and is inti-mately aware of the critiques of organized religion, but she argues, "You can't just dismiss religion." For Stoner, spiritual experience and religious tradition are inseparable. In her personalized meditation practices, Stoner began to focus on two of the Benedictine tenets that identify her order: stability and conversion. While seemingly opposing themes, Stoner suggests that conversion is quite different from the common conception of a dramatic moment in which a new religion is adopted. Instead, conversion—literally meaning a "continual turning"—is dependent upon a sense of stability. The imagined community of historical Benedictine predecessors, as well as the long traditions of Catholic rituals, provides personally potent sources of stability, infusing deeper meaning to individual spiritual practices that she suggests would otherwise seem "free floating or ephemeral." Stoner reflected, "Maybe the only way for me to sustain ongoing conversion is if I have a stable point in my life where I can face change." And in many ways it is stability in a transcendent reality that allows for a solid base, from which creativity and innovation often arise.

Through feelings of efficacy and the ontological security for change, spirituality moves beyond the motivations found within practice alone and allows for active engagement. Active extensions of spirituality are qualitatively different—although not necessarily better—than other forms of secular motivations, such as ethics and morality, that derive from legal or rational claims. Spirituality provides a feeling of something beyond that has an ontologically different status for effecting change.[40]

William James noted the qualitatively unique power of religiously based sentiments. Although James, a psychologist and social philosopher, was most concerned with individual transformations, his discussion of the emotional or feeling side of religious experience resonates with the contemporary examples of the way individuals overcome barriers or constraints to actively engage the social world as they see it. James concluded, after reviewing multiple stories of profound personal transformation, that the effect of secular morality in resolving internal existential turmoil "appears but as a plaster hiding a sore it can never cure." James goes on to suggest that it was often only the addition of religious experience—or spiritual experience—which has the potential to provide an adequate cure to these paralyzing afflictions. According to James, "Religion comes to our rescue and takes our fate into her hands. . . . The time for tension in our soul is over, and that of happy relaxation, of calm deep breathing, of an eternal present, with no discordant future to be anxious about, has arrived. Fear is not held in abeyance as it is by mere morality, it is positively expunged and washed away."[41] Much like James's "sick souls" for whom religious experience eliminates the fears and barriers to a well lived life, the activists, volunteers, and civic leaders interviewed here similarly find that a transcendent component enables them to expunge their fears in order to act upon the world in ways that promote change.

The embedded place of spirituality in the entire process of social service requires that one caveat be reiterated. At the beginning of this chapter I indicated the limitation of language in capturing spiritual feelings. While typologies of spiritual forms, functions, and feelings are necessary for conveying the spiritual connections to social transformation, individual experience is often irreducible to these typologies. Even though most of the stories excerpted above come from people who have been profoundly articulate in expressing their ideas on spirituality, others stumbled in equally profound ways, indicating the complexity of spirituality within social service, and, perhaps, it is through the examples that escape words that the purest and simplest statements arise.

For example, one of the most intimate roles that Father Kennedy enacts is providing meditation, counseling, and legal intervention for incarcerated teens at Juvenile Hall in Los Angeles. During the interview, he tellingly vacillated as he tried to pin down what it is that ultimately brings about personal and lasting change among his often gang-affiliated charges. While spirituality is important, the context in which that spirituality is engaged is crucial.

> [W]hat really counts is the relationship between you and the other person in the group. . . . Obviously this particular [Ignatian meditation technique] of bringing people to God and each other is important. It's like if I went in there and was just someone interested in doing meditation with them; it doesn't work. But it's much more than that. It's who they are. "Eldering," "mentoring," "father figure"—to me those [terms] are irrelevant. But, to really be there for people? That's what counts. So if you can have something in your bag and have enough spirituality to add to it, that's richer. But if someone else comes in and does this other type of practice, and doesn't really connect to them . . . I don't know. Love is what transforms us.

Cultivating Emotion

Adding to Kennedy's concise conclusion about love would only "muddy it up," to borrow a phrase from Pastor Alton. And this is the paradox around mobilizing emotion for engaged spirituality. Love is undoubtedly one of the common emotions that runs through these interviews, along with compassion, unity, wonder, humility, and even strength and conviction. Taken purely as human emotion, these innate capacities wax and wane depending upon circumstances that somehow naturally give rise to an emotional response. But more than merely human capacities for innate responses, emotions are social constructions carried and transmitted socially through communities, feelings rules, and always-shifting circumstances in which even feelings rules do not consistently

apply. The affective components of spirituality—the feelings and passions—
are shaped, much like the original spiritual experiences and repertoires of practice, by various and shifting influences, including family, peers, faith traditions,
role expectations, gender, sexuality, socioeconomic status, politics, and ethnic-
ity, among others.[42] The answers to questions such as to whom do we extend
our sympathy and compassion and against what do we direct our indignation
are answered in part through the interpretive funneling of these institutional
and social frameworks.

The role of engaged spirituality has a unique contribution to the social
and political feelings that often mobilize social action. James Jasper clarifies
that emotions vary across a continuum based upon their scope of application
and their duration.[43] For example, certain emotions such as anger or fear are
reactive emotions that have a specific target or are a relatively short-term response to new information or a dramatic change in one's surroundings. These
emotions can prompt social action in ways that seem almost involuntary.[44]
On the other end of this spectrum, emotions are affective and long term. Feelings such as optimism, loyalty, and moral outrage are held within as templates
for how we approach the world across different issues and across time.[45] While
moral shocks are one way that individuals are mobilized to act, the affective,
longer term feelings of community, empowerment, and transcendent connection remain linked to moral mandates for changing the world through ongoing
spiritual practice. By sustaining these longer-term feelings in practice, it is easier
to call up and direct the reactive feelings that spark action and facilitate change.

Rabbi Beerman's evocative definition of Jewish Optimism is based deeply in
his religious tradition and provides an example of long-term, affective spiritual
feelings: "Jewish optimism is rooted in the profound contempt for life as it
is . . . because you can imagine the way of life different from the one you live in,
that's optimism." For those who see religion or spirituality as a social opiate,
numbing the impulse to make a change, this idea alone is where experience
and motivation both begins and ends; perhaps the better world lies beyond or
is unchangeable by human means. Yet for those in this sample, once their spiritual motivations were matched with resources, organizational outlets, or funneled into creative alternatives for action, they engaged directly in bringing
about images of a different world. Indeed, there is a crucial asterisk to the rabbi's
definition that compels action. Rabbi Beerman warned, "Dissatisfaction about
which you do nothing is the source of impoverishment, but dissatisfaction
about which you do something is the source of all human progress." These
deeply rooted codes, whether from sacred texts, spiritual practices, or religious
community adages such as this one, lay the emotional groundwork for action.

Of course, action is always the necessary step for the engaged spiritualist and requires the reactive emotions that get people moving. Sister Chittister makes the point that motivations are important but that social action typically must go beyond the traditional religious practice that sustains feelings about changing the world but places action in other hands, such as God's. Chittister says she often hears from other well-intentioned, devout Catholics, "'Oh, pray, Sister, that nuclear weapons will be eliminated.' Well, I do of course. But I don't pray that *God* will eliminate nuclear weapons. God didn't make them. We did. We can eliminate them tomorrow."

As we have seen, in the case of engaged spirituality, the spectrum of emotion ranges from long-standing rules about the application of spiritual feeling to newly emergent feelings of creativity that spark changes to these rules or their application. The feelings of engaged spirituality are always in the process of being produced and reproduced between institutional religious and social influences, on the one hand, and the powerful spiritual impulses that fall outside these expected boundaries, on the other.[46] As spiritual motivations move into the realm of public debate and action, leaders, organizations, and interpersonal networks will have to guide this emotion management, inducing emotions that are perceived as beneficial to their goals (moral outrage, excitement, joy, hope, solidarity, and commitment) while inhibiting or preventing those deemed detrimental (fear, anxiety, depression, hopelessness, boredom, or even violent anger). What's more, if an engaged spirituality is to be implemented to its full potential, organizers must support and foster the creative impulses that may not always seem feasible or that break with the accepted patterns of the way things are done. These negotiations are delicate and not always self-evident. However, when done correctly, they have a significant effect on recruitment, efficacy, sustainability, and longevity in social change.

Chapter 6	Degrees of Social Integration

Toward a Theory of
Engaged Spirituality

REVEREND JIM CONN served for decades in a small but progressive Methodist church in a beachside community in Los Angeles. He has always been involved in social service work and activism through his congregation and elsewhere and recently accepted an offer to leave his church and commit full time to community development work. Now working for the Urban Strategic Initiative, Conn is in the trenches with religious leadership and clergy, seeking ways to reinvigorate congregations as active agents within urban neighborhoods throughout Los Angeles. As he put it, "Trying to help churches see themselves as the center of their communities—How can they connect with their neighborhoods? How can they build relationships?"

When Conn was initially told about the possibility of shifting to development work, he dismissed the idea outright. After all, he thought, what right would he—a white, middle-aged minister from a tony seaside town—have in advising the community involvement of mostly ethnic, urban churches facing unimaginable struggles in the city's core? But the idea kept returning to him and tugging at the recesses of his mind. Although always socially active in progressive politics in his professional role as pastor, he felt this might be an opportunity to serve in a new capacity. This nagging feeling forced Conn to reconsider his primary motivation for doing what he does. "I am a social activist because Jesus said to his disciples, 'There is only one commandment that I give to you and that is to love your neighbor as yourself,'" Conn said. He had to square this opportunity, like others in his life, with that simply stated yet often complexly applied calculus.

This spiritual calculus emerged slowly and sporadically across Conn's life—at times in an explicitly secular manner, while at other times in a way that was tinged with spiritual experience, a distinction Conn no longer maintains. What is clear is that in Conn's formative years, spiritually committing to social change was never a straightforward or foregone conclusion. Conn described a childhood like many other white childhoods in America prior to the civil rights movement. Racism was an unquestioned and even unnamed cultural framework with which the world appeared as ordered, fixed, and taken for granted. Social institutions reflected this social reality, including the churches Conn belonged to as a youth. The religion he remembers was much more concerned with individual salvation and therefore saw the church's role as instilling the right principles in order to ensure that ultimate end. When a social gospel of loving one's neighbor was mentioned in the congregations, Conn recalled, it was never implied that it would include such a radical proposition as equality among the races or even the thought of integrated religious communities.

His early socialization both religiously and socially was undone, as it was for many idealistic youth, by the waves of social change that washed through the 1960s.[1] Conn admits to being "radicalized in a secular way" through the tumultuous decade from civil rights to feminism. His internal struggles with making meaning in the world came to a crux when he was eighteen or nineteen years old, a time that Conn calls his "period of agnosticism." College was unhinging a lot of assumptions about how the world worked and asking questions that otherwise would not have been asked. History, philosophy, and even biology offered new ways of looking at the world that differed enough across a wide range of topics to get the wheels of critical introspection turning in Conn's head. Existentialism in particular produced what he called "a deep emotional and spiritual vacuum in my life in which I questioned everything, including the value of my own existence. I thought, 'Why not suicide,' as Camus said." Conn's questions about ultimate meaning and existence inevitably became tinged with theological leanings and finally evolved into the direct confrontation of religious "Truth," with which many other youths involved in the political and ideological movements of the time grappled. "I threw out the Bible. That's not a source book for me anymore, what is? God? Don't know about God. Not a source of wisdom, comfort. Don't get it. Jesus? Completely lost. What's the difference between Jesus and Mohammed or Buddha and I don't know?" he said.

Questions mounted while Conn was living at home and attending a local college. He was caught between the traditionally comprehensible security of the past and the challenging intellectual, social, and political assaults of the present. About five blocks from the Conn family home was a local park that was shaped like a natural amphitheater. The large grassy bowl gently sloped down to a small lake in the center. Late at night, when the existential questions would rattle in his head, Conn would escape to the park and circle the lake until the questions waned or his mind tired enough to return home and sleep. For nearly nine months Conn made these nocturnal getaways three to four times a week. Most nights the walks were angst driven more than peacefully contemplative. Conn described, "I would just break out of the house, run those five blocks thinking, 'What's the world about? What's life about . . . I was trying to put it together but also what's my value? What am I here for?"

Finally, one night the questions seemed to have won out. Conn was very depressed and disturbed by not being able to properly arrange all the right answers anymore. Relativity and the unknowable had become too much to bear. "I burst out of the house, ran to the park and had decided that I would just walk into the middle of this lake in the middle of the night and they would find my body the next day," he said. When he reached the edge of the park he slowed his pace and began slowly descending the slope. As he made his way down, the wind picked up and rustled the leaves of the trees ringing the lake. Before, Conn had tuned out the sound of the environment, but on this night he heard the leaves rustling and thought they sounded unmistakably like laughter. All of a sudden, Conn said, everything seemed clear. In the sound of those trees, he heard, "Why do you think that your life is so insignificant or so valuable that you think you should just end it? This is really ridiculous." He added, "It was sort of a cosmic giggle." As Conn reached the perimeter of the lake, he turned and walked around the edge. Now he heard the trees saying, "You got it." As he walked through the trees and around the lake he realized that the trees, the grass, the sky all had the right to be there and therefore why shouldn't he? From that "cosmic giggle" on, Conn never again questioned the value of life or his responsibility in the world.

Once this existential crisis was resolved, Conn turned back in earnest to the politics of the time only to notice that the social supports of the activist cultures had started to fray. Identity politics and social justice paradigms weighed heavily upon Conn's perceptions of the way the world should work. During his developmental years as an activist, movements built bonds, solidarities were struck, and minds were changed. Yet the movements ultimately fell apart. Looking around, Conn, echoing Hope's observation, saw that only the faith-based folks and Marxists stayed committed to many of the social causes that had been championed.[2] When seeking ways to sustain the commitments he had internalized, Conn found himself turning back to a faith that during this period had been shaken to its core and then finally dismissed. With a fresh perspective and curious vigor, Conn again asked, "So what is God? Why do most of the people of the world believe in something they call God?" This time, however, Conn felt security—an ontologically secure base born out of sustained participation in the movements of the 1960s and 1970s, from which he could ask these questions within a framework of theology and faith.

In fact it was only long after Conn's experience in the park that night that he could reinterpret it as spiritual. At the time, Conn put no spiritual labels on the experience. Now, however, he believes it undoubtedly contributed to the image he now holds of God, deconstructed most often as a force that reveals itself through nature. Courses on process theology while in seminary helped provide a vocabulary for that very personal experience, just as that experience produced a deeply personal affinity for that strain of theology.[3] God, so goes the theology, flows through everything, opening up the fluid and permeating essence of spirituality for all aspects of life. "What else would we call this but a religious experience?" Conn asked.

Today, Conn stays in touch with the early intellectual and cultural influences that caused such internal turmoil in his early adulthood by drawing upon a variety of spiritual practices from nearly all religious and contemplative traditions. He also incorporates natural elements, such as stones, into his everyday life to remind him of the omnipresence of God. This connection extends to the most mundane objects, including a unique doormat at his home that was produced by a cooperative of indigenous women working in the depressed regions of northern New Mexico. The coop incorporates various microeconomies such as weaving and recycling that put a stamp of holistic business practices, environmental sensitivity, and social justice on their products. This simple yet colorful doormat is one of the small and incremental reminders that literally keep Conn's commitments visible throughout everyday life.

As Conn's experience illustrates, spiritual experience, biographical twists and turns, social commitments, and institutional or social structures can swirl around throughout a lifetime, producing a spiritually informed commitment to social activism and change. For Conn, secular intellectualism, agnosticism, spiritual encounters, social activism, and denominational seminary-based theology all project subtle casts upon each other to produce a personally resonant and uniquely meaningful way of understanding the world. In retrospect, he admits, his decision to enter the seminary was tenuous and he could have turned in a different direction in his life. In fact, Conn said that if he had not been offered the pastor position in Los Angeles he probably would have joined a vast majority of other seminarians who had looked elsewhere for fulfilling careers. However, each of these influences, from the most intimately personal to the most bureaucratically anonymous, impinged upon each other in ways that gelled for Conn and in ways that have been maintained and enhanced in the subsequent decades.

Matrix of Engaged Spirituality

The following matrix of engaged spirituality is based upon the typologies discussed earlier—the various types of roles for social engagement or the forms that practice takes—and provides a framework through which to read the development, application, and maintenance of engaged spirituality. For example, using the narrative account of Conn's life experiences, one can trace the multiple social and interpersonal components that affected his spiritual development and its connection to his ongoing social actions.

From left to right, the matrix recounts the main points of the preceding chapters. Spiritual sources dramatically affect the spiritual and social commitments of practitioners either on one extreme through a sudden and indescribable moment of transcendence or on the other extreme through a slow socialization and commonsense understanding that spirituality and social action are inseparable. Roles funnel the spiritual motivations based upon various resources and expectations that are socially established by being an advocate, an imam, or even a concerned mother. In Conn's case, the experience in the park led him to grapple again with his theological questions as a politically active college student. These questions led him to seminary, where his success in his professional role as a student ultimately resulted in his own congregation. Yet while the role expectations of certain positions affect the direction of spirituality, spirituality affects the boundaries of those expectations, often transforming their taken-for-granted parameters. To this day, Conn's mark is evident upon his former church. It remains one of the few Methodist congregations that celebrate the summer solstice as part of the liturgical calendar.

Maintaining spiritual and social motivations also requires the benefits of ongoing spiritual practice and, following Conn's process theology and personal experiences, his practices also involve strong connections to nature. Categorical benefits such as the sense of purpose that Conn derives from his practice emerge across traditions and are present at the time of spiritual practice as well as far beyond, as a sense of purpose and sustainability. Finally, the feelings produced in this practice fuel the ongoing social commitments, sustain the somewhat fleeting or ephemeral spiritual encounters, and promote creativity and innovation. As such, Conn was propelled into a new set of responsibilities and duties when presented with the option to change careers after decades of leading a congregation. Through reflection Conn realized that in order to carry out

Matrix of Engaged Spirituality

Spiritual Sources	Roles	Benefits	Practice	Feeling
Inherited Engagement	Private Quest	Ego Adjustment	Daily Practice	Solidarity
Learned Engagement	Good Neighbor	Vessel	Eclectic Improvisation	Moral Mandate
Social Encounter	Volunteer	Purpose	Habitual Worship	Spirit as Action
Spiritual Epiphan	Professional	Sustainability	Communal Connection	Physical Force
	Advocate		Spontaneous Connection	Supernatural Sensation
	Visionary			Existential Clarity
	Monastic			Efficacy
				Ontological Security

the mandate to love his neighbors he would have to follow his feelings and expand his roles. Guilt certainly played a role in pushing Conn beyond the caring and comfortable zone that he created for himself while serving his congregation for so many years. While Conn's narrative provides certain insights into the workings of spirituality and social action, various experiences, both individual and collective, could be similarly plotted across each of the typologies. Depending upon the varying degrees or frequencies of different experiences and practices, these connections will undoubtedly fluctuate with each example. It is precisely this variation that reveals spirituality's potential for social change.

Taking into consideration the personal stories told here, the matrix should not only be read from left to right. Engaged spirituality does not simply follow a stepwise formula. An unexpected feeling of empathy experienced on the way to work may revive a particularly salient point in which spirituality and social action were fused earlier in life. In turn this experience might energize or shape one's spiritual practice, providing additional insight or certainty regarding the parameters of his or her professional position. Of course, not all elements are in play at all times. People might reflect upon the spiritual sources of their social commitment only occasionally or when specifically asked. As mentioned earlier, the emotional components of spiritual practice and experience are unpredictable and somewhat elusive. Furthermore, some individuals pick and choose their practices according to other timetables and pressing commitments. Clearly, then, engaged spirituality should be read as multidirectional and highly interactive rather than unilinear and static. This being the case, what affects the way spirituality is used and what affects the outcome it has for social engagement?

Understanding the social role of spirituality for social change requires attention to both the individual and the institutional effects on social action, trends that have been traced throughout the stories in this book. Individual effects—the effects of agency—reveal part of the story, just as institutional effects—the effects of social structure—reveal another. In everyday life individuals probably move back and forth between both these different lenses without much thought. However, neither of these on their own completely captures the fluid way that spirituality works in the lives of leaders, volunteers, and activists leaving social analysts seeking a reasonable balance between the interactive effects of agency and structure on social life.[4] The typologies mapped out above are one attempt at acknowledging the many meanings and applications of spirituality and engaged spirituality. While specific spiritual experiences may appear unique and singular, they are actually always part of these much larger and denser networks of meaning, the through line of which is reaffirmed in and by practice, community, social role expectations, memories of other transformative moments, organizational outlets, and, among this group, the experiences of social action itself. All of these consolidate the meanings of spiritual experiences and reinforce them as actionable experiences. In other words, engaged spirituality has to be understood as simultaneously individual and social, emotional and structural, and reflective and motivating. The lived reality, at least as revealed through these narratives, always vacillates somewhere in between.

Cultural Models

Spirituality can be very pragmatic. Individuals can amplify spiritual narratives to express authenticity, share empowering experiences to strengthen collective resolve, and reference sacred texts for guidance or moral authority. At other times they might just as easily tone down or self-edit their spiritual jargon. Spirituality in this sense is far from an all-determining ideology that dictates thoughts, actions, and words without social filters or without individual discretion. Rather, for the vast majority of the individuals interviewed here, an engaged spirituality is a social and cultural resource, much like other skills and values, that can be drawn upon at different times and to different degrees depending upon the appropriateness of a situation or the perceived fit or need. This pragmatic negotiation was often consciously and strategically calculated to derive personal strength and courage, to appear more palatable to a secular public, or to overcome perceived barriers to funding a project or effecting change.

Man Yee used her spiritual practice directly for internal energy, Javier Stauring excised explicit religious rhetoric from his scathing editorial about juvenile justice, and Naim Shah Jr. admits that the Muslim influence in Go Beyond the GAME is exhibited only through example by the volunteers or the clearly identifiable Muslim names of the professional athletes who headline the project.[5]

Beyond the literal definition of pragmatism as a practical approach to situations, pragmatism, as a renewed lens for viewing culture, takes on a much more subtle form. In the recent past, theorists viewed culture as a canopy that stretched across all of society in similar ways, containing the stories, the feelings, the Truths, and the rituals that made life meaningful for all who stood under it. Culture was collective and people drew upon this common source as they navigated their daily lives.[6] However, this presumed consistency and homogeneity of culture no longer fits. We all use culture differently, even those who presumably share this common canopy.

Culture from an active perspective is not a static collective pool that individuals draw upon in similar ways; instead, it is the complex combinations of skills, meanings, and resources that one collects, assembles, and employs differently at different times.[7] The process by which people use culture is relatively the same, but the outcomes and the specific strategies that they come away with may be quite different. It is this view of culture that turns up again and again through people's spiritual stories. Even within denominations and families, as the DeLeon brothers of Templo Calvario illustrate, there is variation in the ways that one's own set of accumulated ideas, tastes, and practices are engaged across settings and for different purposes. Every day individuals are faced with shifting situations, some new and some recurring. They experience challenges, and are presented with new information. As meaning-making creatures, humans try to make sense of these realities. They draw upon and utilize stocks of knowledge that they have accumulated over time in ways that put their everyday lives into meaningful patterns that fit snugly with the way they believe the world works.[8] From this perspective, the pragmatic way that humans use culture and thus spirituality may not always be conscious. Instead, they intuitively pull up elements of these accumulated ideas, skills, and beliefs that constitute their culture. Their meaning is reinforced and re-created through their use and application. Spirituality is one particularly salient component of this view of culture.

Instead of an all-encompassing canopy, spirituality can be thought of as a tool kit.[9] People accumulate new perspectives, alternative practices, different narratives, changing policy positions, or theological concepts, not to mention the lived experiences that become part of a spiritual repertoire or reservoir of emotionally resonant memories. Throughout a lifetime, spiritual practitioners accumulate a wide array of skills, habits, and spiritual insights or they sharply hone a few types of practice so that they become reliable resources—or quite often they do both. In various circumstances, these reservoirs are repeatedly drawn upon or passed over for others in ways that constantly affect the way they use them in the future, either by reinforcing what they know or pushing along familiar boundaries through innovations.[10] In each of these cases, the spiritual passions that fill individuals and drive them to promote change within their communities vary in shape, application, and degree.

Therefore, even though these skills and practices are activated individually, they are constantly held accountable to greater or lesser degrees to the particular context in which they are used. When Conn had his initial experience in the park, he did not identify it as spiritual. Spirituality and religion in his cultural tool kit had slipped out of reach, below the more accessible existentialist riddles and revolutionary social politics that ordered his world at the time. A spiritual interpretation might not have been accepted as a viable alternative given the particular circumstances of that place and time in his life—not only would this interpretation sit poorly with him, it would have been equally discredited by his peers who ascribed to a similar worldview that constrained Conn's role as a student activist. Later, of course, as Conn added new tools and achieved greater dexterity with a new guiding principle of process theology, he was able to draw upon that transformative moment and this time rekey it in terms of a new cultural and spiritual framework that was now reinforced by those around him in his new role as a religious professional.[11] Indeed, changing patterns of cultural practice and contextual influences have consequences in our lives.

Shifting the Patterns:
The Case of Immanuel Presbyterian

The Reverend Frank Alton is currently the pastor of one of the most diverse congregations in the heart of Los Angeles's sprawling Koreatown. Koreatown, it should be explained, is something of a misnomer. While the commercial interests throughout this neighborhood are predominantly Korean owned, as indicated by the barrage of signs in Korean script, the majority of the residents are Latino. Alton's congregation reflects this diversity as well as retaining a remnant of the church's Anglo roots, even though many of the aging members have now dispersed to other suburban communities across southern California. The congregation currently is one-third Latino, one-third white, and one-third black and Asian.

Pastoring such a congregation presents a series of hurdles for Alton, a white

American pastor who speaks fluent Spanish. Complicating the obvious differences in ritual and music is the more difficult barrier to bridge—language. The language divide segregates the church community into smaller constituencies who may only cross paths with the other members of their religious congregation as one group cycles out of the sanctuary on a Sunday morning and the next one cycles in. While part of the same religious and geographic family, their experiences in worship and, to some extent, everyday life are markedly divergent. Such social and cultural influences divide the congregation through distinctive services that pit groups against each other over the most desirable Sunday-morning time slot. Yet, as with similarly composed congregations across the country, this segregated solution makes practical sense.[12] Part of the religious visual landscape now includes signs posted outside of churches announcing various service schedules and their corresponding languages—oftentimes written in their own language. Church resources, such as the building, electricity, music, Bibles, candles, and volunteers, are all strategically organized in patterned ways that allow for the seamless progression of culturally sensitive services over the course of any given weekend.

While these patterns appear reasonable and even necessary, Pastor Alton is moved and sustained by a lifetime of experiences that produce a different vision for his church. When Alton was twenty-three he spent a year working in an economically poor community in a remote area of Colombia. During that year, he read the Bible straight through from beginning to end; a difficult and time-consuming task in and of itself, but Alton also read it in Spanish. His pragmatic intention was not only to brush up on the Bible but also to improve his language skills. Alton was also actively becoming a part of the community, establishing for the first time in his life friendships with people who were truly economically poor. "Those two things happening together in a foreign land for me really made something click," he said.

For Alton, the social context of being in Colombia, the structural economic realities of living within the developing world, and the spiritual discipline of thoroughly reading the Bible alerted him to particular realities in the sacred text that he may not have otherwise experienced in the same way had he been reading the same passages in English in the sheltered confines of his seminary classrooms in the United States. "You can't read three chapters of the Old Testament every day for a year without reading something about the poor and justice and oppression and injustice," he said. His readings were relevant, "especially [then] in my social life I had a category for those things also. So that the hooks were there so that when those [Bible passages] went through they stuck." In terms of an accumulation of skills, experiences, and beliefs, the unique interplay of context, structure, and spiritual practice impacted Alton deeply and reinforced a new cultural lens as a substantial basis for the way he utilized a very socially committed spirituality throughout his life. Looking back over so many years to the real lived connection between sacred text and social injustice, Alton commented, "I think that [connection] became an inevitable part of my spiritual pilgrimage."

The orientation Alton carried with him from his time in Colombia rearranged his previously established preferences for revelation through scripture (to use a theological term) instead of life experiences or spiritual encounter—a preference he formed through his earlier seminary training where the emphasis fell squarely on divine revelation through scripture. "In my life, experience has pretty much gone right up there along with revelation," he said. Now additional hooks are in place based on lived experiences, spiritual encounters, and Alton's interpretation of sacred texts. As he continued accruing emotional and spiritual skills and experiences over the years in Latin America, they built a hefty reservoir from which he could draw experiences for his new role as pastor.

Today in Los Angeles Alton's past experiences, ongoing practices, and commitments allow him to reconsider, based upon his spiritually directed feelings regarding the nature of community, the taken-for-granted pattern of segregation in his own congregation. Using contemplative practices to seek discernment produced a solution to this divide, and Alton now orchestrates a bilingual two-and-a-half-hour church service on Sunday mornings at Immanuel Presbyterian. The first segment of the service is held in Spanish, then a middle interlude is conducted in both languages, and finally a section is concluded in English. The service has an easy flow to it and members may slip in and out at various times. While this new organization of the service is frustrating and disruptive to some members, Alton admits that the vast majority of congregants strongly support the continuation of the three-year-old experiment.

Using the matrix of engaged spirituality, one can map Alton's experiences, innovations, and practices, as well as their effects. Considering spiritual practices alone, the dual process of nurturing a spiritual life through sacred texts and historical teachings—which is illustrative of the structural influences of culture and spirituality—as well as Alton's use of past experiences for contemporary problems—which illustrates the pragmatic tool kit approach—complement each other in producing a positive solution. Moreover, Alton's role as pastor allowed him to reorganize the resources of the church in ways that would not be possible for a volunteer alone, especially when the decision was not received warmly by everyone.

By heeding too closely to cultural models that consider the dialectic between structural aspects and the personal choices, one risks missing out on the consequential role of spiritual feelings and transcendent moments that are often the pivotal points to seeing the world differently and acting accordingly. Alton's lifetime of work and practice illustrates the synergy between very institutional frameworks and organizational resources, individual choices, and pragmatic decisions, while calling attention to the very intimate personal experiences and spiritual feelings that break out of this-worldly considerations, adding meaning, power, and legitimacy to change.

Engaged Spirituality

In order to make sense of overlapping influences, an analytic framework of engaged spirituality explicitly considers three overlapping levels of social life: individual agency; the influences of social structures; and the dynamic, experiential nature of spirituality itself.

INDIVIDUAL AGENCY

First, the activists, leaders, and volunteers I spoke with were all active agents in piecing together a subjectively meaningful practice and worldview. They were by no means passive recipients of either scripted spiritual routines or social circumstances and a rote schedule of expected activities. Even the patterned practices of daily practitioners were infused with particular meaning and directed toward the very real and pressing needs that they or their community faced. In other words, they were passionately *engaged in* their spirituality by personalizing and retooling practice along their individual habits, everyday situational contexts, biographical peculiarities, and simply what felt right at the time.

While quite often individuals select spiritual practices because of the influence of family, friends, or religious leaders or because of familiarity through past experiences,[13] conservative influences on spiritual practice are still shot through with individual agency that tweaks the edges of these practices or routines. The same is true regarding the way in which most of these activists interpret their experiences, both secular and spiritual, and forge or reinforce strong connections between the two. Past experiences as well as interaction with friends, family, or spiritual leaders may facilitate (or hinder) the connections between spirituality and social commitment. For instance, the DeLeon brothers each wanted to follow the example of their parents by living a socially responsible spiritual life in concert with their community. Both brothers stayed true to their parents' faith tradition, going well beyond the informal roles that their parents spliced together to serve the working migrant laborers who passed through their town. Although sparked by family influences, the brothers chose different paths for their professional roles in the ministry. Dan founded an exponentially expanding church within his parents' denomination, and Lee drew upon his talents and interests to create one of the most successful models of social service ministries in the country. Their individual choices even spill over into their subtly different styles of individual worship. The process of engaging in one's own spirituality, exploring the edges in intended and unknowing ways, continually intersects with future experiences, resulting in personally distinct variations in the arrangements of otherwise institutional practice.

The skill with which people are able to pick up, put down, and reassemble the cultural and spiritual resources they already have at their own disposal, along with the new practices they acquire along the way, strengthens their overall ability to deal with changing environments or to promote change in other environments. Everyone interviewed came to social activism or social service work with—to greater or lesser degrees—an extensive, particular, preexisting repertoire from which they could draw from in shaping their strategies for change.[14] The DeLeons in part brought their emotional connection and learned skills from their family, Assistant Imam Shah brought his football experience from his athletic career, and Rabbi Shapiro brought his accumulated knowledge of ancient Jewish mystical texts. People's cultural capacities are vast, and they carry around much more culture—both spiritual and other—than can be used at any given moment.[15] While Shah may not draw upon his capacity to discuss football minutiae during an interfaith dialogue on homelessness and the DeLeons may not always dip into the emotional supply of their upbringing, these deep reservoirs allow for endless variability within constellations of meaning-making, affecting the way that actions are organized, the way that new experiences are interpreted, and the way that creative ideas are developed. In fact, an engaged spirituality that combines agency, structure, and experience often connects capacities, such as football and Islam that might not otherwise be connected.

SOCIAL STRUCTURE

While engaging in spirituality provided for personal choice, direction, and complex combinations of spiritual practice for the participants in this study, individualized repertoires of practice and the experiences they may produce are also always *engaged within* the context of broader social relations and structures that affect its interpretation and application in action. Social structures are made up of enduring external patterns such as economic class struggles or theological institutional strictures that enable actions at some times and constrain them at others. Spiritual experience alone is made meaningful through myriad resources and interpretive frameworks.[16] Spirituality is engaged within frameworks of preexisting cultural codes, both particular, such as Orthodox Jewish or Charismatic Catholic, and general, such as Protestant individualism or filial piety. These cultural codes are often not accounted for when analyzing the successes and failures of individual or collective action.[17] However, culture still exists in the broadest sense as a set of collective meanings, supported by and bound up in social institutions that carry these codes, as well as multiple manifestations of this set of meanings as they are created and re-created within various communities, organizations, and social networks.

Religious institutions, often introduced through families during childhood socialization, are the earliest carriers of these cultural codes that act as interpretive boundary markers, indicating what is appropriate in constructing meaning in life and what to take action against (or not). The structural influences of religious institutions are never exclusively spiritual but are mingled with the cultural contexts of a particular time and place. The influences may be very direct and may include the racist theologies that some of these activists were raised with as late as the middle part of the last century.

At other times codes function under the radar, so to speak. The ubiquitous religious worship styles and spiritual practices of particular religious institutions are picked up and carried along as the way in which religion and spirituality are done, leaving other options invisible or off in the margins. This can go unexamined throughout a lifetime or it can change as other forms of practice are introduced along the way. Moving from one synagogue to another will slightly alter the way certain rituals are performed or the way songs are sung. Such low-level shifts create differences in the way individuals and communities experience spirituality and can produce dramatic shifts, as in Brother Dunn's case, for the way in which spirituality is acted upon for social change.

Beyond the meaning-making significance of structures such as religious institutions and even faith traditions, the options available for acting upon interpretations of spiritual experience are also influenced by a broader structured environment. After all, humans are social beings who live in community. It makes a difference whether they are rich or poor and whether or not they are treated with dignity regardless of color. Patterned opportunities and barriers include minor annoyances and major social frameworks such as institutional discrimination. On the one hand, social context may prevent someone from being unable to meditate in a noisy area. On the other hand, more embedded forms of social structure, such as gender or racial discrimination in ordination practices or limitations on participation in collective social action because of scarce material resources or organizational outlets, are much more systemic and difficult to overcome.

The Reverend Glenda Hope's experience of gender barriers to full-time congregational ministry at the crucial point in her life when her career was determined is a telling example of the way that structural barriers affect the shape of spirituality and social change. Seeing an opportunity for service in the Tenderloin while having no experience in direct service providing among the poor and the addicted—that was not yet part of her cultural repertoire— Hope transposed the congregational strategies that she learned through her ministry training and modified them according to the new resources that were available to her within this new context.[18]

While Reverend Hope is an unusual example of subverting and reimagining social structural barriers as structural opportunities, institutional access and organizational outlets for spiritually informed social action similarly affected individual experience across a wider array of narratives. On a more operational level, participation can be hampered by lack of organizational opportunity or institutional channels through which individuals can act. In extreme cases such as Rabbi Shapiro's Metivta, strong visionary leaders who do not perceive any other viable options than striking out on their own create organizations or revolutionize institutions.

Others feel stifled in their motives until an acceptable outlet is found. Yasser Aman affectively felt the moral mandate from his Islamic faith to actively engage in civic participation, but he did not see adequate local openings in the Muslim American service communities of which he was part. It was not until UMMA Free Clinic opened its doors in South Central Los Angeles that he was finally able to act upon his spiritual motivations and have them supported, reaffirmed, and sustained through a community of volunteers and professionals who were similarly motivated.[19] He said, "Finally I had an avenue of actually doing something and also setting an example for Muslims and non-Muslims that we're human too, we care."

In addition to organizational outlets, organizational resources including creative and innovative staff, mobilizing leaders, buildings in which to gather, organizational skills, and financial funding affect the extent to which these motivations can be carried out. Not surprisingly, all of the professionals I spoke with, while encouraged by the accomplishments they were achieving, dreamed of reaching more people and effecting broader change—even if it simply meant getting beat-up old bicycles for migrant laborers—if only there were more available funds.

Of course, for the most part people do not dramatically reconfigure the structural patterns of everyday life, but their actions, in subtle ways, have cumulative effects. Those in positions of leadership may reorganize these patterns and resources more handily and with broader consequence. With engaged spirituality added to the mix, perceived social mandates based in a transcendent worldview hold significant potential for seeing social patterns in a different light and for motivating action to change patterns that no longer fit within the new worldview. By drawing upon this unique perception that individuals have of their spiritual lives, they can effect change.

These first two influences of engaged spirituality correspond with pragmatic and structural approaches to culture. Built into these approaches are implicit notions of social change. Since humans are all active agents in retooling culture and since social structures can be thought of as dual—both enduring external resources as well as patterns of collective actions and agreed-upon but negotiable rules—the structures or patterns of society always have within them the potential to shift and fluctuate depending upon the ways collective meanings and practices are recombined.[20] It makes sense that changes throughout life will engender other changes and that individuals for whom spirituality matters will draw upon their accumulated spiritual skills and beliefs as one way of making sense of these changes. In the moment, the intersection between personal capacities and understanding of social structures influence the paths individuals chart.[21] These junctures can be unpredictable and people constantly find themselves bound up within situational circumstances that have fluctuating effects on what types of decisions they make.[22]

While individuals may reflect back upon decisions that they make during fluctuating circumstances and reconstruct these decisions in ways that match their overarching values and self-perceptions as rational, intelligent actors, in reality the situational circumstances in the moment can pull out their capacities for acting in ways that they may not expect.[23] In addition to the momentary experiences or accidents of daily life that produce these potential moments for change, spirituality—through practice and experience—also wends its way between the cracks of individual choices and social structural influences.[24] One African American minister, community leader, and member of the Southern Christian Leadership Conference in Los Angeles explained that from time to time people ask, "Where did you come up with that idea?" He often shrugs his shoulders, not knowing himself. "This is what I call rearview mirror spirituality," he explains. "I don't realize it's the influence of God until I turn back and see what He did." Engaged spirituality can act as a powerful lubricant for seeing the world differently or allowing oneself to be open to the ambiguities of life and as such adds unique value and unshakable meaning to an otherwise accidental cultural model of social change.[25] It is here that an engaged spirituality can have its greatest effect.

EXPERIENTIAL BREAKS

The third and final influence of engaged spirituality is the dynamic nature to directly transform both individual perceptions of efficacy and individual relationships to one's perceived structural opportunities or constraints. Throughout this volume there have been reports of being *engaged by* spiritual forces, feelings, and powers that transcend secular imagination in sometimes subtle and sometimes vivid ways. Whether these experiences are real in some metaphysical sense is not the point; they are perceived as real and have a transformative effect on how people live their lives, serving as the creative engine for innovation and producing real, demonstrable consequences.[26]

Taken as experience, spirituality is much more than the analytical constituent parts of self, practice, and social context; it combines into an experience that is wholly other.[27] Engaged spirituality in experience is irreducible to the singular functional benefits, the boundaries of social roles, or the compendium of practices outlined in the matrix. Instead, it is a transcendence that, while varying in degree, is experienced as a cognitive, emotional, or physical break from everyday reality. This transcendence might mean emotionally speaking in tongues, it might mean recalling the spiritual lesson of economically poor communities around the globe, or it might entail realizing, late at night in reflection back upon the day, that a simple conversation with a homeless person was actually the voice of God. These kinds of experiences are subjectively felt as universal or divinely connective. The otherworldly element of spirituality provides the greatest contribution to understanding the persistence and passions many people have for bringing about a better world.

Being engaged by spirituality is a qualitatively distinct contributing factor in social action and change. It is in spirituality that the ineffable realities of religion are manifest. William James was particularly attuned to the possibilities embedded in spiritual experience. He suggested that just as religion provides one salient source for certain socially shared morals and values—the conservative function of religion in society still today—it also holds one key for broader change. Religious experiences, by altering individual perceptions, alter the appearance of the world. This perspective lays the foundation for what James referred to as religious (or what has been referred to here as spiritual) experience as more than a private individualistic phenomenon; rather, it has real consequences for social action and change.[28] Spiritual experience, following William James, not only colors a person's view of the world but also profoundly affects their being in that world. It shifts their relationships to that world and, in doing so, shifts the perceived expectations for acting that can, or often should, be taken.

In similar ways, social historian Robert Orsi describes the way that subjective and experiential elements of religious practice are bound up in and are consequential for the social world rather than designated as private and therefore
uninteresting phenomena. Prayer, for example, allows one to switch between
the social world and one's imaginations, in which "the taken for granted quality
of reality is dissolved and humans encounter the fictive nature of what they call
real, in the sense that they apprehend the radical contingency of their world."[29]
This is the social power of engaged spirituality. Spiritual experiences provide alternative perceptions of available resources or at least alternative perceptions
of the way these resources are put together or patterned.[30] In addition, these
experiences of radical contingency may provide a perceived sense of efficacy or
certainty in new strategies for acting. In short, engaged spirituality—through
this final influence of being engaged by feeling and experience—changes perceptions of social barriers, enhances the scope of perceived options, and increases
the viability of a range of subsequent actions, not to mention inciting indignation and empathy for those in need.

Perhaps no other story as neatly encapsulates the potential of engaged
spirituality as defined here as the Reverend Hope's story of erecting an apartment building in the Tenderloin. Having no accumulated experience in super-
vising such an aggressive project, no sense of city ordinances or knowledge
about building codes, and having few economic resources to devote to this,
Hope, with the existential clarity that her biannual spiritual retreat conferred,
forged ahead undaunted and remarkably succeeded in the process.

The UMMA Free Clinic in South Central Los Angeles similarly epitomizes
the remarkable creativity and fortitude that engaged spirituality can facilitate.
When the idea for this clinic was first conceived by a handful of idealistically
motivated Muslim medical students at UCLA, the practicalities of moving the
idea from their heads to a brick-and-mortar health clinic seemed little more
than fantasy. Substantial barriers separated the dream from the reality, not the
least of which was money. Yet with some scouting and persistence, motivated
and sustained through spiritual drives to serve locally while promoting religious
identity and representation in the community, these students acquired a rundown building that sheltered little more than people looking for a quick place
to shoot up. The city allocated some Housing and Urban Development money
to get the physical structure into working order, but the students still needed
operating costs, community outreach support, and medical supplies. They were
shocked at the outpouring of corporate and private donations that made a
reality out of this spiritually inspired dream to serve the local community.

Finally, Pastor Alton adds that spirituality does not always appear valor-
ous, riding in on pure intentions, existential clarity, or pious faith. Often, spir-

ituality is the last-ditch effort of people who have exhausted all other resources and options and have nothing left to lose. But Alton is a realist who turns to the Christian gospels and points out that in many passages where Jesus names something as faith, one "could substitute desperation and it would fit the scene." He explained that the only thing Jesus might know about those who came to see him was that they had reached the point of desperation. Instead of casting them off as unworthy, Jesus understood their visits to be an act of faith, telling them, "Your faith has made you well." Alton argues that at these points of desperation, "we often choose to check out or give up or become passive victims. And to take a desperate action that I don't even really believe will work but the only alternative is being a victim, then I'll go ahead and do that . . . that's an important piece of the discernment process."

Taking leaps of faith or turning to engaged spirituality, as many of these individuals did in their service and in their careers, provided persistence and creativity out of desperation. These leaps must be taken seriously to understand the cultural process of subjectively motivated and sustained social change.

Tandem Frameworks

Since the creative spiritual dimension does not operate on the same plane as strategizing pie charts, optimizing efficiency, or narrow fiscal accountability, how do the folks interviewed for this study manage, much less succeed, in the calculating modern world of local politics, economic policy, and community development? The simple answer is that they manage in the same ways as everyone else. Everyone carries around a large array of cultural capacities in their tool kits, and because of this they are able to move seamlessly between the different realities they pass through in everyday life—nurturing and unguarded at home, for example, while efficient and professional at work. Each of these roles require different capacities and different affect. While this juggling act may be difficult at times, society is well beyond the point of arguing that nurturance is incompatible with or undermining to public or professional lives. Instead, these different strategies work together. Those interviewed here simply add one other capacity to the mix, the otherworldly guiding touch of how they perceive the divine. And they merge these different realities in innovative ways that do not discount or displace the other capacities they must incorporate into the proper functioning of their temple, their shelter, or their advocacy network.

The individuals here are neither interest-driven automatons, utilizing a one-dimensional rationality, nor ineffectual lotus eaters, detached from the constraints and opportunities of the structural realities around them. Engaged spirituality functions in tandem with, but separate from, other rational decision-making calculations, allowing practitioners to move effortlessly between two frameworks—at times seeing very little difference between the two, while at other times claiming the distinctively transcendent benefits of spirituality. In fact, when pressed on the matter, it was these transcendent spiritual elements rather than (or in conjunction with) rational sociopolitical ends that leaders and activists consistently gave as the primary contributing factor in their daily work.[31]

To sum up, the engaged model proposed here pays particular attention to the affective level of spiritual experience while not relinquishing the impact of either individual agency or the structural contexts in which experience occurs. While spirituality is enabled by individually accumulated capacities as well as funneled through the structural frameworks in which people must act, the strength of spirituality as a resource is found in the interstices of individual experiences and social structures. From this model, spiritual experience contributes to social action and change no less than individual agency and social structures.[32] Perceived transcendence allows for and encourages fluctuations and motivates ongoing change, nudging community agents to exceed realistic expectations or to achieve seemingly unimaginable goals. The subjectively perceived spiritual experiences that allow for variability, that spark creativity, and that make endurable the unexpected outcomes as well as the disappointments and failures of community development or activism is engaged spirituality's hidden capacity for successful, enduring social action for change.

Fields of Engagement

Just as engaged spirituality as a whole varies according to individual experiences, sources, practices, and roles, so does the degree to which individuals actively engage their social worlds. Moving further into the ways in which these frameworks are integrated, there are two orienting dimensions that run through engaged spirituality: aspects of spirituality and aspects of social engagement. The first concerns the way in which spirituality is subjectively experienced and practiced. At one end of this continuum are individual practices and experiences that are interior, contemplative, and reflective, such as silent unscripted prayer, solitary meditation, and feelings of centeredness.[33] On the opposite end of the continuum are collective practices and experiences that are externalized, community based, and socially connective, such as group worship or collective prayer. Various practices fall at various points along the continuum. For example, salat, or the five Muslim prayers, and the Daily Office are both forms of (relatively) silent and internalized conversations that follow regulated patterns and are imagined to take place (and sometimes physically do) with a greater community of others. These examples are neither wholly individual nor always collective and, depending upon the particular circumstance in which, say, a Muslim prays to Mecca, will fall at different points along the continuum. Worshipping in a large mosque with hundreds of others, although still praying internally, will differ from praying alone in a hotel room at five in the morning, even though the same collective patterns will be followed and the same others will be imagined doing the same thing at the same time in both scenarios.

The second dimension concerns the degree to which spirituality is actively employed or connected to bringing about social change. On the one end of this second continuum are spiritual experiences and practices that are engaged in solely for their benefits to the individual practitioner. These include exercises for personal development or solely for transcendent connection or individual salvation. Spirituality in this sense is perceived as something set aside and different from the mundane elements of everyday society. On the other end of this continuum are the practices that see no separation between spirituality and social change. These practices involve activist spiritualities concerned with improving conditions throughout society as a profound form of spirituality itself. As with spiritual practice, spiritual connection to social change also varies along this continuum. A Pentecostal minister relies upon a very individual and emotional form of spiritual practice to secure his salvation but still feels compelled to help those around him because of his interpretation of the scriptures.

When these two continuums are connected as the dominant axes of a field of engaged spirituality, various examples can be plotted along endless points within the four different quadrants set up by this typology. The field of engagement table arranges these ideas visually, illustrating the different degrees of social engagement across two axes—one depicting the continuum from individual to the collective, the other from disengaged to engaged.[34]

Quadrants 1 and 3 can be labeled as fields of disengaged spirituality, very broadly defined. In their extreme variations, individuals represented in these

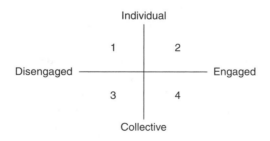

quadrants would include what critics commonly malign as solipsistic spirituality. Within the scope of this study, quadrants 1 and 3 apply to the Private Quest and the Monastic, which I separated out conceptually from the more engaged social roles. The far upper-left corner of quadrant 1 represents the purely private, individualist quest for self-edification or enlightenment, while the far lower left corner of quadrant 3 represents the collective spiritual spectacles that provide individual or communal, therapeutic benefits through group or collective ritual. Certain new-age communes or new religious movements that segregate themselves from the rest of society in order to attain individual or exclusive group enlightenment would fit in the farther corners of this quadrant.

Quadrants 2 and 4, on the other hand, comprise the engaged spirituality discussed in earlier chapters. Each of the five social roles discussed in chapter 3 can be placed at various points within this half of the grid. The Good Neighbor, for example, would fall somewhere within quadrant 2, since he connects his spirituality with social action through random, nonorganized, individual acts of fellowship. The volunteer, on the other hand, would be located within quadrant 4, following the same reasoning; the spiritually motivated actions she takes to serve her community take the form of a scheduled and collective act that is dependent upon a larger degree of social organization and interdependence with other volunteers and organizational leadership. Levels within these two quadrants move from the individualist philosophy of change, one person at a time, as the basis for social change to the revolutionary movement leader who mobilizes thousands through sweeping ideas of a right and just society. Intermediate levels bring about change within religious bodies, neighborhood communities, civic institutions, or political initiatives.

Those familiar with Max Weber's work will see the impetus of this diagram. In constructing a vast treatise on world religions, Weber devised a four-part typology arranged around two similar axes. The first distinguished between asceticism and mysticism—the two categorical forms of religious engagement that he believed were dominant in the world. Ascetics seek salvation through action, whereas mystics seek salvation through contemplation. The second axis in Weber's model considered the locus of salvation. Religions could be either inner-worldly in their orientation, working through their sacred duties and obligations in this world, or world-rejecting, in which they would shun both the privileges and responsibilities of the material world. Weber's agenda was to categorize whole cultural systems—from American Protestantism to Japanese Shintoism—along these quadrants or types. Although the details of Weber's theory are difficult to substantiate through empirical support,[35] some of the core conceptual contributions of his model, with some alterations, remain insightful for a discussion on engaged spirituality. Rather than a static set of quadrants, this updated field is more freely flowing. American Protestant piety, for example, can no longer be generalized always as inner-worldly asceticism, which is the typification Weber placed upon it. Today, spiritual practices in the arena of engaged spirituality are more likely to be shared and appropriated across faith traditions where common ground is constructed around social policy rather than theology. Similarly, individual identity and practice spill across the boundaries containing these four ideal types.

Weber was particularly interested in the ideas and values within these quadrants as active switchmen shifting the course of economies and politics; my conception of spirituality as a pragmatic aspect of culture requires a different view of ideas. Religious ideas do provide the motivating impetus behind social engagement. Beliefs and feelings are intensely felt and hold the potential to redirect action, as Weber suggested, especially when there are friends, family, colleagues, and institutional channels that support and reinforce these ideas over time. However, strong resonance with a set of values does not include the emphasis on action proposed here. This is partly why I have kept the focus throughout on the experiential forms, functions, and feelings, and on the applications of spirituality rather than the ideational values or theological components alone. While values do help shape action, it is the learned habits and skills that are acquired in conjunction with these ideas that enable corresponding actions across situations.[36] The engaged spirituality of the stories here depends upon the cultural repertoires that are picked up in certain situations and utilized in various others, as well as the ideas and values that are such crucial and emotional foundations for this work.

By looking at actions and ideas, some might suggest that, by definition, all individuals living an engaged spiritual life are inner-worldly ascetics, seeking their worth or salvation through the work that they do within this world. If this is true, did one Weberian type win out? Considering engaged spirituality, the answer is both yes and no. In order to fall within the engaged spirituality quadrants in this new field, individuals must act. They have to actively employ their spiritual feelings within society. In this sense, they are inner-worldly ascetics. However, with the exception of the extreme outlier on this map, whose position is structurally entrenched or individually guarded, it is important to note that most people's particular position within this field changes. At any given time it is merely a momentary snapshot of their overall behaviors and actions. Much like Heisenberg's Uncertainty Principle, when people shine a light or focus their attention on one frozen element of a fluidly engaged lifestyle, they can only understand one slice or one aspect of that lifestyle.

Placement within this diagram is constructed in practice rather than by organizational affiliation, denominationalism, political platform, or social role.

Placement involves the degree to which individual actors interpret their other-worldly experiences as directly affecting their actions in this world. Moreover, placement involves the particular activity that they are engaging at one particular moment. This grid then should be read as a field in which individual and even institutional actors have greater autonomy to move from one quadrant to the next. In fact, individuals may move across this grid multiple times throughout their lives, depending upon their spiritual motivations and opportunities for acting. Considering the social roles that people cycle through during any given day alone, the variability in their placement on this grid is easy to imagine. Advocates may speak through international media outlets periodically throughout the year but still maintain a rigid schedule of weekly volunteer work at a synagogue. As they move from one role to the other, their vertical placement within the engaged quadrants moves as well. Similarly, practicing Tai Chi alone in a garden each morning changes one's horizontal position from the community church service performed on the steps of city hall the evening before. This horizontal shift can be beneficial.

Disengaging

Many of the people interviewed here spent most of their time within the engaged spirituality quadrants. However, they also spent some time in the disengaged quadrants, which provided crucial incubation periods where they developed the spiritual practices and relationships necessary for acting in the engaged quadrants. Reverend Wendy Taylor, for example, explained that every year she visits a Buddhist monastery in the mountains for a week at a time. Each visit is a silent retreat in which she says she is allowed to listen. The retreat experience for Taylor is profoundly different from her everyday life working with immigrant and migrant farm families along the northern California coast. Even though these silent retreats are restful for Taylor, they are also quite challenging for a self-described talker. However, the silence and the listening provide a needed respite. After a week, "it feels as if I've been gone for twenty years if I have a real silent break," she said.

An overachiever and constant worker, Taylor suggests that those weeks are times where the space is carved out and defined for her to reconnect. "I can really check with God and make sure things are going the way they're supposed to be going, and I can just soak in it," she said. Stepping outside of her own Christian faith tradition is helpful as well. It allows her in her own mind to be off the hook. In a Buddhist setting, she does not feel the pestering need to read every piece of contemporary theology and exposition on Buddhist thought, as she might feel at a Christian retreat. "I've done that. I'm a grown up now. I don't need to keep pouring in other words. I need to settle in and figure out how to rejuvenate to stay alive," she said.

Taylor's straightforward discussion has none of the tensions and paradoxes of shifting from a contemplative mode in which salvation is sought through cultivating an uninterrupted communion with her God to an inner-worldly mode of seeking salvation through the empowerment of her community. These are permeable membranes and interdependent scaffoldings—each necessary for the sustenance of the other. There are many points at which spiritual practice does not appear to directly fit social commitments or engagement. How is speaking in tongues, for example, really tied to affordable housing issues? How is having a vision of purple lotuses or praying the Divine Office directly related to spousal abuse advocacy or feeding the homeless? Taylor's example of switching locations across this grid as well as across disciplines helps indicate how and why. Spirituality cannot only be articulated through serving those in need, let alone by storming windmills. While often it is, at times it appears to simply and profoundly be about finding meaning, finding a place, and sometimes even finding comfort and respite in order to keep those other actions alive.

Once this switching between quadrants is achieved, it transpires seamlessly, becoming part of a new repertoire. Taylor no longer has to think through the self-imposed contradictions of attending a Buddhist retreat—how do I act, is this consistent with Christian theology, shouldn't I be doing something, do I belong? Now the Buddhist retreat and how to enact contemplative recharging is part of her tool kit. The same is true of the connection between spirituality and social action for change. Reskilled as an engaged spirituality, this pattern of acting—this way of being—is more than a combination of spiritual motivations and social action.[37] These become fused and understood, even if only in the way this feels, as one. This new fusion can be called up independently of reconstructing it anew each time a different situation arises or the seed of a new project takes root. This is not a rational calculation, nor does it require the negotiation between what is spiritual and what is social. Once strategies are integrated they become a new lens for orienting oneself, evaluating situations, and acting.

While initially this engaged spirituality model appeared highly variable and individually contingent, as illustrated through the matrix, maintaining this engaged spirituality through action requires a range of individual as well as interactive and organizational social components. Especially during the early stages of engagement, a strong sense of spiritually informed social commitment may generate a deepening spiritual practice, and this in turn may strengthen commitments or fuel a perceived exigency to do something. This spiritually driven commitment might get a volunteer through the door of a service agency or it might spark creative ideas to fill a perceived need in the community. Over time, however, these connections between experience and action must be sustained individually as well as within a social context of interactive and organizational support.

Chapter 7   Conclusion

Lived Spirituality and the Gamut of Social Action

WHAT IS THE ADVANTAGE for understanding spirituality from an engaged perspective? This question can be read in many different ways—theologically, personally, epistemologically, and/or politically—each with a pragmatic ring for the present as well as a projective implication for the future. One thing that can be concluded is that spirituality is not going away any time soon. Even though it may not always be explicitly expressed publicly or analyzed scientifically, it is still often at work as the motivating, sustaining, and meaning-making engine of social change. In this role, spirituality gives one avenue for understanding, in a qualitatively different way, the creative and transformative actions—large and small, local and global—that have effected change throughout history and most likely will continue well into the future. The stories contained in these pages attest to that empirical reality. And yet the simple acknowledgment that spirituality and religion continue to affect the social world is far too shortsighted if left simply at that. Spirituality is also a deeply personal yet complexly social phenomenon that takes many forms as it intersects with social structures, interpersonal networks, and subjective interpretations. Moreover, spiritually motivated social action is part of human culture. It is part of the way people filter, select, utilize, and reposition available options. Finally, spirituality is a resource in and of itself that people draw upon for comfort, strength, and endurance. Addressing the various ways in which engaged spirituality functions raises questions about its social and more practical potential.

There are three spheres of lived experience in which engaged spirituality may have effects. First, engaged spirituality is a personal, local, and everyday element that often goes unnoticed but has the potential for incremental repercussions in society. These everyday aspects dance around the edges of institutions, revealing a hidden cultural power in the ways that people make meaning, find motivations, and act creatively within their given situations. Second, engaged spirituality moves beyond these beneficial but limited individual meanings and actions to reveal the broader social and structural webs such as economic inequality, political power, and organizational access that are both cause and consequence of spirituality. Third, engaged spirituality is a latent social resource among larger constituencies that do not have a viable outlet for this personal commitment. Tapping this resource can lead to significant change, as it has done periodically throughout social history. In addressing each of these spheres, I will turn one last time to the individual stories of the people who live and breathe these experiences each day.

Under the Big Top

Perhaps the most nontraditional and fun interview that I conducted for this project was with Sister Dorothy Fabritze, a circus nun.[1] Fabritze's story has many similarities with other young women who joined religious orders over a generation ago. Sister Dorothy left her Italian American home when she was thirteen years old and entered the aspirancy, a high school program for girls drawn to serving the religious order. By 1965, she had graduated with no doubt in her mind that she would continue in the novitiate program of the Missionary Sisters of the Most Sacred Heart of Jesus, and she had a clear vision of where she wanted to go. Fabritze's childhood congregation developed a mission in 1900 specifically targeting remote island communities throughout Papua New Guinea. After years of listening to the exotic stories of mission life on the islands, Fabritze knew that was exactly where she belonged. However, when she first applied, Papua New Guinea was going through a turbulent fight for independence and she was denied entry. Committed to the idea of foreign service, Fabritze tried African missions but was again denied visa approval. She interpreted this second denial as a sign to reapply to Papua New Guinea, which had by then resolved its struggle for independence. In 1977, Fabritze was on a plane bound for the South Pacific.

In her sixteen-year tenure along the archipelago, Fabritze traveled the islands in canoes and four-wheel drives, walking through mountains, swamps, and mud, and living in huts in order to reach the 150 schools that were under her religious educational jurisdiction. Although this could be difficult and isolating work, Fabritze thrived under the substantial autonomy of the field and eventually rose to the second in authority among the nuns in the mission. Throughout her time in Papua New Guinea, there was, in her estimation, a justifiable political move to localize the mission and train indigenous leaders. Accordingly, each time Fabritze moved up in rank, she would train a younger woman from the islands to take her place. Fabritze felt a pride and a sense of fulfillment with every trainee, keeping in mind a nagging caution that her time at this mission would be limited. In the 1970s, Fabritze had attended a missionary convention where she heard an African Bishop proclaim, "You European and American missionaries are great. You come to our country. You educate us. You give us health services, social services—wonderful. You do a great job. Proclaim the love of God. But you make one mistake. You don't know when to go home." During her sixteen years in Papua New Guinea, she prayed, "Lord, let me know when it's time for me to go home."

In 1993, she felt that her prayer was answered and she returned to the States. "It was the most traumatic time of my whole life," Fabritze recalled. Back in the States, Fabritze found herself in a society that had changed significantly since she had been gone. She had no idea in which direction to turn with her spiritual motivations. She missed the commitments and the intimate camaraderie of the families in the villages and the different pace of life that the islands provided. One thing was certain; Fabritze would seek a nontraditional role here in the United States.

Having spent nearly all of her adult years abroad, where she learned only secondhand about the social shifts of the Western world during the 1970s and 1980s, she felt little connection with stateside social problems. Then one day, at a religious service work convention, a nun gave Fabritze a manual about teaching circus children. For weeks following that meeting, whenever she opened the drawer containing her mission options—including working with Native Americans, Appalachian communities, or Habitat for Humanity— "that little circus file had lights on it. It just blinked out at me." According to Fabritze, God was up to his tricks in trying to sway her decision.

Eventually Fabritze called the priest who organized the circus ministry, if for nothing else than to close off an option that was taunting her. The priest cut her off when she called, saying, "You don't want to do circus ministry. . . . This is another culture and you don't know anything about working in another culture and . . . it's a mud show and you're going to be traveling in mud and your travel trailer is small and the beds are hard." Indignant, she countered, "Excuse me! You don't know." This was the challenge that Sister Fabritze needed to spark her interest. Defiant, Sister Fabritze, along with Sister Bernard, whom she had worked with for years in Papua New Guinea, bought a trailer. For the past three circuses, they have been erecting tents, selling souvenirs on the midway, and, most meaningfully to the sisters, teaching English as a second language to the circus members.

The feelings Sister Fabritze experienced from the priest who tried to dissuade her prompted her to take the position. Indeed, at times perceived barriers can become motivating impulses and challenges that spark innovative responses or the redirection of energies. It seems reasonable to suggest that if each and every door was opened for these people working for change, there would be little reason to draw upon spiritual resources to sustain their unending successes. For Fabritze, the challenges throughout her service life have sustained her work, her faith, and her identity.

Fabritze feels most enriched spiritually by "being with a people who are journeying, struggling, surviving." In marginalized communities where people make deep personal struggles as part of their life and their faith, Fabritze sees the significant presence and future of the church. "I really think the solution is going to come from the grassroots. The solution is going to come from us, simply living what we know is right and what we believe. Historically that's where this solution has always come from," she said.

On a local level, one solution is having a chapel on the road with the sisters, a significant resource for Fabritze. "If it wasn't for the spiritual life, if it wasn't for that chapel, we wouldn't be here," she said. When Fabritze first developed a credible interest in the circus ministry, she thought she could have a chapel in her own trailer. Even though other sisters with the circus have a chapel in a separate truck that pulls a smaller trailer, Fabritze did not like to be separated from her spiritual touchstone. "I like Jesus right with me," she said with a smile. The plans were in place to purchase a larger trailer, and Fabritze knew exactly where and how the chapel would fit into this new design. However, as the time approached, the overseeing advisory group suggested that her request might be denied, claiming that the church does not allow the chapel to be housed in living quarters, let alone the living quarters of two nuns on the road. "No chapel in my trailer, no MSC Sisters on the road," Fabritze replied. With some last-minute negotiations with the mission priest as a mediator, Fabritze was allowed to construct her chapel.

In the front bedroom of the trailer, separated by a small door, is a fairly stark room, meaningfully adorned along the rear wall with a shell light—reminiscent of her time in the South Pacific—flowers, an incense holder, a prayer candle, and stylized wooden figurines of Mary and a resurrected Jesus. On the makeshift altar lays a photo album containing pictures of friends and family who guide her prayers and intentions. When asked why it was so important to have the chapel in her trailer, Fabritze replied, "It's this presence of Jesus with us. And the opportunity to come away, step away and have a relatively quiet space where we can take the scriptures and discern the will of God and to feed this love relationship I have . . . with Jesus, to bring the worries and the issues of life and bring them here before the Lord. This is absolutely important. . . . Personally, I don't know how anyone else does it . . . but I know how I can live, how I can survive, how I can grow, and how I can be happy."

With the chapel in the trailer the nuns cultivate a mutual understanding about their identity and their perceived role as members of the circus. The circus subculture does not openly ask questions about a person's past but rather focuses on the present. Fabritze is sensitive to that culture and tries to fit in by living in the now, a shift that has affected her spiritual course. Gone are the nostalgic arcs of local empowerment and decades-long struggles of questioning when to leave the mission field. Instead, Fabritze incorporates her newfound worldview and seeks God and service in the present.

Each morning the sisters pray, keeping the door to their trailer closed. While this prayer time is central to Fabritze's sense of identity and growth, her fellow workers and performers assume the sisters are late sleepers. "It's very hard for people sometimes to understand that part of our ministry is our prayer life as well, and it should be the main part of it." For this reason, the altar in the trailer is open for anyone to use at other times of the day, and some circus members have learned to appreciate and take advantage of this spiritual space in an unexpected location.

As Fabritze's story illustrates, while some of the most consequential social and cultural decisions are being hammered away in the public sphere, others are being put into action without fanfare. Engaged spirituality is very much a combination of biography, changing social milieus, and a sense of personal and collective identity, all of which produce a particularly tailored understanding of how to experience spirituality and how to embed it into the everyday lives of communities for change.

At the beginning of this book I suggested that spirituality and social change were potentially mutually beneficial. In the case of Sister Fabritze, it can be seen on a very complex level the way that this is true. Although Fabritze's requirement for a chapel in a circus trailer is a direct and local example of navigating through bureaucratic authority, her story also implies much deeper issues of institutional gender resistance and the transference of personal experiences of relative autonomy in remote islands of the South Pacific to the more pervasive patriarchal authority within the Catholic church.

Sister Fabritze understands her spiritual connections in part through a close physical proximity to the symbolic representations of her relationship with God and with Jesus. This closeness sustained her commitments while in cultures and situations that were not originally her own in the South Pacific, and it was incomprehensible to move into another foreign environment—this time geographically closer but still socially very distant—without the physical proximity to the symbolic representations of her faith. Spirituality provided strength, comfort, and motivation to sustain her work, and, as a fluid and malleable resource, found the cracks in the structures where change could be effected, not only with the chapel but also among the immigrant and domestic workers who spent months away from their families or tried to raise their children in a transient environment. But the changes that Fabritze's redefinition of chapel placement made in Catholic policy, although local, are by no means inconsequential. Sister Fabritze successfully overturned the institutional barriers that limited her access to spiritual connection.

Interestingly, never once did Sister Fabritze use the word "feminism" or speak strategically about the gender politics of the Catholic church. In fact, she sees the different opinions about the chapel as a minor bump in the road toward her more consequential concerns of developing an active circus ministry. Fabritze does not articulate the chapel decision through personal politics. Rather, her commitment to a personally meaningful spiritual presence guided her actions and continually reshaped her interpretation of the institutional arrangements of the Catholic church, resulting in significant local changes. The new parameters Fabritze achieved were motivated by and now sustain her spiritual practice and the service work that she envisioned for the circus.[2] Today, the circus ministry is thriving. Along with teaching English as a second language and erecting tents, Fabritze facilitates Bible studies and prayer meetings, leads catechism classes, and organizes services under the big top in ways that transform the presence of the chapel from a personal resource into traveling spiritual service for a unique and underserved population.

The type of change an engaged perspective facilitates is indicative of the type of change that spirituality has always informed over time and throughout the world. For example, nineteenth-century missionaries, men and women alike, often directed their spiritual passions in ways that shook the standard organizational model of otherwise pietistic religious institutions. These missionaries' passion propelled them around the globe and provided them with the emotional and transcendent resources that shaped European imperialism in complicated ways.[3] However, this same passion at times became an organizational headache for remote mission administrators whose responsibility it was to funnel fervent energies in systematic ways for productive ends.[4] Local negotiations in the missionary field allowed for a happy medium between individual spiritual passions and the missionary societies' organizational requirements. Part of the significant contributions of engaged spirituality is this passionate, central place that it has for personal identity and motivation, effecting local changes in individual lives that ripple out to affect others.

Pink and Fluffy Nothingness vs. Structural Inequality

If spirituality has been utilized by some people as part of local and incremental, if not at times momentous change throughout history, it has been wielded by others with direction and force, hoping to carry a surge of others in their wake. Oftentimes these individuals ask the same questions about the social world, but they tend to come away with different and more widely transformative suggestions or solutions. Addressing these differences through an engaged spirituality model moves them in application beyond personal problems to consider instead the social context of networks, resources, and opportunities that supplement changes in interpretation and action. Typically, Professionals and Advocates reveal this second sphere in which the contributions of engaged spirituality function as part of a broader critique of social structural processes and social change. While Sister Fabritze's Catholic spirituality is in line with a historical legacy of missionary change, albeit at times local and circumscribed, Sister Joan Chittister forthrightly embraces the social shifts of the past forty years and pushes them further.

Chittister is a member and former prioress of the Benedictine Sisters of Erie, Pennsylvania. She is also the founder and executive director of Benetvision, a research and resource center for contemplative spirituality. The mission of Benetvision is, in Chittister's words, to find the "bridges between public and private spirituality . . . Benetvision is designed to look at both of those levels of the person in the relationship to the religious impulse." This vision and her active role in the International Peace Council have taken her to thirty-nine countries as an outspoken leader and activist for human rights. It has also inspired numerous books as well as a monthly column for Beliefnet, an interfaith online community and journal..

As an outspoken voice for radical change within the Roman Catholic church and the rest of society, Chittister may have as many enemies as she has friends. However, she embodies Benedictine hospitality and is warm, welcoming, and at ease with answering questions about her beliefs and her advocacy. Chittister's spirituality is tough and critical and is in no way tolerant of definitions that are private or egoistic, definitions she claims lead to a notion of the "spiritual Jacuzzi." Chittister's spirituality compels as much, if not more than, it comforts.

A significant part of Chittister's criticism looks squarely at institutional and structural influences upon economics, politics, and doctrinal religion through a spiritual filter of social justice. "I raise questions about process and politics and legislation, about the fact that the richest country in the world has forty-four million uninsured people tonight, and ten million of whom are children.

I can't believe that somehow or another I have a moral right to do less," she said. Chittister's spirituality is shaped by her knowledge of and placement within social, economic, and political structures, and it actively reinterprets those structures for fulfillment of what she believes the scriptures call believers to do. "You don't have to take any issues into [contemplation of the scriptures]. The issues are all there," she explained. Chittister is adept at stringing together passages that illustrate an inherent biblical agenda of social justice, and she is quick to answer the ways in which it translates into socially responsible action. In this sense, engaged spirituality helps her reimagine and reinterpret otherwise impervious and abstract social structures as the focus for action and change rather than inaction or passivity.

Religious institutions—including her own—are not immune to her critiques. She cautions that without such a critical spiritual lens, the veneer of religious institutions could turn a blind eye to social injustices within our own communities and throughout the world. "I will do my best to keep the alternative questions alive in this society, because when they die, we die morally. We'll die as a spiritual people, no matter how religious this country thinks it stays," she said. Of course, Chittister's juxtaposition of spiritually driven critical questions with a potentially impotent religion does not completely separate spirituality and religion in practice. Spirituality grounded in religion and community establishes a base, while religion infused with spirituality sparks an actionable mandate. Transcendent mandates are carried through religious institutions and reactivated through spirituality.

Chittister's approach supports the notion that when considering the patterned regularities for interpreting the transcendent aspect of engaged spirituality, one must consider religious institutions. While other forms of transcendence may be available in society—taking drugs or being in love, for example—they are not codified in the same way within communities and with definitive texts that guide the experience.[5] Transcendence is almost exclusively relegated or culturally interpreted as the domain of religion and, more specifically, spirituality. The spark of transcendence is acknowledged, fostered, or cultivated in society in religious terms. Otherwise, inexplicable moments, such as being given a book on circus ministries, are not instances of cosmic and mysterious confluence but simply happenstance. While religious interpretations are the primary guidelines for understanding and seeking transcendence, they by no means determine the way spirituality will be perceived or acted upon. Much like the effect between social issues and spirituality, religion as a structural element both affects and is affected by spirituality. Religion provides the lines, but when spirituality provides the color it does not always stay within the lines, producing different but recognizable results.

Moreover, time and place affect institutional patterns of influence on spirituality. While institutional codes of the Catholic church hold substantial influence over the shape and eschatological understanding of spirituality for Fabritze and Chittister, they do not dictate the final shape of spiritual understandings and social applications that these two women ultimately made. Chittister's spiritual and political formation was galvanized by the social changes taking place in the United States and worldwide that radically repositioned the place of women, in particular Catholic women religious. Increased pluralism, identity politics, feminism, and new structural understandings of the way the world works are at the core of Chittister's interpretation of Catholic doctrine and practice. In fact, it was the sweeping cultural changes of Vatican II that Chittister cites as the point at which her political conscience awoke and latched onto her spiritual passions. Alternatively, Fabritze was abroad in remote island cultures throughout this period of social readjustment and, while obviously aware of the transformations in society, she had a very different vantage point from which to view them and a constrained environment in which to employ the changes herself. Differences in time and place intervened and affected both women's networks, institutional relationships, and interpretations of emotion and Catholic feelings.

Finally, religious institutions such as the Catholic orders also carry history as another patterned lens through which to view the world and one's place in it. Chittister looks to the spiritual exemplars of the past as models for acting on their spiritual principles. "They stepped outside the establishment boxes. They just could not be contained by a class or a country or a type of civil thought," she said. To Chittister, it is clear that these women and men were motivated primarily by transcendent understanding. "You began to realize that they weren't standing up telling you about the glories of the French Revolution and the new parliament and the constitution. They were always talking to you about the life of Jesus and what this meant and how somehow or another it demanded that you be in the leprosariums and it demanded that you be with the poor. It demanded that you be with the refugee. It made great non-conventional, unconventional demands on you," she said.

For Chittister, these women and men, whose shoes she is currently filling, were not working within or primarily for a secular, progressive, political agenda. Although these influences shaped the environment in which spirituality became tangibly understood, first and foremost it was spiritual motivation that was the source of intentions and actions. As Rev. Glenda Hope stressed earlier, the spiritual energy that motivates social action is not merely a reflection or private accessory to a more fundamental politics. Both these women make clear that spiritual foundation not only shapes beliefs but also insists on action.

The spiritual demands for action are intimately tied to the legacy of Chittister's religious order, which calls for women to always be responsive to local structural conditions. "If hospitality is what [Benedictines are] about, and stability, which is one of our vows, is what we're about, then we rise and fall with Erie, Pennsylvania. We can't live outside this neurotic, romantic notion that somehow or another you can be religious, which means you are less human and less responsible for the humanity around you" she said. In fact, spirituality is incomprehensible for Chittister without this component of social engagement. "Such a warped notion of what concentration or contemplation of the way God is working in the world now, what are you contemplating? Pink and fluffy nothingness?" According to Chittister, the aim of contemplation and the more meaningful understanding of God's role in the world is how to confront structural injustices each and every day. "You contemplate what God wills for the world. You see what is going on in the world and you fill the gap between what is going on and what is willed for all people."

Sister Joan Chittister argues that her service work is a lifestyle, not a job. And that is one of the reasons she believes the Benedictine order to which she belongs endures while others dwindle. "You have religious orders that were founded, for instance, to teach, or to nurse, or to take care of orphans, or to ransom captives during the crusades. Now when they ran out of captives, they didn't seem to know what to do next, so we haven't heard from that particular order," she said. In contrast, Chittister defined her work—her lifestyle—as an "ordinary life seeking to be lived extraordinarily well." Her lifestyle does not include working for one platform agenda or one policy goal—although she often devotes her lifestyle toward those objectives. "Every act becomes part of the great religious rhythm of compassion and creativity. That's all you exist for."

Organizational Development

Chittister is an organizational entrepreneur of engaged spirituality—demanding innovation within her own religious order and creating new social spaces in which to promote and act upon commitments. Spirituality is at the core of both Chittister's order and her contemplative organization Benetvision. However, neither of these organizations is purely spiritual. They are simultaneously dependent upon social action as the validating and sacralizing element of their missions. While Chittister may not distinguish between spirituality and social action, many denominational religious institutions shy away from either direct emphasis on spiritual experience or active engagement in social change or both.

In American history there are many examples of the cyclical nature of spiritual revival within religious institutions and the civic participation they engender.[6] The routinization of religion is a cyclical process that inevitably requires a flourish of spiritual energy and fervor to reorganize the institutional structures and social dynamics around which certain key debates turn. The dramatic increase in spirituality over the past generation and the changing structures of religious organizations suggest that substantial change is taking place within the United States. While it is unclear whether or not another spiritual awakening is afoot in the United States today,[7] the rise of spirituality as a commodity and a deeply motivating force for social engagement seems to be roiling beneath the cultural surface. Most of the people interviewed here lamented the lack of organized networks or communities that bridge spiritual motivations to make a change in the world with action. The professionals and the advocates often fought this battle on two fronts: one to reinvigorate a spiritual perspective that if spread could have a grassroots effect throughout social service networks and religious institutions; the other to provide organizational outlets for those who possessed this motivation yet did not know where to direct it or how.

There are a range of strategies and tactics for working within monolithic religious institutions or creatively carving out new spaces. Applying a holistic approach to organizational development and interpersonal relationships that boosts morale, values integrity, and provides sustainability to difficult work, for example, are techniques utilized in newly emerging "spiritual workplaces" that, if successfully employed throughout voluntary or service-oriented organizations, could have similar effects upon participation and camaraderie.[8] Creating an environment that acknowledges and supports individual spiritual practice among its members (while not impinging upon others' beliefs and practices or lack thereof) allows for the full utilization of this resource. Whether organizations schedule specific times within the workday routine for reflection or spiritual practice, as Rabbi Shapiro's Metivta does, or whether organizations allow room for spiritually based recommendations is a matter of degree and requires a sensitive understanding of each organization's constituency, leadership, and worker base.

Chittister's Benetvision and her work with the International Committee for the Peace Council position her strategically in ways that increase her power and sustain, through reciprocal relationships, her own engaged life. Many interfaith committees are active in the United States today, some spanning the nation and others working locally to promote tolerance, understanding, and mutual respect among diverse religious populations. An increased network of individuals and organizations engaged in similar work and following a spiritual motivation would provide support, a network for sharing resources, and a visible community of common objectives. The same is true within denominations or religious communities. Some temples have a very active social outreach, while others have negligible programming. This disparity can seem indomitable for community leaders who do not see the connections or networks beyond their own local neighborhoods or denominations. Yet Chittister, the DeLeons, Shapiro, and even the founders of UMMA all fought beyond institutional limitations to forge new networks and connections that strengthened their work.

Spiritual Power, Man

Jim Wallis leads a life of engaged spirituality, encouraging others to notice the social, political, and economic connections to spiritual life. Years ago during the student movements of the 1960s and 1970s, Wallis discovered that the Sermon on the Mount held a "manifesto of a new order of things" that was "more radical to me than Ho Chi Minh or Che Guevara or Karl Marx or anyone else." Today, as a nationwide lecturer and the editor of *Sojourners* magazine, Wallis has a sense of the tangible contributions spirituality has for socially active communities across an array of backgrounds.[9] He sees a new generation already being galvanized by the radical manifestos of spirituality. Quoting former gang members, Wallis made his point: "'We need spiritual power, man, spiritual power to overcome the madness!' And they're right. So that's what we bring as people of faith. So how do you, in your discipline, your practice, how do you stay connected to that hope? That's crucial. Otherwise you just—it becomes all theoretical and academic and rhetorical."

The focus on spiritual power is reminiscent, Wallis believes, of another period when itinerant preachers drew thousands to often-scandalous revivals across a conflicted and divided young America. At these events, emotional, physical, and transcendent experiences fused a vibrant spirituality with the pressing social issues of the day, sometimes indirectly. The altar call most Christians are familiar with today was in part born out of the desire to get the names and addresses of new converts across the country to add them to the roles of the abolition movement.[10] Nineteenth-century revivals were similarly tied to women's suffrage and child welfare reforms. Revival and reform went hand in hand. Although the twentieth century was marked by a spiritual turn inward, Wallis sees this reforming spirit returning to the faces in his audiences again today.

> A lot are young people . . . they're hungry for a very different type
> of faith that really engages the world. So the twenty-first century
> may look more like the nineteenth than the twentieth. I see a lot of
> nineteenth-century young evangelicals in the twenty-first century
> [for whom] it's obvious that faith connects to their concern for the
> environment, for the poor, for resolving conflicts in a peaceful way,
> for human rights, for all kinds of what seems to be just causes. And

they don't see how that's different from their Christian faith, [which] is the motivating force behind their engagement.

Civic life appears on the cusp of change. The nascent connections between spiritual fervor and social commitments for a better world are only the hint of what is yet to come, both constructive and destructive. And this change is occurring not only at the level of the activist and the institutional leaders but also, as Wallis points out, among broader-based constituencies throughout society.

Participating in Change

Spiritual experience and creative emotion merge projects that might not otherwise be connected. For example, Catholic hierarchical rigidity was reinterpreted around a circus trailer altar of a devoted nun; Muslim students financed and built a free health clinic in the inner city; gang members sought spiritual power to fight the madness of the streets. Strikingly, these individuals and groups drew powerful lines between their spiritual experiences and progressive social actions, even where there were no roadmaps, markers, or social leaders.

The shared benefits that connect personally resonant values and social commitments for action galvanize participation. This participation requires the accessibility of frames, or culturally constructed cognitive linkages, that funnel individual values and interests toward certain types of collective action or toward particular types of movements.[11] Union members gather strength and support when they successfully frame a worker strike with the beliefs of workers who feel they are being denied rightful benefits. Identity politics throughout the 1960s and 1970s spread like wildfire as cultural frames were constructed that linked social marginalization—rather than or in addition to economic and political disenfranchisement—with discrimination and inequality, prompting protests, demonstrations, and marches around issues of representation. Even though the current lack of legitimate cognitive frames connecting spirituality and social change in public and institutional discourse has by default erected cultural constraints to the perceived feasibility of spiritually informed, progressive, collective, social action, the stories told here attest to the fact that shared cognitive frames alone cannot explain the ways in which engaged spirituality takes affect.

In certain cases where passions are strong, action is self-generated by individuals or groups that have strong spiritual experiences and interpretations. It is hard to determine the effect that these self-generated actions can have without some form of interpersonal social network and institutional support. However, it seems clear from this research that the grassroots foundations are currently in place within a variety of social and religious sectors across the country. What is missing is the critical mass in progressive social leadership to tap this energy and the institutional or organizational outlets and networks for individuals already motivated by their spirituality. When Wallis called for spiritual power, the hanging question remained: Who will hear this call and toward what type of social action will this energy be mobilized?

Implementing Spirit, Action, and Identity

While it is perhaps easier to believe that spiritual trends follow social trends or that spiritual norms dictate social norms, the reality is most likely that neither spirituality nor social transformation has a unidirectional, predetermined, or predictable effect on the other. Instead, personal and social transformations are entwined in social and spiritual processes that are pregnant with possibilities. While there is a synergy between spirituality and social action, it must be en-acted through practice, through others, through institutions, through social structures, and through direct action to produce change. The application of spiritual motivations for change is strengthened to the extent that five inter-related influences are present.

First and perhaps most obviously there must be some form of individually felt or perceived spiritual connection to making the world—even if only on a very specific and local level—a better place. This social commitment must truly be social, in that it is acted upon rather than only contemplated or be-lieved. Second, sustaining an engaged spirituality requires some spiritual prac-tice that renews or connects one to the motivations and sense of purpose for their work. While the strength of networks for generating social capital is important to consider, what individuals do in their private practice involves ideational work that rekeys issues morally. Third, an organizational outlet that feels spiritually and socially authentic is essential. The current lack of partici-pation stems not from a lack of desire but from the feeling that progressive actors are unable to participate—or at least participate persuasively.[12] Fourth, engaged spirituality requires an internalization of spiritually informed action as an element of personal and social identity. The degree to which this identity becomes central to the individual increases the degree to which it will be acted upon consistently.[13] Finally, reliance by others upon the actions of engaged spirituality strengthens commitments, practices, and an internalized identity. This is true both for the individuals being served and for the other participants who depend on each other for ongoing support.[14]

Even given that these interrelated influences are present, there are other hurdles that the individuals in these pages must overcome, not the least of which are the social fault lines that hinder the implementation of engaged spirituality. One place where spirituality meets resistance is in its tenuous relationship with public policy discourse and action. However, a publicly acknowledged spiritual platform is not required by these individuals for the full functioning of engaged spirituality. Institutional outlets, yes; but explicit articulation, no. In fact, the tension that exists between public pronouncements of spiritual experience and social policy debate may inadvertently facilitate motivations, sustainability, and a sense of social efficacy. In other words, the tension between the rational public sphere and the nonrational motivations of spiritual actors may promote change much more than either a closed rational system or completely nonrational inwardly directed impulses would.[15]

During a conversation about the scriptural compulsion to better the world, Sister Chittister relayed a Gospel story in which Jesus came face to face with this inattention and inaction.[16] Jesus was visiting a healing pool in Bethesda on the outskirts of Jerusalem. The pool had various patios where the sick or disabled waited for an angel to touch the waters, at which time the first to enter the water would be cured of their ailments. For the more severely disabled, others had to assist them to ensure that they would be the first to reach the water after the angel descended. Jesus came upon one crippled man who had lain patiently on the edges of the pool for thirty-eight years. Chittister explained that when Jesus came upon this man, he asked, "'Don't you want to be healed?' . . . and the answer that comes back in scripture is 'Master, there is no one to carry me down.'" Paraphrasing the Gospel story, Chittister took on the exasperated tone that she heard in Jesus' voice when he said, "'Never mind them, I'll cure you myself. My God—thirty-eight years you come to this pool and for thirty-eight years no one has carried you down?'" For Chittister, as well as for others throughout this research, moral mandates are heightened within an apathetic and bureaucratized social context (or even within a passive religious institution) in which spiritually inspired people feel as if they are the only or at least the minority of people who will stand up and fight the battles for equality, justice, and basic social services, and do so through sometimes unconventional means.

Still, caution is palpable for the social change agents discussed here. Public policy advocates and leaders such as the Reverend Sandie Richards, Chaplain Javier Stauring, or Assistant Imam Naim Shah are acutely aware of the negative spillover in utilizing spirituality and not simply because of the public unease over recruitment or coercion. Implementing engaged spirituality is fraught with other tactical dilemmas. For instance, while some limited use of spiritual framing may be helpful for collective identity or constructing transcendent mandates for change among certain pockets of a constituency, what is the tipping point at which spirituality moves from motivating and unifying to alienating and polarizing? The difficulty in implementing this variable within organizations and in public discourse is finding the appropriate ways in which engaged spirituality may be made available for those who wish to take part while not offending those who do not.

A second and perhaps more challenging barrier for broader implementation of engaged spirituality is the danger of falling into patterns of routinization and institutionalization. Heavy-handed attempts that overbureaucratize ventures in spiritually motivated social service run the risk of dulling this sharp experiential edge or politicizing its payouts. But beyond these formidable tactical hurdles, engaged spirituality has more difficult terrain to cross with regard to the long-standing and still current collective social memories of coercive spiritual politics.

The Darker Side of Spirituality

Spirituality, like charisma, is a creative and dynamic force. It is neither stable nor predictable. As such, it can be experienced and interpreted for constructive as well as destructive ends. In fact, one definition of spirituality states that "as with religion, spirituality can take individual and institutional, traditional and nontraditional, and helpful and harmful forms."[17]

While the realities of how and why we live differently are debatable concerning political security policy, it seems fair to admit that after September 11 the United States had to face the lived experience of a violent attack upon innocent and unknowing civilians in ways that Palestinians and Israelis or Catholic and Protestant Irish have experienced regularly. As with other contemporary examples around the globe, spiritual motivation against great odds and the shifting perception of seeing an immutable world as mutable too often move beyond public debate and emerge as brutal realities with severe consequences.

Some will refuse to acknowledge that the energy, power, and transcendent will that sustained Gandhi and inspired Martin Luther King Jr. could also produce the Christian abortion clinic bomber or the Holocaust denier, not to mention the machinations of al-Qaeda or the conspiring of Aum Shinrikyo in Japan. It would be unconscionable to suggest any connections between the nonviolent and violent motivations of individuals at these two extreme applications of spiritually motivated action, but taking spirituality as a contextual, fluid, and malleable lens through which to view the world, the engaged spirituality framework suggests that one must understand spirituality as it is lived in order to understand the power with which it is used. In an artfully crafted presidential plenary address to a conference of religion scholars a year after September 11, Robert Orsi used the occasion to call attention to precisely this point. Religion cannot be reified into denominational monoliths that encapsulate or somehow define the totality of how any religion is experienced, interpreted, or put into action. Rather, religion is always specific, bound up in shared memories, in family networks, in work and school settings, and in sets of practices that vary across intimate relationships. If these influences impact the understandings of people motivated to serve others in ways deemed compassionate and prosocial—through the interpretive, situated perspective of the modern West—one must understand that alternative relationships and influences similarly funnel, shape, and inform the profound spiritual experiences of differently situated social actors.

Others will try to characterize suicide bombers as wholly political rather than religious or spiritual; however, this artificially distinguishes between two lines of thought that are inseparable and when denied will still not go away. Of course, it is important to acknowledge, as many did after the September 11 attacks, that a few Muslim terrorists do not represent all of Islam any more than a few Catholic abortion clinic bombers represent all of Catholicism. At the same time, one should not lose sight of the fact that they do represent some few Muslims and some few Catholics as these religions and spiritualities are lived. Spiritual resources can in fact be used in disruptive ways—or at least in disruptive ways with which most do not agree.[18]

In a thorough analysis of Christian militia movements in the United States, James Aho hones in on the central role of beliefs in the sometimes aggressive acts of what he refers to as Christian Patriots.[19] Much like the complex social and external influences that affect the motivations behind a group such as al-Qaeda—marginalization on the global stage, infractions on traditional everyday life by the always spreading tentacles of Western capitalism, and values including shifting gender roles—Aho notes that similar senses of social and economic disenfranchisement has been attributed to the rise and spread of radical, white, Christian subcultures.[20] Just as the social shifts repeatedly referred to throughout this book had beneficial consequences for engaged spirituality—pluralism, experimentation, fluidity—these shifts were also perceived negatively by other portions of the population. Rather than attributing the relative disenfranchisement of Christian patriots to economics or a nostalgic pining for a lost past, Aho argues that a rise in subversive Christian movements occurred simultaneously with upswings in their economic standing. No longer the sulking losers in the social and economic gambles of life, Aho turned to taking the spiritual lenses through which they viewed the world as real rather than merely compensatory.[21] Christian Patriots felt deeply that there was a cosmic exigency to the battle that they had to wage. The social world, life, and salvation hung in the balance, and the time for action was now.

While the type of engaged spirituality considered here has elements of exigency to serve those in need, the degree to which it is interpreted is by no means as extreme and does not include the conspiratorial ideas held by the Idaho dissidents Aho described. Some participants in this study did feel that the final judgment could come at any time and this constant awareness shaped in part their spiritual experiences and motivations. Yet there is a difference in the extent to which this pushes serving those in need to waging battle on the perpetrators of moral pollution. While I describe this difference in degree, it is a difference that I can only feel rather than one to which I could ascribe a definitive line of demarcation between just enough and too much. The way cultural tolerances are constructed and by whom would be a productive extension of how and when engaged spirituality is deemed socially valuable and when it is charged with exceeding social limits.

Toward this end, there is another difference between the level of engaged spirituality discussed here and the level that sparks violence or destructive tendencies. Mark Juergensmeyer in *Terror in the Mind of God* similarly agrees that while social and economic shifts affect the context in which social actors, almost always men, act out aggressively based on religious or spiritual beliefs, it is these beliefs that correspond with the perception that the world has gone completely awry that instigate action more than the economic or status losses to social competitors such as women or gay men.[22] A spiritual understanding, to stay within the scope of this study, is deeply entwined with the social context and types of networks that these men live within. What Juergensmeyer adds to the discussion is that these men are attempting to extend coercive power, to do harm, and, in doing so, to gain status or empowerment for themselves and their cosmic cause.[23]

Firm Faith, Shaky Ground

Juergensmeyer's thesis provides more of the definitive line between a spirituality that is deployed for coercive violence and one that is employed for serving others' needs. Yet the argument could be made that spiritually motivated people working for social change coercively utilize a type of social power by influencing others in need with their beliefs, the supposition being that the goods or services could be revoked at any time if the recipient was not responsive to the religious worldview of their providers. The two corresponding yet antithetical ideas about spirituality raised in the first chapter—that spirituality is individually private yet social service is unquestioningly what spiritual people do—are prevalent and hinge on precisely these types of concerns. In fact, even though a clear majority of Americans support the idea of government funding of faith-based organizations, more than half agreed that they harbored reservations based solely upon the underlying proselytizing potential of faith-based service providers.[24]

While many of the people interviewed here had few aspirations of converting those they worked with, some did, even if their motivations were never explicitly stated through the services provided but only offered as examples of the right way to live life. Yet even in these cases where religion by example is implicit rather than explicit, a type of religious coercion is intrinsically presumed by those who may benefit from religious social services or is inherent in the power differential between those who disperse goods, services, or even community organizing advice to those who seek it. There is a long history of religious institutions proselytizing and offering solace in return for participation in or at the very least tolerance of religious rituals or prayer. When backed by military and/or political power or material and economic access to resources, proselytizing self-interests can clearly have a coercive effect.

For most of this project's participants, a discursive social politic is used—if anything at all—rather than a physically, religiously, or economically coercive power. Influencing someone to pray as part of receiving a warm bed in a shelter seems innocuous when compared to the violence of other spiritually inspired actors. Similarly, attaining due process for discrimination against services based upon religion or sexual orientation is incomparably better than the cold comfort of reparations to families who have been on the receiving end of religious violence. However, it is still imperative that individuals are cautious when sorting out the profits and perils of spiritually directed social services. Most participants would agree; at the same time, most would unabashedly attest, as some examples above illustrate, that an individual spiritual connection or transformation would benefit those who are in need either economically, emotionally, or physically, and that they would assist those who asked in any way they could with their spiritual journey. To this they would quickly add that they, of course, would never revoke a helping hand for those who did not seek a spiritual transformation.

While it remains true that spirituality may still be understood as a shorthanded concept that can be exchanged in a variety of public and popular ways, this cultural currency obviously has limits that are deeply rooted and stretch far beyond the derisive parodies that characterize spirituality as some innocuous, new age, or narcissistic commodity. Countervailing images of a positive spirituality may also be found, and the engaged spiritualists I spoke with were trying, by example, to promote these images even if it meant in only local and interpersonal ways. Still, these are the questions that civic and religious leadership in the trenches must grapple with if engaged spirituality is to be harnessed for progressive social change.

Common Ground

Further complicating an implementation of spirituality are the various faith traditions or denominations that institutionally imprint the interpretations of experiences and their intended consequences. Attempts to pull together shared threads of interpretation, while difficult, might seem more reasonable between groups that are more closely akin. Interfaith groups are emerging that utilize the common ground between their understandings and experiences of spirituality in ways that lay the groundwork for a spiritual homology or a commonly read, symbolic expression of basic codes regarding the role of spirituality. Moreover, the widely embraced eclecticism within certain institutional religions and the reemergence of past practices or texts or the sharing of insights from other traditions also establishes connection across denominations and faiths.

While discussing some of the most impacting moments of his spiritual life, Rabbi Rami Shapiro explained the impetus that led to his programs in contemplative practice for religious leaders of Jewish, Islamic, Catholic, and Christian traditions. Interfaith contemplation is a practice that he honed at Snowmass, Father Thomas Keating's contemplative and mystical gathering of various traditions in a Benedictine monastery in Colorado. The only rule was that no one could say, "Judaism says X. Catholicism says Y." Instead, participants had to say, "My experience as a practicing Jew is—blank." Such personalization in dialogue calls attention to the lived and experiential aspects of spirituality instead of the codified and alienating authority that speaking for and from an entire religious population and history carries with it. In doing so, it also establishes connection between the contemplative experience that transcends discipline or tradition. Sister Chittister echoes this sentiment from her years of interfaith dialogue and practice around the world when she says, "Though every denomination is a finger pointing at the moon, every denomination leads us to the greater religious reality. That means then that all of the mystical, contemplative dimensions will eventually arrive at the notion that God transcends culture and denomination."

The stories told here might indicate a similar integrative purpose. Rather than just a spiritual homology that produces a shared understanding of sacred communion or religious transcendence, these stories reveal a moral homology that acknowledges and encourages wide variation in the motivations and actions for social change. Components of a moral homology might include ecumenism, pluralism, and nonessentialism, even if just pragmatically understood for the express purposes of undertaking a particular cause, such as reducing gang violence or demonstrating against unfair labor practices.

A moral homology is the legacy of various influences, not the least of which are the identity politics of the 1960s and 1970s that, while demanding specific tangible rewards, were largely motivated by changing social definitions and perceptions about equality and representation as nonmaterial ends for social protest. Through the 1990s and arguably today, segments of the population are motivated by what has been termed postmaterial values—moral or ethical causes of others rather than specific tangible benefits for themselves or their family.[25] This shift toward ideas already draws together practitioners of engaged spirituality who may agree on little more than compassionate service to the poor. The impetus of the United Religions Initiative (URI), the Reverend Charles Gibbs told me, emerged from very simple questions of values changing the world. He explained, "Basically [we asked], 'What does the world you'd like look like? The world you'd like to see your children grow up in and people grow old in?'" These very basic questions generated dialog across faith traditions that, in Gibbs assessment, had "never talked to each other before." Gibbs hopes that through sharing different traditions and stories these conversations will "make this [ideal] world more visible, more real, locally and globally." Moral homologies construct a middle ground apart from doctrine or the voting booth where affective motivations assemble those who otherwise might not join forces.

Moral homologies that neither push one doctrinal truth over another might also be amenable to secular organizing and service work in ways that do not have to deny the resource of spirituality for some participants while not overtly promoting it among others.[26] And this last point is crucial in determining the way that spiritual impulses to change society will be structured over the following years. Spiritual impulses are rising across the country, throughout populations, and independent of political or doctrinal boundaries. Young gay Jews are putting on tefillin, baby boomer Catholics are returning to the spiritual mysteries of the Latin liturgy, and American-born Muslims are ardently fasting during Ramadan. More broadly than these activities convey, Americans are requiring a greater spiritual connection and personal feeling that often spill beyond their religious communities.

In an extensive study on young Christian believers, Colleen Carroll Campbell suggests that as the quest for experience bubbles up among today's youth, they repudiate the moral relativism and all-you-need-is-love religion of their parents. They shun their Madison Avenue upbringing and instead turn to the morals defined by the Madonna of the Bible rather than the Madonna of the

Billboard charts.[27] It is difficult to refute the deeply personal accounts of young adults who seek moral absolutism and demand personal responsibilities. From the understanding of engaged spirituality expressed here, however, one must look further than spiritual spark to the networks that embrace these young Christian adults and the outlets that are available for them and through which they funnel their feelings. Campbell tracks this well, noting that these young adults seek out traditional venues in which strict faith is coupled with strict lifestyles and commitments. They come to challenge what they see as a rudderless culture and hope to live lives that will inspire others to make similar sacrifices of faith.

These stories of a new and growing subculture are interesting because on some level they are counterintuitive and fly in the face of the common liberal secular youth scenario. But there are fewer organizational outlets or shared stories on the left that might funnel or redirect spiritual experiences and motivations of the younger generation toward social action and change. In interviews with community leaders who had cut their teeth in the civil rights movement of the 1960s and the social justice politics of the 1970s and 1980s, I asked them if they foresaw another wave of social justice grassroots organizing that would join the political left with spiritual social politics. While some were more optimistic than others, few saw the commanding leadership required to convene on a mass scale around any particular issue or group of issues. This is unfortunate for the legacy of the left. The influence of religion, God, or experiential spirituality on public social life is an element that individuals often try to downplay publicly. Religion and spirituality are by no means solely private affairs that have little direct impact on the social life of communities every single day. Denying their existence will not remove spirituality from the public sphere but will only mask its contribution. Acknowledging hybrids—the creative connections between spirituality and social change, for example— need not advocate for them but provides a better understanding of these junctures and how they function in the world.

Dichotomies Blurred, Dichotomies Retained

Take any of the cases on any side of the political, social, or religious spectrum and I believe that the typologies of engaged spirituality are descriptive of the process through which subjective experience is funneled through practice, through interpretive schema, and through application toward social action.

Part of the similarities around which certain spiritually inclined individuals and organizations cohere is possible in part because of the particular innerworldly asceticism that is endemic to practitioners of engaged spirituality—in both positive and negative degrees. Inner-worldly asceticism is not always, or at least not only, an attempt for personal salvation in the way the term is often used. Instead the current inner-worldly asceticism described here runs parallel to the broader shifts in American religion that demand personally relevant experiences in everyday life. As spirituality became increasingly personalized and tailored along resonant experiences, biographical peculiarities, networks, and social structures, it simultaneously and necessarily became (or reappeared as) diffuse, manifesting itself in all aspects of life rather than simply attributable to religious referents such as synagogues, prayer schedules, or mantras.

Daniele Hervieu-Leger suggests that part of the reason that religion has survived today is precisely because of the individual trends toward assembling and reassembling its constituent parts in ways that keep belief alive even while the traditional institutional structures may be crumbling, radically reorganizing, or suffering under lost confidences.[28] The participants of this study say much the same, indicating the ways in which deeply personal and varied forms of practice and experience inform and enrich the valued traditions and communities that remain, in their perspectives, necessary elements in a full spiritual life. However, even within their traditions and communities, the pluralism that ultimately diversifies experience is a reflection of increasingly diverse social networks and society as a whole.

Current cultural eclecticism influences the recombining process that Hervieu-Leger suggests, often accentuating the blurred boundaries of social binaries. Spirituality, instead of being one or the other, is a fluid essence in individual lives, slipping between the cracks of otherwise artificially and externally defined divisions. This fluidity is spirituality's strength, although it also makes it difficult to plot one singular direction or predict any specific causal determinacy.

Admittedly, a shift toward an analysis of engaged spirituality may preclude predictions about the patterns in the rational selection of categorical preferences in religious participation or the ups and downs of a spiritual market equilibrium; however, while past interpretations of religion as irrational started a pendulum swinging that beneficially brought religion back into the mainstream fold for legitimate sociological analysis, the contributions that rectified the stigma of irrationality sometimes miss the subjective experiential vigor that motivates, sustains, and transforms perceptions and sparks innovative action. It might be said that the experiential baby was thrown out with the irrational bathwater.[29] Yet while these transcendent experiences may be outlying exceptions in the overall aggregate pattern of religious organization and civic participation, they are by no means anomalies that simply register noise in the data. They are the interpretive stuff of religion and, if one takes the experiential reports in the interview data as any indication, an essential contributing factor in individual motivations for social action and change.

Throughout this book I have tried to add a richer, more descriptive account of cultural meaning-making and creative action that stays close to the lived experiences retold here. In doing so I did not intend to dismiss rational perspectives. Instead, I see spirituality as one of various perceived ontological systems, alongside rationality, that is beneficial to some social actors and allows for new modalities of constructing meaning, creative action, and potentially inspiring individuals to imagine possibilities that exceed realistic and rational expectations. The different ways spiritual individuals see the world—one relating to a transcendent calculus and the other to the rational practicalities of their environment—do not construct a new dichotomy. This is not an either/or distinction in these individuals' minds but rather complementary and intermingling perspectives that are mutually informing. Individuals effortlessly pick up ideas and inspiration from one while simultaneously holding the other.[30]

What is clear from these stories is that spirituality is in everything: the mundane, the intimate, the iconic, and the unexpected. Engaged spirituality ensures acknowledgment of this connection as not only internalized or salvation-bound but also externalized in the works of this world. It is neither exclusively private nor public, sacred nor profane. Spirituality in the minds and actions of these interviewees is in struggle and in service; it is the energy of change. While these dichotomies may be blurred, they are far from collapsed. To different degrees, what drives engaged spirituality for better or worse ends is the palpable tension between what is and what could or, in most cases, what should be. It is this *should* that courageously motivates, tirelessly sustains, and unimaginably inspires. Including spiritual experience and practice as real social factors contributing to social change requires conceptual and theoretical discussion. However, it also requires methodological sensitivity to the meanings that actors carry around in their heads, including their most intimate, profound, and even nonrational realities.

Notes

Introduction

1. Elizabeth M. Rose, John S. Westefeld, and Timothy N. Ansley, "Spiritual Issues in Counseling: Clients' Beliefs and Preferences," *Journal of Counseling* 48 (2001): 61–71; Daniel A. Helminiak, "Treating Spiritual Issues in Secular Psychotherapy," *Counseling and Values* 45 (2001): 163–189.
2. Patricia Sermabeikian, "Our Clients, Ourselves: The Spiritual Perspective and Social Work Practice," *Social Work* 39 (1994): 181.
3. Edward R. Canda, "Spirituality, Religious Diversity, Social Work Practice," *Social Casework* 69 (1988): 238–247; idem, *Spirituality in Social Work: New Directions* (New York: Haworth Pastoral Press, 1998); Toni Cascio, "Incorporating Spirituality into Social Work Practice: A Review of What to Do," *Families in Society* 79 (1998): 523–531; Michael J. Sheridan, "Defining Spiritually Sensitive Social Work Practice: An Essay Review of Spiritual Diversity in Social Work Practice: The Heart of Helping," *Social Work* 46 (2001): 87–92.
4. Gary Charles Davidson, *Spirituality and the Therapeutic Relationship: A Comparative Study of Occupational Therapist Perspectives' in Canada and the United States* (Milligan College, TN: Milligan College Press, 2000); Marc Galanter, "Spiritual Recovery Movements and Contemporary Medical Care," *Psychiatry* 60 (1997): 211–223; Jared D. Kass et al., "Health Outcomes and a New Index of Spiritual Experience," *Journal for the Scientific Study of Religion* 30 (1991): 203–211.
5. Thompson, "Train."
6. Neal, "Work as Service"; Opiela, "Sullivan."
7. Stephen R. Covey, *The 7 Habits of Highly Effective People* (New York: Free Press, 1990); M. Scott Peck, *The Road Less Traveled* (New York: Simon and Schuster, 1978).
8. Burack, "Workplace."
9. Stephen L. Carter, *The Culture of Disbelief: How American Law and Politics Trivialize Religious Devotion* (New York: Basic Books, 1993), 275–276.
10. Laurel Kearns, "Saving the Creation: Christian Environmentalism in the United States," *Sociology of Religion* 57 (1996): 55–70.

Chapter One: Bridging the Gap

1. Wade Clark Roof, *Spiritual Marketplace: Baby Boomers and the Remaking of American Religion* (Princeton, NJ: Princeton University Press, 1999); Richard P. Cimino and Don Lattin, *Shopping for Faith: American Religion in the New Millennium* (New York: Jossey-Bass, 1998).

2. Robert N. Bellah et al., *Habits of the Heart: Individualism and Commitment in American Life* (Berkeley: University of California Press, 1985), 221.

3. Jose Casanova, *Public Religions in the Modern World* (Chicago: University of Chicago Press, 1994), 35–39, provides an excellent synopsis of different branches of secularization theses, one of which is the privatization model in which religion recedes to the family or the bounded space of the church, temple, or synagogue, but has little influence on larger arenas of public life.

4. Penny Long Marler and C. Kirk Hadaway, "'Being Religious' or 'Being Spiritual' in America: A Zero-Sum Proposition?" *Journal for the Scientific Study of Religion* 41 (2002): 289–300; Zinnbauer et al., "Religion and Spirituality: Unfuzzying the Fuzzy," *Journal for the Scientific Study of Religion* 36 (1997): 549–564.

5. Marler and Hadaway, "Being Religious."

6. For example, in one Gallup poll that Marler and Hadaway analyze, respondents were asked only if they were religious but not spiritual (54 percent), spiritual but not religious (30 percent), or neither (9 percent), missing the population who are both religious and spiritual.

7. Zinnbauer et al., "Religion and Spirituality," in an attempt to rectify this, found that 74 percent of Americans reported being both religious and spiritual, whereas 19 percent reported being spiritual but not religious, 4 percent reported being religious but not spiritual, and 3 percent reported neither. See also Zinnbauer et al., "The Emerging Meanings of Religiousness and Spirituality: Problems and Prospects," *Journal of Personality* 67 (1999): 909.

8. Robert Wuthnow, *All in Sync: How Music and Art Are Revitalizing American Religion* (Berkeley: University of California Press, 2003), 15.

9. Robert K. C. Forman, "What Does Mysticism Have to Teach Us about Consciousness?" *Journal of Consciousness Studies* 5 (1998): 185–201; Daniel A. Helminiak, *Spiritual Development: An Interdisciplinary Study* (Chicago: Loyola University Press, 1987); Helminiak, *The Human Core of Spirituality: Mind as Psyche and Spirit* (Albany: State University of New York Press, 1996); Pargament et al., "The Many Meanings of Religiousness"; Zinnbauer et al., "Religion and Spirituality."

10. Kenneth I. Pargament, *The Psychology of Religion and Coping: Theory, Research, Practice* (New York: Guilford Press, 1997).

11. Zinnbauer et al., "Religion and Spirituality," 909.

12. Robert Wuthnow, *Christianity in the Twenty-First Century: Reflections on the Challenges Ahead* (New York: Oxford University Press, 1993), 168–198.

13. Robert A. Emmons, *The Psychology of Ultimate Concerns: Motivation and Spirituality in Personality* (New York: Guilford Press, 1999).

14. Jack. M. Barbalet, *Emotion, Social Theory, and Social Structure: A Macrosociological Approach* (New York: Cambridge University Press, 1998), xvi.

15. Mabel Berezin, *Making the Fascist Self: The Political Culture of Inter-war Italy* (Ithaca, NY: Cornell University Press, 1997) argues that political community building can be constructed through public dramatic performances. Berezin, "Emotions and Political Identity: Mobilizing Affection for the Polity," in *Politics: Emotions and Social Movements* (Chicago: University of Chicago Press, 2001), and Berezin, "Secure States: Towards a Political Sociology of Emotion," in *Emotions and Sociology* (London: Basil Blackwell Publishing, 2002), further addresses the emotional components of political adherence, although not with specific reference to spirituality.

16. I use the term "natural affiliation" in a conscious way that reflects my assumptions about spiritually profound moments, human nature, and the social construction of our lived environments. This is based upon sociological and cultural assumptions rather than personal or theological ones. Peter Berger, *The Sacred Canopy: A Sociological Theory of Religion* (Garden City, NY: Doubleday, 1967); Christian Smith,

Moral, Believing Animals: Human Personhood and Culture (New York: Oxford University Press, 2003).

17. In *America's Crisis of Values: Reality and Perception* (Princeton, NJ: Princeton University Press, 2004), Wayne E. Baker points out that American values such as egalitarianism and individualism are often projected onto an idealized past as a way to critique the contemporary and debatable "crisis" in contemporary American values.

18. In *Protestant Catholic Jew* (Garden City, NJ: Anchor Books, 1955), Will Herberg's classic assessment of mid-twentieth-century American life attested to the religious adherence of this generation and the salience that it had for a nation still experiencing growing pains from the waves of immigration at the turn of the nineteenth to twentieth century.

19. Tom Brokaw, *The Greatest Generation* (New York: Random House, 1998).

20. Robert Orsi's *Thank You St. Jude: Women's Devotion to the Patron Saint of Hopeless Causes* (New Haven: Yale University Press, 1996) is a wonderful account of immigrant women during this period of transition that sensitively unpacks the spiritual lives of devotees of Saint Jude.

21. At different times and influenced by different social constraints or encouragements, this spiritual expression has flourished or been decried as regressive irrationality—and often times both. Jon Butler, *Awash in a Sea of Faith: Christianizing the American People* (Cambridge, MA: Harvard University Press, 1990); Roger Finke and Rodney Stark, *The Churching of America, 1776–1990: Winners and Losers in Our Religious Economy* (New Brunswick, NJ: Rutgers University Press, 1992); Rodney Stark and Roger Finke, *Acts of Faith: Explaining the Human Side of Religion* (Berkeley: University of California Press, 2000); Ann Taves, *Fits, Trances, and Visions: Experiencing Religion and Explaining Religion from Wesley to James* (Princeton, NJ: Princeton University Press, 1999). Peter Berger, *The Desecularization of the World: Resurgent Religion and World Politics* (Grand Rapids, MI: William B. Eerdmans Publishing Co., 1999) assesses the contemporary cycle of religious resurgence.

22. My approach here is cultural and I view spirituality as a particular element of culture that is similarly constituted. By culture, I mean the dual meaningful processes that are both "medium and outcome." Anthony Giddens, *The Constitution of Society* (Cambridge, MA: Polity Press, 1984), 25. The active cultural influence is from Ann Swidler, "Culture in Action: Symbols and Strategies," *American Sociological Review* (1986).

23. Prema Kurien, "Becoming American by Becoming Hindu," in *Gatherings in Diaspora: Religious Communities and the New Immigrants* (Philadelphia: Temple University Press, 1998), suggests that Indian immigrant communities in Los Angeles construct congregational models in order to fulfill the needs of religious and cultural preservation in their new home, pass down traditions to a new generation, and foster networks that were based on religious community rather than solely on business and status groupings.

24. Finke and Stark, *Churching*; Roof, *Spiritual Marketplace*; Stark and Finke, *Acts of Faith*.

25. Wade Clark Roof, *A Generation of Seekers* (San Francisco: HarperSanFrancisco, 1993).

26. Christopher Lasch, *The Culture of Narcissism: American Life in the Age of Diminishing Expectations* (New York: Norton, 1979).

27. *Publishers Weekly* (December 6) notes that in 2004 religion/self-help was the most successful subcategory of books on religion. Micki McGee, *Self Help, Inc.* (New York: Oxford University Press, 2005).

28. Two *New York Times* reviews mirror this divide with Nichiko Kakutani on June 20, 2004, excoriating the "self-serving" mess of reflections by the "avatar of his [baby

boomer] generation," while, three days later, Larry McMurtry lobbed softer comparisons to reflective literary figures admitting that this was the "richest American presidential autobiography."

29. Jana Riess, *What Would Buffy Do: The Vampire Slayer as Spiritual Guide* (New York: Jossey-Bass, 2004). This question riffs off the common "Jesus question" but substitutes the film and television character Buffy the Vampire Slayer, who has attained a cultlike following among some viewers.

30. Colleen McDannell, *Material Christianity: Religion and Popular Culture in America* (New Haven, CT: Yale University Press, 1995).

31. Robert Bellah, *The Broken Covenant: American Civil Religion in a Time of Trial* (New York: Seabury Press, 1975); Richard W. Fox, *Jesus in America: Personal Savior, Cultural Hero, National Obsession* (San Francisco: HarperSanFrancisco, 2004). David Morgan, *Protestants and Pictures: Religion, Visual Culture, and the Age of American Mass Production* (New York: Oxford University Press, 1999) provides a wonderful visual history.

32. In *St. Jude*, Orsi illustrates the profound and complex spiritual relationships women throughout the early to middle parts of the twentieth century often secretly maintained with Saint Jude. Jude became a confidant and receptacle for their concerns and desires that they were unable to legitimately express elsewhere. Harvey Cox, *Fire from Heaven: The Rise of Pentecostal Spirituality and the Reshaping of Religion in the Twenty-first Century* (Reading, MA: Addison-Wesley, 1995), notes the sensation caused by Pentecostals throughout the twentieth century, specifically noting the provocative racial and gender relations at the Azusa Street revival.

33. Bruno Latour, *We Have Never Been Modern* (Cambridge, MA: Harvard University Press, 1993).

34. Ibid., 34. Latour notes that while God is removed, He is not missing in the lives of moderns. Latour states, "His position became literally ideal . . . . He would no longer interfere in any way with the development of the moderns, but He remained effective and helpful within the spirit of humans alone."

35. Benjamin Barber, *Jihad vs. McWorld: How Globalism and Tribalism Are Reshaping the World* (New York: Ballantine Books, 1996) provides empirical examples in which these combinations reemerge and were reacted to and labeled.

36. Distinctions can still be made between religion and spirituality without completely separating the two. The notion that religion increasingly denotes an institutional, substantive, and formal phenomenon, whereas spirituality embodies a separate, individual, functional, and expressive phenomenon is aptly descriptive but does not suggest that these two are mutually exclusive. Brian J. Zinnbauer, Kenneth I. Pargament, and Allie B. Scott, "The Emerging Meanings of Religiousness and Spirituality: Problems and Prospects," *Journal of Personality* 67 (1999): 889–919.

37. Aldon Morris, *The Origins of the Civil Rights Movement: Black Communities Organizing for Change* (New York: Free Press, 1984), 77–99.

38. Christian Smith, *Disruptive Religion: The Force of Faith in Social Movements* (New York: Routledge, 1996), compiled a list of organizational and cultural resources that religious institutions bring to the table in aiding social movements or facilitating social change. These include organizational resources, shared identity, social and geographic positioning, privileged legitimacy, institutional self-interest, and, perhaps most significantly for this conversation, transcendent motivations.

39. Quoted in Morris, *Civil Rights*, 97.

40. Myra Marx Ferree, "The Political Context of Rationality: Rational Choice Theory and Resource Mobilization," in *Frontiers in Social Movement Theory* (New Haven, CT: Yale University Press, 1992), 32, suggests that acknowledging that "all people do behave impulsively and irrationally at times *enriches* the account of rationality

that can be given by including the individual and organizational problems of anticipating, managing, and reacting to such tendencies." Ferree is making the case for anticipating destructive, although emotionally satisfying, episodes of impulsive behavior such as reactions to taunting or beatings. However, I want to suggest that this impulsive experience may also be used constructively in ways that link positive experiences to social change.

41. Fredrick C. Harris, *Something Within: Religion in African-American Political Activism* (New York: Oxford University Press, 1999); Douglas A. Marshall, "Behavior, Belonging, and Belief: A Theory of Ritual Practice," *Sociological Theory* 20 (2002): 360–380; Mark R. Warren, *Dry Bones Rattling: Community Building to Revitalize American Democracy* (Princeton, NJ: Princeton University Press, 2001); Richard L. Wood, *Faith in Action: Religion, Race, and Democratic Organizing in America* (Chicago: University of Chicago Press, 2002).

42. Robert D. Putnam, *Bowling Alone: The Collapse and Revival of American Community* (New York: Simon and Schuster, 2000).

43. Frances F. Piven and Richard Cloward, *Poor People's Movements* (New York: Pantheon, 1977), 12. See also Doug McAdam, *Political Process and the Development of Black Insurgency, 1930–1970* (Chicago: University of Chicago Press, 1999).

44. Social movement literature of the past half century, much like recent analyses of religion, has battled to rationalize collective actions previously explained away by or derided as irrational. For social movement discussions of this critique, see Ferree, *Political Context*; James M. Jasper, "The Emotions of Protest: Affective and Reactive Emotions in and around Social Movements," *Sociological Forum* 13 (1998): 397–424; Laura Pulido, "The Sacredness of 'Mother Earth': Spirituality, Activism and Social Justice," *Annals of the Association of American Geographers* 88 (1998): 719–723. For religion, see Robert Orsi, "Is the Study of Lived Religion Irrelevant to the World We Live In? *Journal for the Scientific Study of Religion* 42 (2003):169–174. And see Smith, *Disruptive Religion*, for a combination of the two.

45. Anthony Giddens, *Modernity and Self-Identity: Self and Society in the Late Modern Age* (Stanford, CA: Stanford University Press, 1991), 3, states, "all knowledge [now] takes the form of hypotheses: claims which may very well be true, but which are in principle always open to revision and may have at some point to be abandoned. Similarly, Michel de Certeau, *The Practice of Everyday Life* (Berkeley: University of California Press, 1984), 179, suggests, "There are now too many things to believe and not enough credibility to go around." It is this lack of credibility that some find fulfilled through action.

Chapter Two: Biography, Behavior, and Belief

1. E. J. Dionne and John J. Diiulio Jr., *What's God Got to Do with the American Experiment* (Washington, D.C.: Brookings Institution Press, 2000); In *Who Will Provide? The Changing Role of Religion in American Social Welfare* (Boulder, CO: Westview Press, 2000), Mary Jo Bane, Brent Coffin, and Ronald Thiemann provide a thorough debate concerning the assumptions and potential for religion and social welfare.

2. Darren Sherkat and John Wilson, "Preferences, Constraints, and Choices in Religious Markets: An Examination of Religious Switching and Apostasy," *Social Forces* 73 (1995): 993–1026.

3. C. Daniel Batson, Patricia Schoenrade, and W. Larry Ventis, *Religion and the Individual* (New York: Oxford University Press, 1993).

4. In *Christianity in the Twenty-First Century: Reflections on the Challenges Ahead* (New York: Oxford University Press, 1993), Robert Wuthnow suggests that for much of the twentieth century religious switching was associated with status mobility within

society. However, as denominations become less status bound in the twenty-first century, this no longer appears to affect motivations or rates for switching. Darren E. Sherkat, "Leaving the Faith: Testing Theories of Religious Switching Using Survival Models," *Social Science Research* 20 (1991): 171–187. In "Social Predictors of Retention in and Switching from the Religious Faith of Family of Origin: Another Look Using Religious Tradition Self-Identification," *Review of Religious Research* 45 (2003): 200, Christian Smith and David Sikkink point out that "*different social factors influence different groups of people in diverse religious traditions in dissimilar ways.*" See also William Kooistra and Kenneth I. Pargament, "Religious Doubting in Parochial School Adolescents," *Journal of Psychology and Theology* 27 (1999): 33–42; Dean Hoge, Benton Johnson, and Donald Luiden, *Vanishing Boundaries: The Religion of Mainline Protestant Baby Boomers* (Louisville, KY: Westminster/John Knox Press, 1994); Darren E. Sherkat and Christopher G. Ellison, "Recent Developments and Current Controversies in the Sociology of Religion," *Annual Review of Sociology* 25 (1991): 363–394.

5. Reginald Bibby and Merlin B. Brinkerhoff, "The Circulation of the Saints: A Study of People Who Join Conservative Churches," *Journal for the Scientific Study of Religion* 12 (1973): 273–283; Reginald Bibby, "On Boundaries, Gates, and Circulating Saints: A Longitudinal Look at Loyalty and Loss" *Review of Religious Research* 41 (1999): 149–164; Darren E. Sherkat, "Tracking the Restructuring of American Religion: Religious Affiliation and Patterns of Mobility, 1973–1998," *Social Forces* 79 (2001): 1459–1492.

6. Stark and Finke, *Acts of Faith*, 115. See also Mark Musick and John Wilson "Religious Switching for Marriage Reasons," *Sociology of Religion* 56 (1995): 257–270; C. Kirk Hadaway and Penny Long Marler, "All in the Family," *Review of Religious Research* 35 (1993): 97–116.

7. Marjorie Gunnoe and Kristin Moore, "Predictors of Religiosity among Youth Aged 17–22: A Longitudinal Study of the National Survey of Children," *Journal for the Scientific Study of Religion* 41 (2002): 613–622.

8. Doug McAdam, *Freedom Summer* (New York: Oxford University Press, 1988).

9. Ibid. McAdam calls this lack of social constraints, such as family responsibilities or economic difficulties, "biographical availability."

10. Robert Wuthnow, *Learning to Care: Elementary Kindness in an Age of Indifference* (New York: Oxford University Press, 1995) makes the point that "caring" in adulthood beyond just the family unit is sometimes a direct result of having parents that participated in formal volunteer work. But for others it may include parents who were simply involved in civic participation not related to formal volunteerism such as PTAs, youth groups, or church councils.

11. Stan L. Albrecht and Tim B. Heaton, "Secularization, Higher Education, and Religiosity," *Review of Religious Research* 26 (1984): 43–56, noted that in the broader American population this decrease in religious participation among college students was prevalent, but this does not imply a decrease in subjective adherence to faith.

12. Emile Durkheim, *The Elementary Forms of the Religious Life* (New York: Free Press, 1915), 218.

13. The combining of worldviews is most often referred to as "framing." William A. Gamson, "The Social Psychology of Collective Action," in *Frontiers in Social Movement Theory* (New Haven, CT: Yale University Press, 1992); David A. Snow and Robert D. Benford, "Master Frames and Cycles of Protest," in *Frontiers in Social Movement Theory* (New Haven, CT: Yale University Press, 1992); Snow et al., "Frame Alignment Processes, Micromobilization, and Movement Participation," *American Sociological Review* 45 (1986): 787–801.

14. James M. Jasper, *The Art of Moral Protest* (Chicago: University of Chicago Press, 1997).
15. Most conversion stories within the Christian traditions retain a similar narrative form. These function as "paradigms by which people interpret their own lives." Lewis Rambo, *Understanding Religious Conversion* (New Haven, CT: Yale University Press, 1993), 158. In *Religious Autobiographies* (Belmont: Wadsworth, 1995), Gary L. Comstock provides interfaith examples of this narrative form.
16. Rambo, *Conversion*, 44–55, discusses this as "crisis."
17. The term "cognitive liberation" is from McAdam, *Political Process*. William A. Gamson, Bruce Fireman, and Steven Rytina, *Encounters with Unjust Authority* (Homewood, IL: Dorsey, 1982) calls this similar process in which the world is redefined as an "injustice frame."
18. In *The Emergence of Liberation Theology: Radical Religion and Social Movement Theory* (Chicago: University of Chicago Press, 1991), Christian Smith provides one notable exception in studying liberation theology. Here he discusses this subjective turn as "insurgent consciousness."
19. Rambo, *Conversion*.
20. Donald J. Gelpi, "Religious Conversion: A New Way of Being," in *The Human Experience of Conversion: Persons and Structures in Transformation* (Villanova, PA: Villanova University Press, 1987); idem, "Conversion: Beyond the Impasses of Individualism," in *Beyond Individualism*, ed. Donald J. Gelpi, 1–30 (South Bend, IN: University of Notre Dame Press, 1989).
21. Pargament, *Religion and Coping*, developed this distinction between religious conversion and spiritual conversion. Religious conversion for Pargament is a radical shift that connects the self to the sacred, whereas spiritual conversion connects the self to a spiritual force.
22. Sharon Erickson Nepstad, *Convictions of the Soul: Religion, Culture, and Agency in the Central American Solidarity Movement* (New York: Oxford University Press, 2004); Sharon Erickson Nepstad and Christian Smith, "The Social Structure of Moral Outrage in Recruitment to the U.S. Central America Peace Movement," in *Passionate Politics: Emotions and Social Movements*, ed. Jeff Goodwin, James M. Jasper, and Francesca Polletta, 158–174s (Chicago: University of Chicago Press, 2001).
23. Jasper, *Moral Protest*, 106, 323.
24. Nepstad, *Convictions*; Nepstad and Smith, "Moral Outrage."
25. Nepstad and Smith, "Moral Outrage."

Chapter Three: Acting on Faith

1. I use "cultural" and "structural" here in a dual sense. Giddens, *Constitution*; William H. Sewell Jr., "A Theory of Structure, Duality, Agency, and Transformation," *American Journal of Sociology* 98 (1992): 1–29.
2. In *Mind, Self, and Society* (Chicago: University of Chicago Press, 1962), George Herbert Mead pointed out that learning social roles such as mother, father, store clerk, or customer were essential building blocks in developing a sense of identity and shared social expectations. However, as socialization continues children must further develop a sense of the values and a diffuse sense of right and wrong that is interpreted as agreed upon by the entire society. Parents, and in this case spiritually motivated service, impact the socialization of shared values.
3. Manuel M. Suarez-Orozco, *Crossings: Mexican Immigration in Interdisciplinary Perspectives* (Cambridge, MA: Harvard University Press, 1998) provides an excellent overview of both historical and contemporary patterns of transnational labor between the United States and Mexico.

4. Donald E. Miller, *Pentecostalism and Social Transformation* (Berkeley: University of California Press, forthcoming).

5. Templo Calvario is an umbrella ministry for various other services. Within Obras de Amor is Family Impact, through which the church "adopts" nearly two hundred families and provides them with food, household products, and even appliances from the distribution center, administers job training, and offers economic and personal counseling. Families are able to stay in the program for up to one year. Templo Calvario also offers an extensive educational ministry that includes formal ministry training through Bible College as well as more general religious education classes aimed primarily at children and some adults, job training, life skills, and English as a second language.

6. In some instances the responsibilities and expectations of certain positions are clearly codified in job descriptions or federal guidelines for social service provision. In others they are dictated by central moral tenets, spiritually informed revelations, or the watchful eye of others.

7. Social networks have various benefits such as sharing information or religious practices or generating constituencies around an issue. The strength of cross-cutting ties, for example, in collective action was essential in the emergence of certain identity politics of the 1960s and 1970s such as the Gay Liberation Front. John D'Emilio, *Sexual Politics, Sexual Communities: The Making of a Homosexual Minority in the United States, 1940–1970* (Chicago: University of Chicago Press, 1983). Along similar lines, in organizational sociology the notion of the strength of "weak ties" has been noted. Mark Granovetter, "The Strength of Weak Ties," *American Journal of Sociology* 78 (1973): 1360–1380. Finally, Robert Putnam, *Bowling Alone: The Collapse and Revival of American Community* (New York: Simon and Schuster, 2000), argues that organized diversity through cross-cutting ties can produce norms of generalized reciprocity.

8. Early, or "primary," socialization from parents produces a view of the world that appears natural and permanent. Peter L. Berger and Thomas Luckmann *The Social Construction of Reality: A Treatise in the Sociology of Knowledge* (New York: Doubleday, 1966).

9. This reciprocal relationship between society and the individual is a common theme throughout classic and contemporary interactionist perspectives on social identity and social action. Just as society creates our sense of self, so does our sense of self then act back upon the nature and composition of that society. Herbert Blumer, *Symbolic Interactionism: Perspectives and Method* (Englewood Cliffs, NJ: Prentice-Hall, 1969); Sheldon Stryker, *Symbolic Interactionism: A Social Structural Version* (Menlo Park, CA: Benjamin Cummings, 1980).

10. Bellah et al., *Habits*.

11. J. Craig Jenkins and Charles Perrow, "Insurgency of the Powerless: Farm Worker Movements, 1946–1972," *American Sociological Review* 42 (1977): 249–268.

12. Daniel Sack, *Whitebread Protestants: Food and Religion in American Culture* (New York: St. Martin's Press, 2000).

13. Smith, *Disruptive Religion*.

14. In *Frame Analysis* (Cambridge, MA: Harvard University Press, 1974), Erving Goffman first coined this term when discussing the way in which ideas are linked to others so as to have broader resonance across groups in society.

15. See, for example, Katherine S. Newman, *Falling from Grace: The Experience of Downward Mobility in the American Middle Class* (New York: Free Press, 1988).

16. Putnam, *Bowling Alone*.

17. Stryker, *Symbolic Interactionism*, claims that this reciprocal relationship between self and social structure saves his theory from a "strict determinism." Engaged spirituality

suggests that spirituality is one of the intervening experiences that further limits this determinism.

18. Ibid. Stryker calls this identity "salience" and argues that commitment increases around those tasks or relationships that have greater affect on one's sense of personal identity or sense of self.

Chapter Four: Keeping the Faith in Action

1. While "spiritual practice" is difficult to define, many definitions cohere around similar ideas. Robert Wuthnow, *After Heaven: Spirituality in America since the 1950s* (Berkeley: University of California Press, 1998), 170, defined spiritual practice as "a cluster of intentional activities concerned with relating to the sacred." For the purposes of this chapter, I will use "spiritual practice" to mean as any act, ritual, or attempt at communication or communion with a socially constructed yet subjectively meaningful ideal, entity, or higher power.

2. I am using the terms "function," "form," and "feelings" broadly here. For a long time within the analysis of religion, there was a split between functional and substantive definitions of religion. Functional accounts sought the basis of religion in the benefits that it provided society or the individual, be those solace or comfort or social control. Substantive approaches analyzed what religion was, over what religion did. Substantive perspectives looked for ways to delineate religion apart from other social processes by describing a set of beliefs and practices or a community of believers. Substantive approaches sought definitions. My phrasing of function, form, and feeling draws somewhat on each but with the intention of synthesizing their contributions.

3. Studies of conversion often stress the importance of social networks that reaffirm and sustain the religious identity of a new convert. While I am not suggesting that the connection between spirituality and social commitments is as strong as the case that is often made regarding conversion to new religious movements, the analytic point of reinforcement through social networks remains valid. Rambo, *Conversion*, 102–123. Similarly, see John Lofland and Rodney Stark, "Becoming a World-Saver: A Theory of Conversion to a Deviant Perspective," *American Sociological Review* 30 (1965): 862–875.

4. Charles Taylor, *Varieties of Religion Today: William James Revisited* (Cambridge, MA: Harvard University Press, 2002), 116, suggests that James's individualist approach to feeling and meaning, while still significant, misses the point that the spiritual intuitions humans experience may be incorporated into formal practices in ways that are significant beyond the moment of conversion or initial inspiration.

5. Interlocking social processes, practices, and networks that reaffirm and sustain everyday realities rely upon plausibility structures of friends, family, or peers. While much of this focuses on others for reinforcement, repeated individual practices can also solidify these commitments or identities. Berger and Luckmann, *Social Construction*, 72–79, 147–163.

6. Kenneth J. Gergen, *The Saturated Self: Dilemmas of Identity in Contemporary Life* (New York: Basic Books, 2000), for example, argues that the complexity of modern global life has irrevocably altered, in pathological directions, the ways in which we interact and subsequently think about ourselves and construct our identities.

7. David A. Roozen, William McKinney, and Jackson W. Carroll, *Varieties of Religious Presence: Mission in Public Life* (New York: Pilgrim Press, 1984).

8. Elmer H. Burack, "Spirituality in the Workplace," *Journal of Organizational Change Management* 12 (1999): 280–291; William David Thompson, "Can You Train People to Be Spiritual?" *Training and Development* 54 (2000): 18–19.

9. This notion of pride versus humility in spiritual practice bridges religious traditions, including Buddhism, Hinduism, Judaism, Islam, and Christianity, and spans time as well. John Wesley is an emblematic figure in Western Christianity who instructed followers to "methodically" temper their enthusiasms through appropriate, pious, and humble expressions. Ann Taves, *Fits, Trances, and Visions: Experiencing Religion and Explaining Religion from Wesley to James* (Princeton, NJ: Princeton University Press, 1999).

10. Robert Wuthnow, *After Heaven*, 180, refers to these "authentic" prayers focused on the joys of worship itself rather than status or marital happiness as the intrinsic rewards of spirituality.

11. Rick Warren, *The Purpose-Driven Life: What on Earth Am I Here For?* (Grand Rapids, MI: Zondervan, 2002) refers to five "purposes": worship, fellowship, discipleship, ministry, and evangelism.

12. Gustavo Gutierrez, *A Theology of Liberation* (Maryknoll, NY: Orbis Books, 1973).

13. Canales later goes on to develop this point in another section of his interview where he cites Henri Nouwen, *Gracias! A Latin American Journal* (San Francisco: Harper and Row, 1983). Canales interprets Nouwen, saying, "When we're helping the poor, we're saying 'thank you' to God."

14. Sarah Brooks, "Catholic Activism in the 1990's: New Strategies for the Neoliberal Age," in *Latin American Religion in Motion: Tracking Innovation, Unexpected Change, and Complexity*, ed. Christian Smith and Joshua Prokopy (New York: Routledge, 1998).

Chapter Five: Experience and Emotion

1. Richard W. Flory, "Toward a Theory of Generation X Religion." In *GenX Religions* (New York: Routledge, 2000); Charles Taylor, *Sources of the Self: The Making of the Modern Identity* (Cambridge, MA: Harvard University Press, 1989).

2. Arlie Hochschild, "Emotion Work, Feeling Rules and Social Structure," *American Journal of Sociology* 85 (1979): 551–575.

3. Much of Hochschild's premise was based on the managed feelings that flight attendants produce as part of their employment. This early analysis was prescient, and today the service industry from Starbucks to Disneyland has well-established guidelines of how to treat customers and what emotions to enact when working. In these bounded arenas of the service industry, this model works quite well, even though, as Hochschild acknowledges, people are actively engaged in negotiating these rules even in these settings. Barbalet, *Emotion*, 23, however argues that in non-institutional settings, these feeling rules are too general to fit individual experiences.

4. Raymond Williams, *Marxism and Literature* (New York: Oxford University Press, 1977).

5. Ann Swidler, *Talk of Love: How Culture Matters* (Chicago: University of Chicago Press, 2001), 71, suggests that individuals learn how to be certain types of people even through the cultural resources that they accumulate through experience. This includes desires, feelings, and moods as much as ways of acting upon these. See also Pierre Bourdieu, *The Logic of Practice* (Stanford, CA: Stanford University Press, 1990).

6. Sheldon Stryker, cited in Verta Taylor, "Emotions and Identity in Women's Self-Help Movements," in *Self, Identity, and Social Movements* (Minneapolis: University of Minnesota Press, 2001), 271–299.

7. Jeff Goodwin, "The Libidinal Constitution of a High-Risk Social Movement: Affectual Ties and Solidarity in the Huk Rebellion, 1946–1954," *American Sociological Review* 62 (1997): 53–69; Jasper, *Moral Protest*; Verta Taylor and Nancy

Whittier, "Analytic Approaches to Social Movement Culture: The U.S. Women's Movement," in *Social Movements and Culture*, ed. Hank Johnston and Bert Klandermans, 163–187 (Minneapolis: University of Minnesota Press, 1995).

8. Robert Wuthnow, *Producing the Sacred: An Essay on Public Religion* (Urbana: University of Illinois, 1994), 24–29.

9. Wuthnow, *All in Sync*.

10. I intend the term imagined here to be understood analytically rather than normatively. In other words, imagined does not mean that these feelings are illusory but rather that these imagined interactions are the perceived realities on which people base their interactions. Charles Horton Cooley, *Human Nature and the Social Order* (New York: Scribners, 1902), 179–185.

11. Smith, *Disruptive Religion*, 9–13.

12. Nancy Ammerman, *Congregation and Community* (New Brunswick, NJ: Rutgers University Press, 1997); R. Stephen Warner and Judith G. Wittner, *Gatherings in Diaspora: Religious Communities and the New Immigrants* (Philadelphia: Temple University Press, 1998).

13. I use the term "creative" since much of Durkheim's second-hand data on Australian Aborigines has been challenged and discounted. Still, the theoretical ideas are inventive and provide some of Durkheim's greatest insights on culture—even if they reveal more about the theorist than the empirical case. For a more in-depth critique of Durkheim's thesis, see W. S. F. Pickering, *Durkheim on Religion: A Selection of Readings with Bibliographies* (London: Routledge, 1975); W. S. F. Pickering, *Durkheim's Sociology of Religion* (London: Routledge, 1985).

14. See Chris Shilling, "The Two Traditions in the Sociology of Emotions," in *Emotions and Sociology* (London: Basil Blackwell Publishing, 2002), 18–20.

15. Helen Rose Ebaugh, *Women of the Vanishing Cloister: Organizational Decline in Catholic Religious Orders in the United States* (New Brunswick, NJ: Rutgers University Press, 1993); John Fialka, *Sisters: Catholic Nuns and the Making of America* (New York: St. Martin's Press, 2003).

16. Daniel Dayan and Elihu Katz, *Media Events: The Live Broadcasting of History* (Cambridge, MA: Harvard University Press, 1992) updated this Durkheimian notion of worshiping a projected sense of our society in a contemporary setting. They argue that mass media provide integrative functions in which the world can come together and experience moments of great emotion collectively.

17. Donald E. Miller, *Reinventing American Protestantism: Christianity in the New Millennium* (Berkeley: University of California Press, 1997), 136–156, makes the point that Christian megachurches decentralize their organizational hierarchy in ways that empower laity within smaller groups, producing a much more intimate and even family-style sense of community. Robert Wuthnow, "How Religious Groups Promote Forgiving: A National Study," *Journal for the Scientific Study of Religion* 36 (2000): 124–137, similarly suggests that small groups generate emotional capital through sharing experiences and supplying support and reassurance. See also Gregory C. Stanczak, "The Traditional as Alternative: The GenX Appeal of the International Churches of Christ," in *GenX Religions*, ed. Richard W. Flory and Donald E. Miller, 113–138 (New York: Routledge, 2000).

18. Having high expectations of individual members counters the "free rider" problem that more liberal religious organizations or social movements face. Free riders are individuals who benefit from membership but might participate only in name. Laurence R. Iannaccone, "Sacrifice and Stigma: Reducing Free-Riding in Cults, Communes, and Other Collectives," *Journal of Political Economy* 29 (1992): 297–310; Laurence R. Iannaccone, "Why Strict Churches Are Strong," *American Journal of Sociology* 99 (1994): 1180–1204; Stark and Finke, *Churching*.

19. Here I am broadly extending a term from Benedict Anderson, *Imagined Communities* (London: Verso, 1983). Anderson's analysis of imagined communities focuses on the emergence and persistence of nationality through issues of capitalism, media, language, and even religion. I am unhooking this sense of "we-ness" from the national base that Anderson employs and instead applying it to other subjectively defined communities.

20. Daniele Hervieu-Leger, *Religion as a Chain of Memory* (New Brunswick, NJ: Rutgers University Press, 2000).

21. Taylor, *Self*, 84, makes the point that we all imagine ourselves as part of greater collectivities through the economy, through the public sphere, through styles of dress, or through nationality. Spiritual practice and religious identity function in similar ways. I would argue that, spiritually, in Taylor's terms, people "grasp [themselves] and great numbers of others as existing and acting simultaneously."

22. Chittister's opinions on a wide range of issues can be found in her ongoing column "From Where I Stand" in the *National Catholic Reporter Newsweekly*.

23. See Bruce Fireman and William A. Gamson, "Utilitarian Logic in the Resource Mobilization Perspective. In *The Dynamics of Social Movements* (Cambridge, MA: Winthrop Publishers, 1979).

24. Ferree, *Political Context*.

25. Jasper, *Moral Protest*, 156. See also Nepstad and Smith, "Moral Outrage"; Jeff Goodwin and Steven Pfaff, "Emotion Work in High-Risk Social Movements: Managing Fear in the U.S. and East German Civil Rights Movements," in *Passionate Politics: Emotions and Social Movements*, ed Jeff Goodwin, James M. Jasper, Francesca Polletta, 282–302 (Chicago: University of Chicago Press, 2001).

26. Michael Young, "A Revolution of the Soul: Transformative Experiences and Immediate Abolition," in *Passionate Politics: Emotions and Social Movements*, 99–114. Michael Young, "Confessional Protest: The Religious Birth of U.S. National Social Movements," *American Sociological Review* 67 (2002): 660–688, discusses the rise of abolition politics among American evangelical Protestants when slavery was redefined affectively and theologically as a sin, and personal redemption was tied to acting against this institution.

27. While this occurs on the individual level, a similar process of emotional rearticulation is possible more broadly. Anne Kane, "Finding Emotion in Social Movement Processes: Irish Land Movement Metaphors and Narratives," in *Passionate Politics: Emotions and Social Movements* (Chicago: University of Chicago Press, 2001), 256–257, notes on a societal level the way that thousands of Irish, during the Land War, reconceptualized emotions of humiliation as emotions of "solidarity, enthusiasm, pride, love, and empowerment."

28. Peter Berger, *The Heretical Imperative: Contemporary Possibilities of Religious Affirmation* (Garden City, NY: Anchor Press, 1979), 31, tracked this trend as ongoing evidence of the secularization of religion in modern Western societies. He notes that as the external authorities and traditions decline, individual practitioners are left to their own reflective experiences for determining religious truth, asking "Just what has been *my own experience of X?*"

29. While these reformulations of "God" can produce a closer sense of connection to the sacred in otherwise or previously marginalized populations, it can additionally produce a new sense of solidarity and feeling of community among those making these claims. Race, class, gender, sexual identity, and nationality—and the inclusive bonds of contemporary pluralism that unites these under a new political perspective—can heighten collective identity and, therefore, action. See, for example, Jeff Goodwin, James M. Jasper, and Francesca Polletta, *Passionate Politics: Emotions and Social Movements* (Chicago: University of Chicago Press, 2001); Francesca Polletta

and James M. Jasper, "Collective Identity in Social Movements," *Annual Review of Sociology* 27 (2001): 283–305.

30. Joan Chittister, *Heart of Flesh: A Feminist Spirituality for Women and Men* (Grand Rapids, MI: Eerdmans, 1998).
31. Barbalet, *Emotion*, xvi.
32. Morgan, *Protestants and Pictures*.
33. Shah had a reserved reflection and subtle sense of humor when discussing this cosmic battle for living a spiritually conscious life. In retelling this one portion of our interview I want to make clear that his public and interfaith theology is not one of fire and brimstone, and although I had had several conversations with Shah before this interview and clearly noticed the devoutly religious convictions that structured his life, I had never heard a single mention of angels or Satan. Even in this interview, this issue came up nearly in passing as he filled me in on the six articles of Islamic faith. I make this distinction in an attempt to contextualize these comments. Shah, much like Sara Desh Arpana or even Kennedy, was not bragging about the wonderful, otherworldly, mystical spectacle of faith that is available to him. Angels were simply part of the ingrained traditions that he followed as part of daily life and spiritual practice. In other words, they were not an end in themselves, but one part of the complex amalgam of beliefs and experiences that made his life and his work in the community meaningful and on track.
34. Barbalet, *Emotion*, xvi.
35. For a more complete discussion of Durkheim's extension of emotional energy, see Shilling, "Two Traditions," 18–20; Pickering, *Durkheim's Sociology*.
36. In "Our Clients, Ourselves: The Spiritual Perspective and Social Work Practice," *Social Work* 39 (1994): 181, Patricia Sermabeikian points out that in social work practice a transcendent power provides clients with "courage, strength, and willpower" when coping with change or conflict and is significant in producing personal transformation. For other applications of this sense of efficacy, see Fredrick C. Harris, *Something Within: Religion in African-American Political Activism* (New York: Oxford University Press, 1999); Marshall, "Behavior, Belonging, and Belief"; Morris, *Origins*.
37. Hans Joas, *The Genesis of Values*, trans. Gregory Moore (Chicago: University of Chicago Press, 2001), 49, in reconsidering William James's argument that religious experiences can produce new ways to view and act in the world, adds that security is part of this bundle of feelings that contribute to a change in perspectives and that is unique to the nonrational claims of religion.
38. Swidler, *Culture*. In *Talk of Love*, Swidler suggests that when our lives feel disrupted or insecure (unsettled, in her terms) we creatively and consciously must draw upon our cultural tools to make meaning and to meaningfully act in new situations. However, if this feeling of ontological security allows the stability from which to explore new possibilities and creative strategies for acting, then there may exist an alternative for when and why we reevaluate these tools and innovatively take them up.
39. Griffith, *God's Daughters*, 79. See also Orsi, *St. Jude*.
40. In the past, Victor Turner used the phrase "the center out there" to describe this sense of the sacred or the transcendent. This captures the flavor of what these stories relate, although, increasingly, this center out there is no longer only out there.
41. William James, *The Varieties of Religious Experience* (Cambridge, MA: Harvard University Press, 1985), 47.
42. W. Bradford Wilcox, *Soft Patriarchs, New Men: How Christianity Shapes Fathers and Husbands* (Chicago: University of Chicago Press 2004), for example, notes the intersection of conservative Protestantism, the family, and gender as the locus of reshaping emotion and interaction.

43. Jasper, "Emotions," discusses the difference between affective and reactive emotions. Theodore D. Kemper, *A Social Interactional Theory of Emotions* (New York: John Wiley, 1978), 47, previously defined the social role of emotions that were "relatively short-term."

44. Jasper, *Moral Protest*, 106.

45. In addition to Jasper, "Emotions," see also Goodwin, Jasper, and Polletta, *Passionate Politics*, 11.

46. Ann Taves, *Fits*, 47, develops the idea of constructed experience by suggesting that meaningful emotional encounters emerge through the interplay of personal experiences and social practices.

Chapter Six: Degrees of Social Integration

1. David DeLeon, *Leaders from the 1960s: A Biographical Sourcebook of American Activism* (Westport, CT: Greenwood Press, 1994).

2. It should be noted that beyond Marxists and religious activists, core members of activist movements—those who maintain the unwavering commitment to "ideological purity"—often sustain the kernel of these agendas even when significant membership drops. This has been particularly well documented in the feminist movement. Jane J. Mansbridge, *Why We Lost the ERA* (Chicago: University of Chicago Press, 1986); Verta Taylor, "Social Movement Continuity: The Women's Movement in Abeyance," *American Sociological Review* 54 (1989): 761–775; Nancy Whittier, *Feminist Generations: The Persistence of Radical Women's Movements* (Philadelphia: Temple University Press, 1995).

3. Process theology is often attributed to the metaphysical philosophy of Albert North Whitehead. The theology has strains in both Judaism and Christianity and was popularized by Harold Kushner, *When Bad Things Happen to Good People* (New York: Schocken Books, 1981).

4. This is an ongoing sociological puzzle that can be traced through the work of the canonical sociological theorists to the present. See Charles Camic and Neil Gross "Contemporary Developments in Sociological Theory: Current Projects and Conditions of Possibility," *Annual Review of Sociology* 24 (1998): 453–476.

5. Part of what sparks public debates around religious social service is the assumption that religious organizations pitch particularly palatable images of themselves in order to acquire federal funding for social services. Arguably, one might assume that there are aspects of this direct, rational calculation within religious social service, but by no means did this appear to be the case with the individuals interviewed here. However, they were savvy readers of what Carter called the culture of disbelief and tailored their presentations of self accordingly. Stephen L. Carter, *The Culture of Disbelief: How American Law and Politics Trivialize Religious Devotion* (New York: Basic Books, 1993).

6. Durkheim, *Elementary Forms*; Robert N. Bellah, *Beyond Belief: Essays on Religion in a Post-Traditional World* (New York: Harper and Row, 1970); Robert N. Bellah, *The Broken Covenant: American Civil Religion in a Time of Trial* (New York: Seabury Press, 1975). Durkheim and Bellah argued across centuries that culture and religion, as one particularly illustrative example of culture, were reflections of the society. Years later, Clifford Geertz, *The Interpretation of Cultures: Selected Essays* (New York: Basic Books, 1973) carried this collective notion by suggesting that culture was a pool from which members of a particular society had equal and common use.

7. Swidler, *Talk of Love*, 79, makes a similar distinction between Geertz's collective view of culture as "ethos" and this active view of culture.

8. Berger and Luckmann, *Social Construction*, 34–46.
9. Swidler, "Culture" and *Talk of Love*.
10. Swidler, *Talk of Love*, 30, suggests that, in general, most people use culture in a more piecemeal way, "tinker[ing] at the edges or to defend their existing patterns of life."
11. The concept of rekeying stretches back to Goffman, *Frame Analysis*.
12. Integrating communities involves significant amounts of commitment and work both by religious leadership and laity alike. Penny Edgell Becker, *Congregations in Conflict: Cultural Models of Local Religious Life* (Cambridge, MA: Cambridge University Press, 1999); Michael O. Emerson and Christian Smith, *Divided by Faith: Evangelical Religion and the Problem of Race in America* (New York: Oxford University Press, 2000). Karen J. Chai, "Competing for the Second Generation: English Language Ministry at a Korean Protestant Church," in *Gatherings in Diaspora: Religious Communities and the New Immigrants* (Philadelphia: Temple University Press, 1998) has noted that the language barrier can similarly divide immigrant congregations along generational lines.
13. Darren Sherkat, "Counterculture or Continuity? Competing Influences on Baby Boomers' Religious Orientations and Participation," *Social Forces* 76 (1998): 1087–1114; Laurence Iannaccone, "Religious Resources and Church Growth," *Social Forces* 74 (1995) 705–731.
14. The term "strategies for action" is from Swidler, "Culture." The term implies the way that cultural tools are organized for use beyond the "unit act" for which they were originally intended.
15. See Paul Dimaggio, "Culture and Cognition," *Annual Review of Sociology* 23 (1997): 263–287; Swidler, *Talk of Love*.
16. Mary Jo Neitz, *Charisma and Community: A Study of Religious Commitment within the Charismatic Renewal* (New Brunswick, NJ: Transaction, 1987); Wayne Proudfoot, *Religious Experience* (Berkeley: University of California Press, 1985).
17. Jasper, *Moral Protest*, makes a similar point about our unacknowledged social codes.
18. R. Marie Griffith, *God's Daughters*, 80–107, points out that women have been working in social service agencies throughout American history with great yet unacclaimed success in part because of the institutional barriers for leadership within Protestant church structures.
19. Marie Cornwall, "The Determinants of Religious Behavior: A Theoretical Model and Empirical Test," *Social Forces* 68 (1989): 572–592, in explicating a cultural broadening theory, suggests that plausibility structures are crucial in maintaining religious worldviews in a highly pluralistic society. See also Berger and Luckmann, *Social Construction*.
20. Sewell, "Theory of Structure," 13, for example, argues that social structures must be sustained by both the informal meanings of individual and collective actors that put resources to use, as well as the materials that allow individuals and groups to enact these meanings. This process sustains certain elements of structure while it simultaneously changes others. Strains of rational choice approaches have appropriated this cultural theory for the religious market. Darren Sherkat, "Embedding Religious Choices: Integrating Preferences and Social Constraints into Rational Choice Theories of Religious Behavior," in *Rational Choice Theory and Religion: Summary and Assessment*, ed. Lawrence A. Young, 65–86 (New York: Routledge, 1997); Sherkat, "Counterculture"; Darren E. Sherkat and John Wilson, "Preferences, Constraints, and Choices in Religious Markets: An Examination of Religious Switching and Apostasy," *Social Forces* 73 (1995): 993–1026; Christopher G. Ellison and Darren E. Sherkat, "The Semi-Involuntary Institution Revisited: Regional Variations in Church Participation among Black Americans," *Social Forces* 73 (1995): 1415–1437.

21. Hans Joas, *The Creativity of Action* (Chicago: University of Chicago Press, 1996), following John Dewey, suggests that goals and means are chosen reciprocally. Dewey states, "Only when we recognize that certain means are available to us do we discover the goals which had not occurred to us before" (154). In this sense, our perceptions or cognitions are part of the phase of action rather than a detached and preconceived formula for carrying out action. Perceptions and cognitions can direct action across various situations, but the situations as they present themselves and one's abilities to act given these situations are a crucial element in understanding one's own perceptions.

22. Sewell, "Theory of Structure," 19, goes on to argue that humans merely have the capacity for agency that is dependent upon, and varies greatly depending on, an actor's social milieu. Agency in this sense is understood as "the actor's capacity to reinterpret and mobilize an array of resources in terms of cultural schemas other than those that initially constituted the array."

23. Swidler, "Culture," argues that cultural tools are useful beyond the "unit act" of singular behavior and instead comprise "strategies for action" that are employed across situations. More recently Swidler, *Talk of Love*, 71–72, suggests that culture "equips persons for action both by shaping their internal capacities and by helping them bring those capacities to bear in particular situations." Sewell, "Theory of Structure," 18, terms this the "transposability of schemas," which translates as an inherent form of agency among members of society that extends the learned rules of action or behavior to unfamiliar cases.

24. Max Weber conjured a wonderful railroad metaphor about the role of ideas in social history. He indicated that the particular sociohistorical context laid the track along which history unfolds; interests fuel the engine of the locomotive, while ideas (and here was particularly concerned with religion) acted as switchmen along the tracks, occasionally redirecting the train while not replacing the engine or derailing it from its tracks. This metaphor, although critiqued for seeing religion and culture as bound to ideas rather than action (see Swidler, "Culture"), still works to some extent today. However, as evidenced throughout these examples, the engaged spirituality model suggested here looks at actions and ideas and structural contexts as recursively constituted.

25. The recursive or dialectic model of social change on which this cultural theory is based can be traced back to its roots in Hegelian dialectics that views these changes as evolutionary and socially natural. I would not dispute that assumption. However, for some people, these spiritual interpretations are the explicit reason for generating or at least accelerating that change.

26. This assertion is a sociological riff on W. I. Thomas, *The Unadjusted Girl* (Boston: Little Brown and Co., 1923). Thomas's maxim was that "if men describe situations as real, they are real in their consequences."

27. Mary Jo Nietz and James V. Spickard, "Steps Toward a Sociology of Religious Experience," *Sociological Analysis* 51 (1990): 17. In secular experience this has been discussed as "flow." Mihaly Csikszentmihaly, *Creativity: Flow and the Psychology of Discovery and Invention* (New York: Harper Collins, 1996); idem, *Finding Flow: The Psychology of Engagement with Everyday Life* (New York: Basic Books, 1997).

28. Hans Joas, *Genesis*, 49, argues that religious experience in William James's sense "expands the possibilities for acting" precisely through these emotional contributions that emerge out of circumstance and make the world seem somewhat different.

29. Orsi, "Lived Religion," 173. See also Orsi, *St. Jude*, for an ethnographic account of this.

30. Jasper, *Moral Protest*, 64–68, calls this creativity in changing the taken-for-granted patterns of our world "artfulness."

31. Resource mobilization analyses, beginning in the 1970s, legitimized social movements as organized rather than disorganized and planned, unlike the spontaneous or emotional outbursts of irrational mobs. While important for countering the deviant view of movements, this line of argument led to what Ferree, "Political Context," 32, has called a "one-dimensional rationality" that only considers a universal, social actor as self-interested and profit driven, devoid of particular biography, race, class, or gender. The inclusion of identity construction and collective meaning making have produced a significant amount of recent scholarship to complement these more organizationally based approaches. See, for example, Enrique Larana, Hank Johnston, and Joe Gusfield, *New Social Movements: From Ideology to Identity* (Philadelphia: Temple University Press, 1994).

32. I do not want to imply that spirituality determines social action any more than I would suggest agency or structures do. Instead I agree with Jasper, who suggests we get around this idea of what social factor is most important in social action and change. He states, "To say or imply that one dimension of protest comes first, in the sense that it is most important, is to foreclose certain paths of research, to predetermine what results one can find." Jasper, *Moral Protest*, 67.

33. Even in the most solitary, individual practices in which someone does not follow a scripted prayer or style of praying—for example, the popular "conversations" with God—I acknowledge that their practices are still bound and relatively determined by rules of syntax, formality, or lack thereof, etc., that shapes prayer and meaning (see Berger and Luckmann *Social Construction;* De Certeau, *Practice*). Glossalalia, or the Pentecostal speaking in tongues, subverts these grammatical and even linguistic rules but clearly supplants them with an alternatively accepted and bounded set of appropriate rules. Cox, *Fire;* Taves, *Fits*, 47–75.

34. I am indebted to Don Miller for suggesting that I pursue this extension of Weber's typology.

35. Weber's cultural generalizations have been taken to task by social historians, sociologists, and cultural theorists who suggest that such gross categorizations reveal more about the power relations between cultures at the time than about any inherent characteristics of either side. See, for example, Edward Said, *Orientalism* (New York: Vintage Books, 1979) and Ian Buruma and Avishai Margalit *Occidentalism: The West in the Eyes of Its Enemies* (New York: Penguin, 2004).

36. Swidler, "Culture." On this level of individual action, the definition of culture moves beyond the shared meanings of a group or society and focuses as well on "informal cultural practices such as language, gossip, stories, and rituals of daily life" (273). These informal cultural practices reveal the "social processes of sharing modes of behavior and outlook" (273), which is central to this level of analysis but often overlooked in the research on religious groups. See also Giddens, *Constitution;* Sewell, "Theory of Structure."

37. Giddens, *Modernity*, coined the term "reskilling" to capture the process of taking one strategy and applying it to other situations that were otherwise unrelated. This process has been similarly defined as "culture work." Swidler, "Culture."

Chapter Seven: Conclusion

1. I am very grateful to Ernestine Avila for the introduction to Sister Dorothy and for her insightful collaboration on this interview.

2. Carol Coburn and Martha Smith, *Spirited Lives: How Nuns Shaped Catholic Culture and American Life, 1836–1920* (Chapel Hill: University of North Carolina Press, 1999).

3. Jon Miller, *Missionary Zeal and Institutional Control: Organizational Contradictions in the Basel Mission on the Gold Coast, 1828–1917* (Grand Rapids, MI: William B.

Eerdmans Publishing Co., 2003), makes this point about the spiritual passions, or "fervor," that sustained missionaries throughout nineteenth century.

4. Ibid. Miller draws these lines of connection between spiritual fervor and institutional negotiations. See also Line Predelli and Jon Miller, "Piety and Patriarchy: Contested Gender Regimes in Nineteenth-Century Colonial Missions," in *Gendered Missions: Women and Men in Missionary Discourse and Practice*, ed. Mary Taylor Huber and Nancy C. Lutkehaus, 67–112 (Ann Arbor: University of Michigan Press, 1999).

5. Clearly today's popular culture is rife with interpretive grids for understanding love and drug use, and literature has provided guidelines for both for centuries. Yet these are not doctrinal foundations in the same sense as religion is for spiritual transcendence.

6. Finke and Stark, *Churching*, analyze these cycles utilizing an economic model of competition for practitioners. Jon Butler, *Awash*, views these cycles as examples of American religious syncretism.

7. Miller, *Reinventing*.

8. Judi Neal, "Work as Service to the Divine: Giving our Gifts Selflessly and with Joy," *American Behavioral Scientist* 43 (2000): 1316–1333; Nancy Opiela, "Mary K. Sullivan: Soul Stories" *Journal of Financial Planning* 13 (2000): 156–158.

9. Jim Wallis, *God's Politics: Why the Right Gets It Wrong and the Left Doesn't Get It* (San Francisco: HarperSanFrancisco, 2005).

10. Young, "Confessional"; Taves, *Fits*.

11. Gamson, "Social Psychology"; Snow et al., "Frame Alignment."

12. The alternative is the isolated practitioner who finds energy and social motivation in spiritual practice yet does not know how to utilize this resource to its full potential. Yasser Aman of the UMMA Free Clinic epitomizes the increasing need for social and institutional outlets for this rise in spiritual energy. Desperately seeking an outlet for the spiritual mandates to serve the needy in his community, Aman finally found an avenue through UMMA. In a telling reversal of who the clinic serves, Aman says, "I was here from when the clinic opened up and it instantly sparked something as a realization of 'Well, I'm kind of on the receiving end of what they were wanting to do for Muslims.'"

13. Stryker, *Symbolic Interactionism*, refers to this as identity salience, which determines which type of "self" is invoked in different situations. This depends upon context but also upon the way one sees oneself in different contexts.

14. Ibid. See also Rick Fantasia, *Cultures of Solidarity: Consciousness, Action, and Contemporary American Workers* (Berkeley: University of California Press, 1988); Alberto Melucci, *Nomads of the Present: Social Movements and Individual Needs in Contemporary Society* (Philadelphia: Temple University Press, 1989); Alberto Melucci, "The Process of Collective Identity," in *Social Movements and Culture*, ed. Hank Johnson and Bert Klandermans (Minneapolis: University of Minnesota Press, 1995); Verta Taylor and Nancy Whittier, "Analytic Approaches to Social Movement Culture: The U.S. Women's Movement," in *Social Movements and Culture*, ed. Hank Johnson and Bert Klandermans (Minneapolis: University of Minnesota Press, 1992).

15. Ann Swidler, foreword, *The Sociology of Religion*, by Max Weber (Boston: Beacon Press, 1993), ix–xvii.

16. John 5:1–9.

17. Zinnbauer et al., "Emergent Meanings," 909.

18. Religion as a disruptive force, as noted throughout this book, is often valued. See Morris, *Origins*, for the use of religion and spirituality in the civil rights movement. See Gutierrez, *Theology*, for Liberation Theology in Central America. See Erik

Erikson, *Gandhi's Truth on the Origins of Militant Nonviolence* (New York: Norton, 1969) for Gandhian nonviolence. All are examples of socially acceptable religious disruption.

19. James Aho, *Politics of Righteousness: Idaho Christian Patriotism* (Seattle: University of Washington Press, 1990).
20. Gore Vidal, *Perpetual War for Perpetual Peace: How We Got to Be So Hated* (New York: Thunder's Mouth Press, 2002).
21. Kristin Luker, *Abortion and the Politics of Motherhood* (Berkeley: University of California Press 1985) is another powerful example through which religious lenses are taken as real and substantial elements of mobilization for social and political stances.
22. Mark Juergensmeyer, *Terror in the Mind of God: The Global Rise of Religious Violence* (Berkeley: University of California Press, 2001), 201.
23. Juergensmeyer, *Terror*, 188, notes that this empowerment is mostly symbolic since the efforts will surely never overcome the David and Goliath battle that they have set before them. Rather the empowerment was being part of the battle at all.
24. A report published by the Pew Forum on Religion and Public Life Research Center for the People and the Press suggests that "three-quarters [of Americans] think that churches and other houses of worship contribute significantly to solving America's social problems." "Faith-Based Funding Backed, Church State Doubts Abound."
25. Ronald Inglehart, *The Silent Revolution: Changing Values and Political Styles among Western Publics* (Princeton, NJ: Princeton University Press, 1977).
26. Courtney Bender, *Heaven's Kitchen: Living Religion at God's Love We Deliver* (Chicago: University of Chicago Press, 2003).
27. *The New Faithful: Why Young Adults Are Embracing Christian Orthodoxy* (Chicago: Loyola Press, 2002).
20. Hervieu-Leger, *Religion as a Chain*.
29. Robert Orsi, "Lived Religion," 171, has explicitly acknowledged the "juncture of fear and power" that many scholars feel as they raise the specter of nonrational or irrational and unpredictable energies that spirituality, or in his terms, "lived religion," foments. And as a secular scholar who is not personally spiritual, on some level I must agree. However, as Orsi chastised scholars for not facing this fear, I also believe that grounded qualitative work that does not address these deeply subjective and potentially transforming elements in everyday social life and social action is not only committing a disservice to our subjects but also missing a salient analytical piece of the puzzle.
30. Swidler, *Talk of Love*, 24–40, makes a similar point when she suggests that humans often and seamlessly change frames.

Bibliography

Aho, James. 1990. *Politics of Righteousness: Idaho Christian Patriotism*. Seattle: University of Washington Press.

Albrecht, Stan L., and Tim B. Heaton. 1984. "Secularization, Higher Education, and Religiosity." *Review of Religious Research* 26:43–56.

Ammerman, Nancy. 1997. *Congregation and Community*. New Brunswick, NJ: Rutgers University Press.

Anderson, Benedict. 1983. *Imagined Communities: Reflections on the Origin and Spread of Nationalism*. London: Verso.

Bane, Mary Jo, Brent Coffin, and Ronald Thiemann. 2000. *Who Will Provide? The Changing Role of Religion in American Social Welfare*. Boulder, CO: Westview Press.

Barbalet, Jack M. 1998. *Emotion, Social Theory, and Social Structure: A Macrosociological Approach*. New York: Cambridge University Press.

Barber, Benjamin. 1996. *Jihad vs. McWorld: How Globalism and Tribalism Are Reshaping the World*. New York: Ballantine Books.

Baker, Wayne E. 2004. *America's Crisis of Values: Reality and Perception*. Princeton, NJ: Princeton University Press.

Bateson, C. Daniel, Patricia Schoenrade, and W. Larry Ventis. 1993. *Religion and the Individual*. New York: Oxford University Press.

Becker, Penny Edgell. 1999. *Congregations in Conflict: Cultural Models of Local Religious Life*. Cambridge, MA: Cambridge University Press.

Bellah, Robert N. 1970. *Beyond Belief: Essays on Religion in a Post-Traditional World*. New York: Harper and Row.

———. 1975. *The Broken Covenant: American Civil Religion in a Time of Trial*. New York: Seabury Press.

Bellah, Robert N., Richard Madsen, William M. Sullivan, Ann Swidler, and Steven M. Tipton. 1985. *Habits of the Heart: Individualism and Commitment in American Life*. Berkeley: University of California Press.

Bender, Courtney. 2003. *Heaven's Kitchen: Living Religion at God's Love We Deliver*. Chicago: University of Chicago Press.

Berezin, Mabel. 1997. *Making the Fascist Self: The Political Culture of Inter-war Italy*. Ithaca, NY: Cornell University Press.

———. 2001. "Emotions and Political Identity: Mobilizing Affection for the Polity." In *Politics: Emotions and Social Movements*, ed. Jeff Goodwin, James Jasper, and Francesca Polleta, 83–98. Chicago: University of Chicago Press.

———. 2002. "Secure States: Towards a Political Sociology of Emotion." In *Emotions and Sociology*, ed. Jack Barbalet, 33–52. London: Basil Blackwell Publishing.

Berger, Peter L. 1967. *The Sacred Canopy: A Sociological Theory of Religion*. Garden City, NY: Doubleday.

———. 1970. *A Rumor of Angels: Modern Society and the Rediscovery of the Supernatural*. Garden City, NY: Anchor Press.

———. 1979. *The Heretical Imperative: Contemporary Possibilities of Religious Affirmation*. Garden City, NY: Anchor Press.

———, ed. 1999. *The Desecularization of the World: Resurgent Religion and World Politics*. Grand Rapids, MI: William B. Eerdmans Publishing Co.

Berger, Peter L., and Thomas Luckmann. 1966. *The Social Construction of Reality: A Treatise in the Sociology of Knowledge*. New York: Doubleday.

Bibby, Reginald. 1999. "On Boundaries, Gates, and Circulating Saints: A Longitudinal Look at Loyalty and Loss." *Review of Religious Research* 41:149–164.

Bibby, Reginald, and Merlin B. Brinkerhoff. 1973. "The Circulation of the Saints: A Study of People Who Join Conservative Churches." *Journal for the Scientific Study of Religion* 12:273–283.

Blumer, Herbert. 1969. *Symbolic Interactionism: Perspectives and Method*. Englewood Cliffs, NJ: Prentice-Hall.

Bourdieu, Pierre. 1990. *The Logic of Practice*. Stanford, CA: Stanford University Press.

Brokaw, Tom. 1998. *The Greatest Generation*. New York: Random House.

Brooks, Sarah. 1998. "Catholic Activism in the 1990's: New Strategies for the Neoliberal Age." In *Latin American Religion in Motion: Tracking Innovation, Unexpected Change, and Complexity*, ed. Christian Smith and Joshua Prokopy. New York: Routledge.

Burack, Elmer H. 1999. "Spirituality in the Workplace." *Journal of Organizational Change Management* 12:280–291.

Buruma, Ian, and Avishai Margalit. 2004. *Occidentalism: The West in the Eyes of Its Enemies*. New York: Penguin.

Butler, Jon 1990. *Awash in a Sea of Faith: Christianizing the American People*. Cambridge, MA: Harvard University Press.

Camic, Charles, and Neil Gross. 1998. "Contemporary Developments in Sociological Theory: Current Projects and Conditions of Possibility." *Annual Review of Sociology* 24:453–476.

Campbell, Colleen. 2002. *The New Faithful: Why Young Adults Are Embracing Christian Orthodoxy*. Chicago: Loyola Press.

Canda, Edward R. 1988. "Spirituality, Religious Diversity, Social Work Practice." *Social Casework* 69:238–247.

———, ed. 1998. *Spirituality in Social Work: New Directions*. New York: Haworth Pastoral Press.

Carter, Stephen L. 1993. *The Culture of Disbelief: How American Law and Politics Trivialize Religious Devotion*. New York: Basic Books.

Casanova, Jose. 1994. *Public Religions in the Modern World*. Chicago: University of Chicago Press.

Cascio, Toni. 1998. "Incorporating Spirituality into Social Work Practice: A Review of What to Do." *Families in Society* 79:523–531.

Chai, Karen J. 1998. "Competing for the Second Generation: English Language Ministry at a Korean Protestant Church." In *Gatherings in Diaspora: Religious Communities and the New Immigrants*, ed. R. Stephen Warner and Judith G. Wittner, 295–332. Philadelphia: Temple University Press.

Chittister, Joan. 1998. *Heart of Flesh: A Feminist Spirituality for Women and Men*. Grand Rapids, MI: Eerdmans.

Cimino, Richard, and Don Lattin. 1998. *Shopping for Faith: American Religion in the New Millennium*. New York: Jossey-Bass.

Coburn, Carol, and Martha Smith. 1999. *Spirited Lives: How Nuns Shaped Catholic Cul-*

ture and American Life, 1836–1920. Chapel Hill, NC: University of North Carolina Press.

Comstock, Gary L. 1995. *Religious Autobiographies*. Belmont, CA: Wadsworth.

Cooley, Charles Horton. 1902. *Human Nature and the Social Order*. New York: Scribners.

Cornwall, Marie. 1989. "The Determinants of Religious Behavior: A Theoretical Model and Empirical Test." *Social Forces* 68:572–592.

Covey, Stephen R. 1990. *The 7 Habits of Highly Effective People*. New York: Free Press.

Cox, Harvey. 1995. *Fire from Heaven: The Rise of Pentecostal Spirituality and the Reshaping of Religion in the Twenty-first Century*. Reading, MA: Addison-Wesley.

Csikszentmihaly, Mihaly. 1996. *Creativity: Flow and the Psychology of Discovery and Invention*. New York: Harper Collins.

———. 1997. *Finding Flow: The Psychology of Engagement with Everyday Life*. New York: Basic Books.

Davidson, Gary Charles. 2000. *Spirituality and the Therapeutic Relationship: A Comparative Study of Occupational Therapist Perspectives' in Canada and the United States*. Milligan College, TN: Milligan College Press.

Dayan, Daniel, and Elihu Katz. 1992. *Media Events: The Live Broadcasting of History*. Cambridge, MA: Harvard University Press.

De Certeau, Michel. 1984. *The Practice of Everyday Life*. Berkeley: University of California Press.

DeLeon, David. 1994. *Leaders from the 1960s: A Biographical Sourcebook of American Activism*. Westport, CT: Greenwood Press.

D'Emilio, John. 1983. *Sexual Politics, Sexual Communities: The Making of a Homosexual Minority in the United States, 1940–1970*. Chicago: University of Chicago Press.

Dimaggio, Paul. 1997. "Culture and Cognition." *Annual Review of Sociology* 23:263–287.

Dionne, E. J., and John J. Diiulio. 2000. *What's God Got to Do with the American Experiment?* Washington, D.C.: Brookings Institution Press.

Durkheim, Emile. 1965 [1915]. *The Elementary Forms of the Religious Life*. New York: Free Press.

Ebaugh, Helen Rose. 1993. *Women of the Vanishing Cloister: Organizational Decline in Catholic Religious Orders in the United States*. New Brunswick, NJ: Rutgers University Press.

Ellison, Christopher G., and Darren E. Sherkat. 1995. "The Semi-Involuntary Institution Revisited: Regional Variations in Church Participation among Black Americans." *Social Forces* 73:1415–1437.

Emerson, Michael, and Christian Smith. 2000. *Divided by Faith: Evangelical Religion and the Problem of Race in America*. New York: Oxford University Press.

Emmons, Robert A. 1999. *The Psychology of Ultimate Concerns: Motivation and Spirituality in Personality*. New York: Guilford Press.

Erikson, Erik. 1969. *Gandhi's Truth on the Origins of Militant Nonviolence*. New York: Norton.

Fantasia, Rick. 1988. *Cultures of Solidarity: Consciousness, Action, and Contemporary American Workers*. Berkeley: University of California Press.

Ferree, Myra Marx. 1992. "The Political Context of Rationality: Rational Choice Theory and Resource Mobilization." In *Frontiers in Social Movement Theory*, ed. Aldon D. Morris and Carol McClurg Mueller, 29–52. New Haven, CT: Yale University Press.

Fialka, John. 2003. *Sisters: Catholic Nuns and the Making of America*. New York: St. Martin's Press.

Finke, Roger, and Rodney Stark. 1992. *The Churching of America, 1776–1990: Winners and Losers in Our Religious Economy*. New Brunswick, NJ: Rutgers University Press.

Fireman, Bruce, and William A. Gamson. 1979. "Utilitarian Logic in the Resource

Mobilization Perspective. In *The Dynamics of Social Movements*, ed. Mayer N. Zald and John D. McCarthy. Cambridge, MA: Winthrop Publishers.

Flory, Richard. 2000. "Toward a Theory of Generation X Religion." In *GenX Religions*, ed. Richard W. Flory and Donald E. Miller, 231–249. New York: Routledge.

Forman, Robert K. C. 1998. "What Does Mysticism Have to Teach Us about Consciousness?" *Journal of Consciousness Studies* 5:185–201.

Fox, Richard Wrightman. 2004. *Jesus in America: Personal Savior, Cultural Hero, National Obsession.* San Francisco: HarperSanFrancisco.

Fuller, Robert C. 2001. *Spiritual, but Not Religious: Understanding Unchurched America.* New York: Oxford University Press.

Galanter, Marc. 1997. "Spiritual Recovery Movements and Contemporary Medical Care." *Psychiatry* 60:211–223.

Gamson, William A. 1992. "The Social Psychology of Collective Action." In *Frontiers in Social Movement Theory*, ed. Aldon D. Morris and Carol McClurg Mueller, 53–76. New Haven, CT: Yale University Press.

Gamson, William A., Bruce Fireman, and Steven Rytina. 1982. *Encounters with Unjust Authority.* Homewood, IL: Dorsey.

Geertz, Clifford. 1973. *The Interpretation of Cultures: Selected Essays.* New York: Basic Books.

Gelpi, Donald J. 1987. "Religious Conversion: A New Way of Being." In *The Human Experience of Conversion: Persons and Structures in Transformation*, ed. Francis A. Eigo. Villanova, PA: Villanova University Press.

———. 1989. "Conversion: Beyond the Impasses of Individualism." In *Beyond Individualism*, ed. Donald J. Gelpi. South Bend, IN: University of Notre Dame Press.

Gergen, Kenneth J. 2000. *The Saturated Self: Dilemmas of Identity in Contemporary Life.* New York: Basic Books.

Giddens, Anthony. 1984. *The Constitution of Society.* Cambridge, MA: Polity Press.

———. 1991. *Modernity and Self-Identity: Self and Society in the Late Modern Age.* Stanford, CA: Stanford University Press.

Goffman, Erving. 1974. *Frame Analysis.* Cambridge, MA: Harvard University Press.

Goodwin, Jeff. 1997. "The Libidinal Constitution of a High-Risk Social Movement: Affectual Ties and Solidarity in the Huk Rebellion, 1946–1954." *American Sociological Review* 62:53–69.

Goodwin, Jeff, James Jasper, and Francesca Polleta, eds. 2001. *Passionate Politics: Emotions and Social Movements.* Chicago: University of Chicago Press.

Goodwin, Jeff, and Steven Pfaff. 2001. "Emotion Work in High-Risk Social Movements: Managing Fear in the U.S. and East German Civil Rights Movements." In *Politics: Emotions and Social Movements*, ed. Jeff Goodwin, James Jasper, and Francesca Polleta, 282–302. Chicago: University of Chicago Press.

Granovetter, Mark. 1973. "The Strength of Weak Ties." *American Journal of Sociology* 78:1360–1380.

Griffith, R. Marie. 1997. *God's Daughters: Evangelical Women and the Power of Submission.* Berkeley: University of California Press.

Gunnoe, Marjorie, and Kristin Moore. 2002. "Predictors of Religiosity among Youth Aged 17–22: A Longitudinal Study of the National Survey of Children." *Journal for the Scientific Study of Religion* 41:613–622.

Gutierrez, Gustavo. 1973. *A Theology of Liberation.* Maryknoll, NY: Orbis Books.

Hadaway, C. Kirk, and Penny Long Marler. 1993. "All in the Family." *Review of Religious Research* 35:97–116.

Harris, Fredrick C. 1999. *Something Within: Religion in African-American Political Activism.* New York: Oxford University Press.

Hatch, Nathan O. 1991. *The Democratization of American Christianity*. New Haven, CT: Yale University Press.

Helminiak, Daniel A. 1987. *Spiritual Development: An Interdisciplinary Study*. Chicago: Loyola University Press.

———. 1996. *The Human Core of Spirituality: Mind as Psyche and Spirit*. Albany, NY: State University of New York Press.

———. 2001. "Treating Spiritual Issues in Secular Psychotherapy." *Counseling and Values*. 45:163–189.

Herberg, Will. 1955. *Protestant Catholic Jew*. Garden City, NJ: Anchor Books.

Hervieu-Leger, Daniele. 2000. *Religion as a Chain of Memory*. New Brunswick, NJ: Rutgers University Press.

Hochschild, Arlie Russell. 1979. "Emotion Work, Feeling Rules and Social Structure," *American Journal of Sociology* 85:551–575.

———. 1983. *The Managed Heart: Commercialization of Human Feeling*. Berkeley: University of California Press.

Hoge, Dean, Benton Johnson, and Donald Luiden. 1994. *Vanishing Boundaries: The Religion of Mainline Protestant Baby Boomers*. Louisville, KY: Westminster/John Knox Press.

Hunter, James Davison. 1991. *Culture Wars: The Struggle to Define America*. New York: Basic Books.

Iannaccone, Laurence R. 1992. "Sacrifice and Stigma: Reducing Free-Riding in Cults, Communes, and Other Collectives." *Journal of Political Economy* 29:297–310.

———. 1994. "Why Strict Churches Are Strong." *American Journal of Sociology* 99: 1180–1204.

———. 1995. "Religious Resources and Church Growth." *Social Forces* 74:705–731.

Inglehart, Ronald. 1977. *The Silent Revolution: Changing Values and Political Styles among Western Publics*. Princeton, NJ: Princeton University Press.

James, William. 1985. *The Varieties of Religious Experience*. Cambridge, MA: Harvard University Press.

Jasper, James M. 1997. *The Art of Moral Protest: Culture Biography and Creativity in Social Movements*. Chicago: University of Chicago Press.

———. 1998. "The Emotions of Protest: Affective and Reactive Emotions in and around Social Movements." *Sociological Forum* 13:397–424.

Jenkins, J. Craig, and Charles Perrow. 1977. Insurgency of the Powerless: Farm Worker Movements, 1946–1972." *American Sociological Review* 42:249–268.

Joas, Hans. 1996. *The Creativity of Action*. Chicago: University of Chicago Press.

———. 2001. *The Genesis of Values*. Trans. Gregory Moore. Chicago: University of Chicago Press.

Juergensmeyer, Mark. 2001. *Terror in the Mind of God: The Global Rise of Religious Violence*. Berkeley: University of California Press.

Kane, Anne. 2001. "Finding Emotion in Social Movement Processes: Irish Land Movement Metaphors and Narratives." In *Passionate Politics: Emotions and Social Movements*, ed. Jeff Goodwin, James Jasper, and Francesca Polleta, 251–266. Chicago: University of Chicago Press.

Kass, Jared. D., Richard Friedman, Jane Leserman, Patricia C. Zuttermeister, and Herbert Benson. 1991. "Health Outcomes and a New Index of Spiritual Experience." *Journal for the Scientific Study of Religion* 30:203–211.

Kearns, Laurel. 1996. "Saving the Creation: Christian Environmentalism in the United States." *Sociology of Religion* 57:55–70.

Kemper, Theodore D. 1978. *A Social Interactional Theory of Emotions*. New York: John Wiley.

Kooistra, William, and Kenneth I. Pargament. 1999. "Religious Doubting in Parochial School Adolescents." *Journal of Psychology and Theology* 27:33–42.

Kurien, Prema. 1998. "Becoming American by Becoming Hindu." In *Gatherings in Diaspora: Religious Communities and the New Immigrants*, ed. R. Stephen Warner and Judith G. Wittner. Philadelphia: Temple University Press.

Kushner, Harold. 1981. *When Bad Things Happen to Good People*. New York: Schocken Books.

Larana, Enrique, Hank Johnston, and Joe Gusfield, eds. 1994. *New Social Movements: From Ideology to Identity*. Philadelphia: Temple University Press.

Lasch, Christopher. 1979. *The Culture of Narcissism: American Life in the Age of Diminishing Expectations*. New York: Norton.

Latour, Bruno. 1993. *We Have Never Been Modern*. Cambridge, MA: Harvard University Press.

Lichterman, Paul. 1996. *The Search for Political Community: American Activists Reinventing Commitment*. New York: Cambridge University Press.

Lofland, John, and Rodney Stark. 1965. "Becoming a World-Saver: A Theory of Conversion to a Deviant Perspective." *American Sociological Review* 30:862–875.

Luker, Kristin. 1985. *Abortion and the Politics of Motherhood*. Berkeley: University of California Press.

Mansbridge, Jane J. 1986. *Why We Lost the ERA*. Chicago: University of Chicago Press.

Marler, Penny Long, and C. Kirk Hadaway. 2002. "'Being Religious' or 'Being Spiritual' in America: A Zero-Sum Proposition?" *Journal for the Scientific Study of Religion* 41:289–300.

Marshall, Douglas A. 2002. "Behavior, Belonging, and Belief: A Theory of Ritual Practice." *Sociological Theory* 20:360–380.

McAdam, Doug. 1988. *Freedom Summer*. New York: Oxford University Press.

———. 1999. *Political Process and the Development of Black Insurgency, 1930–1970*. 2nd ed. Chicago: University of Chicago Press.

McDannell, Colleen. 1995. *Material Christianity: Religion and Popular Culture in America*. New Haven, CT: Yale University Press.

McGee, Micki. 2005. *Self Help, Inc.* New York: Oxford University Press.

Mead, George Herbert. 1962. *Mind, Self, and Society*. Ed. C. Morris. Chicago: University of Chicago Press.

Melucci, Alberto. 1989. *Nomads of the Present: Social Movements and Individual Needs in Contemporary Society*. Philadelphia: Temple University Press.

———. 1995. "The Process of Collective Identity." In *Social Movements and Culture*, ed. Hank Johnston and Bert Klandersmans. Minneapolis: University of Minnesota Press.

Miller, Donald E. 1997. *Reinventing American Protestantism: Christianity in the New Millennium*. Berkeley: University of California Press.

———. Forthcoming. *Pentecostalism and Social Transformation*. Berkeley: University of California Press.

Miller, Jon. 2003. *Missionary Zeal and Institutional Control: Organizational Contradictions in the Basel Mission on the Gold Coast, 1828–1917*. Grand Rapids, MI: William B. Eerdmans Publishing Co.

Morgan, David. 1999. *Protestants and Pictures: Religion, Visual Culture, and the Age of American Mass Production*. New York: Oxford University Press.

Morris, Aldon D. 1984. *The Origins of the Civil Rights Movement: Black Communities Organizing for Change*. New York: Free Press.

Musick, Mark, and John Wilson. 1995. "Religious Switching for Marriage Reasons." *Sociology of Religion* 56:257–270.

Myers, Scott. 1996. "An Interactive Model of Religiosity Inheritance: The Importance of Family Context." *American Sociological Review* 61:858–866.

Neal, Judi. 2000. "Work as Service to the Divine: Giving our Gifts Selflessly and with Joy." *American Behavioral Scientist* 43:1316–1333.

Neitz, Mary Jo. 1987. *Charisma and Community: A Study of Religious Commitment within the Charismatic Renewal.* New Brunswick, NJ: Transaction.

Neitz, Mary Jo, and James V. Spickard. 1990. "Steps Toward a Sociology of Religious Experience." *Sociological Analysis* 51:15–33.

Nepstad, Sharon Erickson. 2004. *Convictions of the Soul: Religion, Culture, and Agency in the Central American Solidarity Movement.* New York: Oxford University Press.

Nepstad, Sharon Erickson, and Christian Smith. 2001. "The Social Structure of Moral Outrage in Recruitment to the U.S. Central America Peace Movement." In *Passionate Politics: Emotions and Social Movements,* ed. Jeff Goodwin, James Jasper, and Francesca Polleta, 158–174. Chicago: University of Chicago Press.

Newman, Katherine S. 1988. *Falling from Grace: The Experience of Downward Mobility in the American Middle Class.* New York: Free Press.

Nouwen, Henri. 1983. *Gracias! A Latin American Journal.* San Francisco: Harper and Row.

Opiela, Nancy. 2000. "Mary K. Sullivan: Soul Stories." *Journal of Financial Planning* 13: 156–158.

Orsi, Robert A. 1996. *Thank You St. Jude: Women's Devotion to the Patron Saint of Hopeless Causes.* New Haven: Yale University Press.

———. 2003. Presidential Address 2002. "Is the Study of Lived Religion Irrelevant to the World We Live In? *Journal for the Scientific Study of Religion* 42:169–174.

Pargament, Kenneth I. 1997. *The Psychology of Religion and Coping: Theory, Research, Practice.* New York: Guilford Press.

———. 1999. "The Psychology of Religion *and* Spirituality? Yes and No." *International Journal for the Psychology of Religion* 9:3–16.

Pargament, K. I., Sullivan, M. S., Balzer, W. K., Van Haitsma, K. S., and Raymark, P. H. 1995. "The Many Meanings of Religiousness: A Policy Capturing Approach. *Journal of Personality* 63:953–983.

Peck, M. Scott. 1978. *The Road Less Traveled.* New York: Simon and Schuster.

Pickering, W. S. F. 1985. *Durkheim's Sociology of Religion: Themes and Theories.* London: Routledge.

———, ed. 1975. *Durkheim on Religion: A Selection of Readings with Bibliographies.* London: Routledge.

Piven, Frances F., and Richard Cloward. 1977. *Poor People's Movements.* New York: Pantheon.

Polletta, Francesca, and James M. Jasper. 2001. "Collective Identity in Social Movements." *Annual Review of Sociology* 27:283–305.

Predelli, Line, and Jon Miller. 1999. "Piety and Patriarchy: Contested Gender Regimes in Nineteenth-Century Colonial Missions." In *Gendered Missions: Women and Men in Missionary Discourse and Practice,* ed. Mary Huber and Nancy Lutkehaus. Ann Arbor: University of Michigan Press.

Proudfoot, Wayne. 1985. *Religious Experience.* Berkeley: University of California Press.

Pulido, Laura. 1998. "The Sacredness of 'Mother Earth': Spirituality, Activism and Social Justice." *Annals of the Association of American Geographers* 88:719–723.

Putnam, Robert D. 2000. *Bowling Alone: The Collapse and Revival of American Community.* New York: Simon and Schuster.

Rambo, Lewis. 1993. *Understanding Religious Conversion.* New Haven, CT: Yale University Press.

Riess, Jana. 2004. *What Would Buffy Do: The Vampire Slayer as Spiritual Guide.* New York: Jossey-Bass.

Roof, Wade Clark. 1993. *A Generation of Seekers: The Spiritual Journeys of the Baby Boom Generation.* San Francisco: HarperSanFrancisco.

———. 1999. *Spiritual Marketplace: Baby Boomers and the Remaking of American Religion*. Princeton, NJ: Princeton University Press.

Roozen, David A., William McKinney, and Jackson W. Carroll. 1984. *Varieties of Religious Presence: Mission in Public Life*. New York: Pilgrim Press.

Rose, Elizabeth M., John S. Westefeld, and Timothy N. Ansley. 2001. "Spiritual Issues in Counseling: Clients' Beliefs and Preferences." *Journal of Counseling Psychology* 48:61–71.

Sack, Daniel. 2000. *Whitebread Protestants: Food and Religion in American Culture*. New York: St. Martin's Press.

Said, Edward. 1979. *Orientalism*. New York: Vintage Books.

Sermabeikian, Patricia. 1994. "Our Clients, Ourselves: The Spiritual Perspective and Social Work Practice." *Social Work* 39:178–183.

Sewell, William H., Jr. 1992. "A Theory of Structure, Duality, Agency, and Transformation." *American Journal of Sociology* 98:1–29.

———. 1996. "Historical Events as Structural Transformations: Inventing the Revolution at the Bastille." *Theory and Society* 26:245–280.

Sheridan, Michael J. 2001. "Defining Spiritually Sensitive Social Work Practice: An Essay Review of Spiritual Diversity in Social Work Practice: The Heart of Helping." *Social Work* 46:87–92.

Sherkat, Darren E. 1991. "Leaving the Faith: Testing Theories of Religious Switching Using Survival Models." *Social Science Research* 20:171–187.

———. 1997. "Embedding Religious Choices: Integrating Preferences and Social Constraints into Rational Choice Theories of Religious Behavior." In *Rational Choice Theory and Religion: Summary and Assessment*, ed. Lawrence Young, 65–86. New York: Routledge.

———. 1998. "Counterculture or Continuity? Competing Influences on Baby Boomers' Religious Orientations and Participation." *Social Forces* 76:1087–1114.

———. 2001. "Tracking the Restructuring of American Religion: Religious Affiliation and Patterns of Mobility, 1973–1998." *Social Forces* 79:1459–1492.

Sherkat, Darren E., and Christopher G. Ellison. 1999. "Recent Developments and Current Controversies in the Sociology of Religion." *Annual Review of Sociology* 25: 363–394.

Sherkat, Darren, and John Wilson. 1995. "Preferences, Constraints, and Choices in Religious Markets: An Examination of Religious Switching and Apostasy." *Social Forces* 73:993–1026.

Shilling, Chris. 2002. "The Two Traditions in the Sociology of Emotions." In *Emotions and Sociology*, ed. Jack Barbalet, 10–32. London: Basil Blackwell Publishing.

Shupe, Anson, and David G. Bromley. *Strange Gods: The Great American Cult Scare*. Boston: Beacon Press, 1981.

Smith, Christian. 1991. *The Emergence of Liberation Theology: Radical Religion and Social Movement Theory*. Chicago: University of Chicago Press.

———, ed. 1996. *Disruptive Religion: The Force of Faith in Social Movements*. New York: Routledge.

———. 2003. *Moral, Believing Animals: Human Personhood and Culture*. New York: Oxford University Press.

Smith, Christian, and David Sikkink. 2003. "Social Predictors of Retention in and Switching from the Religious Faith of Family of Origin: Another Look Using Religious Tradition Self-Identification." *Review of Religious Research* 45:188–206.

Snow, David A., and Robert D. Benford. 1992. "Master Frames and Cycles of Protest." In *Frontiers in Social Movement Theory*, ed. Aldon D. Morris and Carol McClurg Mueller, 133–155. New Haven, CT: Yale University Press.

Snow, David A., Burke E. Rochford, Steven Worden, and Robert Benford. 1986. "Frame

Alignment Processes, Micromobilization, and Movement Participation." *American Sociological Review* 45:787–801.

Stanczak, Gregory C. 2000. "The Traditional as Alternative: The GenX Appeal of the International Churches of Christ." In *GenX Religions*, ed. Donald E. Miller and Richard Flory. New York: Routledge.

Stark, Rodney, and Roger Finke. 2000. *Acts of Faith: Explaining the Human Side of Religion*. Berkeley: University of California Press.

Stryker, Sheldon. 1980. *Symbolic Interactionism: A Social Structural Version*. Menlo Park, CA: Benjamin Cummings.

Stryker, Sheldon, Timothy J. Owens, and Robert W. White, eds. 2001. *Self, Identity, and Social Movements*. Minneapolis: University of Minnesota Press.

Suarez-Orozco, Marcelo M., ed. *Crossings: Mexican Immigration in Interdisciplinary Perspectives*. Cambridge, MA: Harvard University Press.

Swidler, Ann. 1986. "Culture in Action: Symbols and Strategies." *American Sociological Review* 51:273–286.

———. 1993. "Foreword." In *The Sociology of Religion*, by Max Weber. Boston: Beacon Press.

———. 2001. *Talk of Love: How Culture Matters*. Chicago: University of Chicago Press.

Taves, Ann. 1999. *Fits, Trances, and Visions: Experiencing Religion and Explaining Religion from Wesley to James*. Princeton, NJ: Princeton University Press.

Taylor, Charles. 1989. *Sources of the Self: The Making of the Modern Identity*. Cambridge, MA: Harvard University Press.

———. 2002. *Varieties of Religion Today: William James Revisited*. Cambridge, MA: Harvard University Press.

Taylor, Verta. 1989. "Social Movement Continuity: The Women's Movement in Abeyance." *American Sociological Review* 54:761–775.

———. 2001. "Emotions and Identity in Women's Self-Help Movements." In *Self, Identity, and Social Movements*, ed. Sheldon Stryker, Timothy J. Owens, and Robert W. White, 271–299. Minneapolis: University of Minnesota Press.

Taylor, Verta, and Nancy Whittier. 1995. "Analytic Approaches to Social Movement Culture: The U.S. Women's Movement." In *Social Movements and Culture*, ed. Hank Johnston and Bert Klandermans, 163–186. Minneapolis: University of Minnesota Press.

Thomas, W. I. 1923. *The Unadjusted Girl*. Boston: Little Brown and Co.

Thompson, William David. 2000. "Can You Train People to Be Spiritual?" *Training and Development* 54:18–19.

Vidal, Gore. 2002. *Perpetual War for Perpetual Peace: How We Got to Be So Hated*. New York: Thunder's Mouth Press.

Wallis, Jim. 2005. *God's Politics: Why the Right Gets It Wrong and the Left Doesn't Get It*. San Francisco: HarperSanFrancisco.

Warner, R. Stephen, and Judith G. Wittner. 1998. *Gatherings in Diaspora: Religious Communities and the New Immigrants*. Philadelphia: Temple University Press.

Warren, Mark R. 2001. *Dry Bones Rattling: Community Building to Revitalize American Democracy*. Princeton, NJ: Princeton University Press.

Warren, Rick. 2002. *The Purpose-Driven Life: What on Earth Am I Here For?* Grand Rapids, MI: Zondervan.

Whittier, Nancy. 1995. *Feminist Generations: The Persistence of Radical Women's Movements*. Philadelphia: Temple University Press.

Wilcox, W. Bradford. 2004. *Soft Patriarchs, New Men: How Christianity Shapes Fathers and Husbands*. Chicago: University of Chicago Press.

Williams, Raymond. 1977. *Marxism and Literature*. New York: Oxford University Press.

Wood, Richard L. 1999. "Religious Culture and Political Action." *Sociological Theory.* 17:307–332.

———. 2002. *Faith in Action: Religion, Race, and Democratic Organizing in America.* Chicago: University of Chicago Press.

Wuthnow, Robert. 1993. *Christianity in the Twenty-First Century: Reflections on the Challenges Ahead.* New York: Oxford University Press.

———. 1994. *Producing the Sacred: An Essay on Public Religion.* Urbana: University of Illinois.

———. 1995. *Learning to Care: Elementary Kindness in an Age of Indifference.* New York: Oxford University Press.

———. 1998. *After Heaven: Spirituality in America since the 1950s.* Berkeley: University of California Press.

———. 2000. "How Religious Groups Promote Forgiving: A National Study." *Journal for the Scientific Study of Religion* 36:124–137.

———. 2001. *Creative Spirituality: The Way of the Artist.* Berkeley: University of California Press.

———. 2003. *All in Sync: How Music and Art Are Revitalizing American Religion.* Berkeley: University of California Press.

Young, Michael P. 2001. "A Revolution of the Soul: Transformative Experiences and Immediate Abolition." In *Passionate Politics: Emotions and Social Movements,* ed. Jeff Goodwin, James Jasper, and Francesca Polleta, 99–114. Chicago: University of Chicago Press.

———. 2002. "Confessional Protest: The Religious Birth of U.S. National Social Movements." *American Sociological Review* 67:660–688.

Zinnbauer, B. J., and K. I. Pargament. 1998. Spiritual Conversion: A Study of Religious Change among College Students." *Journal for the Scientific Study of Religion* 37: 161–180.

Zinnbauer, Brian J., Kenneth I. Pargament, B. Cole, M. S. Rye, E. M. Butter, T. G. Belavich, K. M. Hipp, Allie B. Scott, and J. L. Kadar. 1997. "Religion and Spirituality: Unfuzzying the Fuzzy." *Journal for the Scientific Study of Religion* 36:549–564.

Zinnbauer, Brian J., Kenneth I. Pargament, and Allie B. Scott. 1999. "The Emerging Meanings of Religiousness and Spirituality: Problems and Prospects." *Journal of Personality* 67:889–919.

Index